Indigenous Activism

Published by Lexington Books
An imprint of The Rowman & Littlefield Publishing Group, Inc.
4501 Forbes Boulevard, Suite 200, Lanham, Maryland 20706
www.rowman.com

6 Tinworth Street, London SE11 5AL, United Kingdom

Copyright © 2021 by The Rowman & Littlefield Publishing Group, Inc.

All rights reserved. No part of this book may be reproduced in any form or by any electronic or mechanical means, including information storage and retrieval systems, without written permission from the publisher, except by a reviewer who may quote passages in a review.

British Library Cataloguing in Publication Information Available

Library of Congress Cataloging-in-Publication Data

Library of Congress Control Number: 2021931402

ISBN: 978-1-7936-4542-5 (cloth)
ISBN: 978-1-7936-4541-8 (electronic)

To American Indian Grandmothers, Mothers,
Aunties, Daughters, and Sisters

Women Who Changed Our Lives

Contents

Preface	ix
Introduction	1
1 Red Power in the Northwest: Ramona Bennett *Vera Parham*	17
2 Being Mary Crow Dog: It Isn't Easy: Mary Crow Dog *Renae M. Bredin*	25
3 Power of Voice, Power in the Land: Ada Deer *Theodor Gordon and Michael Seager*	41
4 Cheyenne and Hodulgee Muscogee Activist: Suzan Shown Harjo *Michelle Lorimer*	51
5 Strikes with *Puha*—Power! Comanche Activist, LaDonna Harris *Clifford E. Trafzer*	57
6 Tribal Community and National Activist: Wilma Mankiller *Jeffrey Allen Smith*	69
7 *Numakshi Mihe*: The Lead Woman of the Three Affiliated Tribes: Alyce Spotted Bear *Daniel Archuleta*	75
8 Navajo Judge, Ramah and Crownpoint Districts: Irene Toledo *Thomas Long*	85
9 "In Unity There Is Strength," Writer and Activist: Marie Potts *Daniel Stahl-Kovell*	93

10	Cultural Activist: Zitkala-Ša, Gertrude Simmons Bonnin *Benjamin Jenkins*	99
11	Where Is Victory? Harriette Shelton Dover *Richard A. Hanks*	107
12	Ending Termination in Indian Country: Lucy Covington *Benjamin Jenkins*	117
13	Good-Hearted Woman: Cecilia Fire Thunder *Joshua Thunder Little*	123
14	The Necessary Evil: Dolly Smith Cusker Akers *Shannon M. Smith*	129
15	Champion of the National Congress of the American Indian: Ruth Muskrat Bronson *Julia Coates*	135
16	Seeking Justice through Storytelling: Leslie Marmon Silko *Amanda K. Wixon*	145
17	Native American Scholar Activist: Bea Medicine *Elvia Rodriguez*	151
18	Literary Activist, Political Voice of Native America: Elizabeth Cook-Lynn *Susan M. Wood*	157

Index	163
About the Editors	171
About the Contributors	173

Preface

Ada Deer, Suzan Harjo, Wilma Mankiller, Mary Crow Dog, and Leslie Silko are among the thousands of Native American women who were activist leaders during the twentieth-century West. A generation ago, few of these women were known outside their American Indian communities. The publication of *ndigenous Activism: Profiles of Native Women in Contemporary America* addresses this oversight by introducing eighteen enlightening essays about Native American women who were political activists during the last century. Here are short biographies of Wilma Mankiller, Leslie Silko, Suzan Harjo, Alyce Spotted Bear, and others who fought for social justice for Native Americans. These women and other Indigenous women fought to maintain and grow tribal sovereignty, preserve cultural traditions, fight for Indian rights, and enhance the general well-being of life in Indian Country. As the United States becomes increasingly more diverse in the twenty-first century, understanding the efforts, the trials and tribulations, successes and failures of Native American women of the last century will expand the meaning of being American.

During the past few decades, scholars have researched the lives of significant Indigenous women in the history of the American West. For generations, historians of the American West primarily focused on rugged individualists who reportedly raised themselves up by their bootstraps to contribute to the "winning of the West." In the past, historians focused on a male-conceived, oriented, and dominated story. Men were at the center of most past histories of the West with women and children tagging along as backdrops to the "real" West. Except for Pocahontas, Sacagawea, and Sarah Winnemucca, few other Indigenous women who lived in the eighteenth and nineteenth centuries appeared in the pages of American History and Western History surveys of the eighteenth and nineteenth centuries. Those women acknowledged in this masculine literary world were primarily white Euro-American wives and daughters of early settlers. Later writers noted the stereotypes: the "Madonna" of the prairies and their sisters, the sunbonneted helpmates, the "wild women outlaws" and those "soiled doves," the prostitutes. Native American women received little scholarly attention, far less than Indian men. However, far too often, scholars depicted Native American women as "squaws," drudges, or Indian princesses. Writers found in *Indigenous Activism: Profiles of Native American Women in Contemporary Society* have researched the activism of a select number of American Indian women to offer illuminating accounts that will inform and delight readers.

Serious study of Native American women from the American West is a relatively new subfield of the larger history of women in America. Gender history evolved in the 1960s in the unsettled, and unsettling, social, political, and economic movements then convulsing the nation. By the mid-1970s, the new scholarship triggered the birth of an impressive number of publications, journals, conferences, workshops, and women's studies departments that focused on the lives of women, asserting correctly that their stories are an integral part of American history, too long silenced in American history. These early studies focused primarily on women whose stories were already part of American mythology, but scholars slowly addressed other women. However, during the 1960s–1970s, most accounts of women still focused on the histories of white Euro-American women and a few African American women. Most scholars ignored the rich activism of Native American women scattered across the West. However, among Native American communities, women held and hold central roles as traditional doctors, midwives, dancers, singers, advisors, healers, and teachers. Sometimes, as was the case of Palouse Collesta or Apache female warriors, they served their people as patriots, fighting as warriors against tribal enemies. In many Native American communities, women maintained the history and culture of their people. Sandy Dixon, Vivienne Jake, Malissa Minthorn, Mary Jim, Pauline Murillo, and Lorena Dixon spent their lives preserving tribal knowledge and standing up for their people as tribal leaders and representatives. They taught the younger generation in the political arts at home, in the state, and in the nation.

During the 1970s, historians of the American West and Native America began to research diverse communities of women, including Native American women. In a journal article published in 1980, historians Joan Jensen and Darlis Miller pointed out the need to reexamine the history of women in the nation's western region and most especially, the history of minority women. Their seminal essay, "Gentle Tamers Revisited: New Approaches to the History of Women in the American West," argued for new and deep studies of women of the American West. Their work and others led to a thriving and productive field of study that remains robust today. Jenson and Miller asked historians to "explore new possibilities for analysis," to broaden their accounts to include analyses of gender, class, race, and ethnicity.

The confluence of Native American cultures in the West and women's history offers a fertile field for studying diversity and the intersection of race, ethnicity, and gender. The life histories of Native American women offer a window into the values, traditions, goals, and aspirations of unique women of the American West. Studies of American Indian women have brought forth new understanding of their communities and world views. When class, gender, ethnicity, religion, age, sexual orientation, and countless other factors are added to the racial mix, the "face" of the West becomes increasingly lined with complexity. The anthology you are reading marks a contribution to the growing number of accounts about Native American women who have made substantial contributions to their communities, professions, and/or fields.

Most often, professors and biographers offer studies describing and analyzing the significant role Native American women have played in local, state, national, and international spheres. Historians have provided accounts of Pocahontas and Sacagawea, but integrated histories of women are too often ancillary to male-dominated historical events. This volume intends to expand this limited view by sharing stories of known and little-known Native American women. In *Indigenous Activism: Profiles of Native American Women in Contemporary Society*, we showcase examples of women who were or are political activists. Readers will know or have heard of some of these women, but not all of them. Members of particular Native communities or regions of the American West will know more obscure women who are well-known in Indian Country.

The women addressed in this volume came from varied backgrounds and experiences. They include wives, mothers, daughters, sisters, and partners. They are all leaders and teachers in the broadest sense. Their distinct identities derive from their Indigenous roots, and their work demonstrates lifelong commitments to the quest for justice for Indian people, to improving the lives of their people, and of giving back to their communities in a unique variety of ways. This volume of essays will introduce readers to these remarkable women.

A common theme permeates the stories found here. On some level—local, tribal, national—these women were—and some remain—political activists, women who have taken action to affect change in their communities, states, and nation. Webster defines activism as the policy of taking positive, direct action, especially for political or social ends. Historically, American Indian women have engaged in activism and volunteerism. Where and how the activism emerges can arise anywhere. Perhaps the need to address a long-ignored and contaminated community water source comes up between members after tribal council meeting; maybe parents want to advocate sobriety, educational opportunities for children, better healthcare, new jobs, and a host of other issues. Women must struggle against barriers erected by majority communities, tribal councils, and government agencies, and national leaders, including presidents, in order to affect change. These Native American women have found ways to be heard, to take action, to persist in overcoming obstacles in their efforts to create healthy, sustainable communities for the benefit of all their people. And many times, their actions impact more than their local communities.

Irene Toledo is one example. Toledo was appointed Navajo District Court Judge in 1989 and brought to the bench the Navajo system of peacemaking, "a collective effort that incorporates the Navajo culture and spiritual belief system." Unlike the adversarial method that characterizes the larger American legal system, Toledo's courtroom is based on ways to reduce conflict that focus on harmony. Applying the Navajo peacemaking approach and methodologies to issues of domestic violence, Toledo has become a nationally known expert in the field of domestic and family law.

Many of the Indigenous women profiled here received their first education at home from their parents and people. With this Indigenous foundation, some of them earned degrees in higher education that helped propel them into leadership positions within their tribes, states, and nation. In an article published in the *New York Times* in 2006, Monica Davey noted the increased number of highly educated Native American women who have returned to their communities to serve as leaders. According to Davey, "Increasingly, women have become the administrators, the teachers, the community organizers, and the ones to receive broader education and work experience beyond the reservation." Alyce Spotted Bear (of Mandan, Hidatsda, and Arikara descent), Wilma Mankiller (Cherokee), Erma Vizenor (White Earth Band of Ojibwe), Cecilia Fire Thunder (Oglala Sioux), and Vivian Juan-Sanders (Tohono O'odham) have all served as tribal chairpersons. Ada Deer (Menominee), the first woman in her tribe to earn a master's degree, was also the first (and to date, only) Native American woman to serve as head of Bureau of Indian Affairs (BIA). In 1993, she took the helm of the troubled agency that has guided national Indian policy for many years. Like other activists, Ada Deer used her position and leadership to improve conditions for Indigenous people. The commitment and determination of Deer and women activists like her serve as compelling examples of the significant role Native American women have played in American history.

Janine Pease Pretty-on-Top (of Crow, Hidatsa, Welsh, and German ancestry), whose schoolteacher parents instilled a love of education in their daughter, became the first woman of Crow descent to earn a doctorate. Shortly after college graduation, she found her "calling" as an activist in promoting the importance of high school degree via the GED. In 1980, Pease was instrumental in the founding of Little Big Horn College on the Crow Reservation and was named president of the college two years later. Still active in academia, she currently serves as Vice President of Academic Affairs at Fort Peck Community College in Poplar, Montana. Pease is also known for her lawsuit, Windy Boy v. Big Horn County, a successful federal case to protect and extend voting rights for Indian people. Other women of note include Allison Hedge-Coke, a remarkable woman best known as an author, poet, and professor at the University of California in Riverside. She has lived a life of activism and is currently leading "Along the Chaparral," a school program, K-University designed to recognize the contributions of military men and women buried in the Riverside National Cemetery and Punchbowl of Hawai'i.

Bea Medicine (Standing Rock Sioux) or "Returns Victorious With A Red Horse Woman" was a much-loved and well-published anthropologist, "the quintessential outsider within a professional anthropology." Medicine was known for her defense of participants in the Wounded Knee protest of 1973 and for her fights for Indian rights in cities and counties of the United States. By the time of her death in 2005, her people of Standing Rock considered her a respected and trusted elder. Like Bea Medicine, other Native American women came of age during the Civil Rights era of the 1960s and 1970s. Mary Crow Dog (Mary Brave Bird, Lakota Sioux) is one of the more well-known and controversial activists of the era, present in 1973 during the Indian occupation of Wounded Knee on the Pine Ridge Reservation. Along with Annie Mae Pictou-Aquash (Mi'kmaw tribe in Nova Scotia), she was a member of the American Indian Movement. Both women fiercely fought for civil rights and Indian sovereignty while committing themselves to the preservation of Native American cultures, sometimes in direct confrontation with the dominant body politic. The political activism of these and other women reflects the important struggles and commitment of contemporary Native American women of the recent past.

The women featured in this work took different routes to their activism. Many of the college-educated women became political leaders on various levels of government. Some women made a decision to remain among their people and work at the grassroots level. But whether women worked on the tribal, state, or national level, all of them took actions to improve the lives of others. According to Cheryl Crazy Bull (Rosebud Sioux), political activism among Native American women was and remains: "For our students, social action is a form of 'coming home' to oneself—we are the children of warriors and survivors, it feels to natural to take action." We hope this anthology will inform and impress you as well as broaden the scope of the history of Native American women in the American West.

FURTHER READING

Akers, Donna L., "Killing Winged Celia: Race and Culture in Indian Territory," in *Women on the North American Plains*, ed. Renee M Laegreid and Sandra K. Mathews, Texas Tech University, 2011, 190–205.
Davey, Monica, "As Tribal Leaders, Women Still Fight Old Views." *The New York Times*, February 4, 2006.
Garceau-Hagen, Dee, ed. *Portraits of Women in the American West*. New York: Routledge, 2005.
Jameson, Elizabeth, "Toward A Multicultural History of Women in the Western United States," *Signs: Journal of Women in Cultural and Society* 13 (Summer 1988): 761–91.
Jenson, Joan M. and Darlis Miller, "Gentle Tamers Revisited: New Approaches to the History of Women in the American West, "*Pacific Historical Review* 49 (May 1980): 173–213.
Learning to be an Anthropologist and Remaining "Native": Selected Writings of Dr. Bea Medicine. Edited with Sue-Ellen Jacobs. Urbana: University of Illinois, 2001.
Ruiz, Vicki L. and Ellen Carol DuBois, eds. *Unequal Women: An Inclusive Reader in U.S. Women's History*. New York: Routledge, 2000.
Schackel, Sandra K., ed. *Western Women's Lives: Continuity and Change in the Twentieth Century*. Albuquerque: University of New Mexico Press, 2003.

Introduction

Since time immemorial, American Indian women have held a special place within the families, villages, communities, and tribes of Native America. They have also contributed greatly to American history through their commitment to many political spheres of activity within the United States and the world. Thousands of years before the Spanish, Portuguese, English, French, Dutch, Swiss, Russians, and other newcomers arrived on the shores of Turtle Island, Native American women played important roles within all Indigenous communities and many Native nations. Tribal people of the Americas recognized women in their oral accounts of origins as creative actors who put the world into motion and kept it moving. Native Americans recognize the importance of women within their communities who serve others as teachers, philosophers, historians, storytellers, songwriters, singers, dancers, providers, artists, nurses, doctors, advisors, chiefs, architects, artists, masons, warriors, seamstresses, chefs, chemists, biologists, ministers, midwives, and many more fields of endeavor. Significantly, women have always served their people as political actors, not just as clan mothers among the Haudenosaunee but among many tribes whether or not they as patrilineal or matrilineal.

Women brought forth generations of children, raised them responsibly, and taught them correct behavior in accordance with tribal traditions. They were and are the mothers, grandmothers, aunts, nieces, and sisters within every Native American community. They passed on knowledge and wisdom to every new generation and kept the diverse cultures alive. Women served families as genealogists, ensuring that their families and people did not break incest laws that governed marriages intra- and inter-tribally. Women are honored in all Native American cultures and people within communities listened to and learned from women. Although the above narrative is cast in past tense, Native American women continue to perform many of these same functions within contemporary Indigenous worlds throughout the Native Universe of North, Central, and South America. The work found herein provides short exposés on a select number of American Indian women of the twentieth century who either grew up in the American West or influenced people of the region through their politics. Readers will readily recognize some of the women featured in this volume but will not know others. All of these women lived compelling lives in the twentieth century, contributing to the history of their Native nations as well as the history of the United States. Some of them are known internationally for their various contributions in several fields of endeavor.

Many women deserve recognition through a publication such as this, but we are limited by topic and space. The editors chose the women found herein as subjects to introduce a diversity of Indigenous women engaged in different forms of political activism. Their examples demonstrate the many ways American Indian women have contributed to the well-being of their people, state, and country. We did not intend to slight any person, any tribe, or area of political activism. We could only research and present a limited number of essays. Many activist Native American women are absent from this book. Knowing this, the editors hope that this presentation will encourage scholars, young and old, to research and publish new and groundbreaking studies of the significant women of Native America. Indigenous women in North American and around the world have not received the recognition they deserve and earned during their activist lives. Indigenous women have a lot to teach us through their experiences and work in the world of social justice. In part, historians have not recognized the contribution of Native American women, because of the emphasis on great men. In addition, too many scholars have only researched historical documents and have not engaged Native American communities and listened to their oral accounts. Too many scholars have not spent time working with Native Americans and participating in and working with the communities they research and write about. Anyone who has worked with tribal communities knows that American Indian women in every Indigenous community are highly significant to the political life of that tribe and past knowledge of the tribe. It has always been that way. We have knowledge of the place and power of women from the beginning of life on earth when women helped create the world and universe. They contributed greatly in establishing and teaching laws by which each Indigenous community has followed since the beginning of time.

Laws helped to order the daily life of Indigenous peoples and reflected their sacred beliefs. Among the Choctaw people and many tribes, laws rested on the consensus of tribal members and were not imposed by a "god" or revelation to a leader. To the Choctaws and other Southeastern Indigenous peoples, maintaining harmony and balance within their society and with other species was paramount. For example, the Choctaws believed that if they did not give proper thanks to animals for sacrificing their lives, the animal spirits might inflict disease on the people. Thus, each time a hunter killed an animal, the hunter had to ask the animal for pardon and give him thanks for providing food for the People. Choctaw hunters always sacrificed a piece of meat from the animal in the sacred Fire, dedicating it to the headman or *miko* of the animal's species.

Several tribes of the American West had similar rules when taking plant and animal life for food and medicine. Many times, when women drew water from a well, stream, or lake, she gave thanks to the water for its life-giving qualities, sometimes leaving a feather or other offering. Creation songs and narratives often provide accounts of the origin of rules of life, including blessings that must be given to plants, animals, and water before it is consumed. Creation songs often place women at the center of American Indian societies. Many examples exist, including the creation account of the *Nuwu* or Southern Paiute. According to Southern Paiute and Chemehuevi elders, *Hutsipamamau'u* or Ocean Woman descended from a sky world and began the creation process of the earth, plants, places, animals, waters, air, and humans. Using skin and oil from her thighs as well as mud from the bottom of a great ocean, she laid on the surface of these elements and stretched out lands that became the Native Universe from the tip of Tierra del Fuego to the Arctic Ocean. Aided by Coyote, Cougar, and Wolf, Ocean Woman formed the length and breadth of the Americas, shaping and contouring mountains, valleys, plateaus, hills, forests, islands, grasslands, lakes, rivers, oceans, and other geographical features of earth.

At the same time that Hutsipamamau'u formed the earth, a network of power known as *puha* encircled the globe, holding the world together and concentrating power in certain places where *puhagaants* or medicine people could access puha to be used in healing, government, hunting, gathering, war, and other pursuits by humans. Thus, with the arrival of Creator Ocean Woman, spiritual power came to earth so that people and animals could access and use it for many purposes. For Southern Paiute people, women may access this power to conduct political work important to them and their people. Southern Paiute say that this power exists today and contributes significantly to the power of people enabling them to contribute to the well-being of the *Nuwuvi* people.

Within diverse communities and for generations, activist women established their own spheres of influence in accordance to tribal laws or rules of life handed down at the beginning of time by creators. However, original roles of Indigenous women have expanded into many areas of political activism, which originated within American Indian communities thousands of years before the arrival of invaders. Women played activist roles within their own communities, contributing in many ways that colonizers did not see or understand. After 1492 and the arrival of Christopher Columbus, invading Europeans left written records of their impressions and observations of Native American women. They based some information on well-informed sources, while other descriptions emerged from ignorance or imaginations of non-Indians, especially men, who knew little about American Indian people. Right or wrong, the written records, including observations from explorers, traders, soldiers, missionaries, and others, provided scholars with the first "evidence" of Indigenous women and their history in North America. Explorers, traders, soldiers, and settlers arrived in the Western Hemisphere with their own preconceived views of the Indigenous peoples based on the patriarchal societies of Europe, which distorted their observations, making it necessary for modern scholars to correct for their biases. Written evidence must, therefore, be used with caution and an understanding of European beliefs at the time, in order to critically analyze and sift through these accounts for useful information.

Some historical accounts portrayed Native American women in a positive light. However, many other accounts depicted Indigenous women in negative ways, offering writings filled with biased, judgmental descriptions of Native American women as drudges. Men from Western European countries treated women from Europe unequally, especially after the Reformation when Protestants sought to undermine elements of equality found in the guilds and wills of Medieval people. Most non-Indians traveling through or settling Indian Country brought with them their Christian biases about Indigenous families, women, "sin," and gender norms that created unequal gender relations in Euro-American societies and families. Christian rules of hierarchy made the subjugation of Indigenous women a necessary part of their writings. Explorers, traders, and soldiers exhibited their own biases when reporting on the everyday lives of Indian people, especially Indian women. Settlers sought to force Indian people to conform with the norms of "civilized" Euro-American society.

Euro-Americans often provided false impressions, uninformed judgments, and inaccurate written accounts about Native American women, which emerged not from reality but from the social, intellectual, and religious biases of newcomers. Settlers and writers used the written word as their historical truths and the historical record has been accepted uncritically by modern scholars without knowing and learning from Indigenous peoples of North America. Their written words became "evidence" that codified for their readers the lowly place of Indigenous women. As a result, documents confirming the insignificant place of American Indian women were not accurate but became part of the canon of conquest, which historians and others still use today. Non-Native men, most of whom could not speak Indigenous languages, wrote most of these biased accounts. They did not understand the division of labor of Native communities nor the gender roles of women and men in these communities.

Euro-American men came from societies that normally subjugated and deprived women of fundamental economic, social, and political equality. They stereotyped all Native American women as they had their own women. However, within Indigenous societies, traditional Native American women were equal to men and esteemed for their place and abilities as members of their communities. Most importantly, Indigenous men honored and valued women for their power in giving and sustaining life, which is often celebrated in creation songs and stories of heroic and powerful women.

European and American men often projected their own biases about American Indian women in their accounts, as if they presented "truths" and historical realities. Many records of Spanish, Dutch, Swiss, French, and English explorers denigrated American Indian women, relegating them as "squaws," as they passed through Indigenous homelands. They often provided false impressions about the role and stature of American Indian women. In the American West, non-Native newcomers passing through Indian Country often recorded that Native American women were weak, unattractive, backward, subservient, and lesser beings. In California, early newcomers referred to Indians as "diggers," a pejorative word akin to the N word but in reference to Native Americans. In sum, people of European descent often held Native American women in low regard, which reflected more about European men than realities about Native American women and their place within their communities and tribes.

Many non-Indian observers spent little time with Native Americans and had little experience living among tribal people of the Americas. Most did not understand the nuances of Native life and society. As a result, many negative views of Native American women exist in the historical record, and contemporary scholars and writers often repeat the older accounts without fully interrogating their sources or learning from contemporary tribal scholars. One such scholar claimed that contemporary Indian people could teach him nothing about the Spanish Mission system. Like this professor, scholars often fail to consult contemporary American Indian women and their communities as part of their assessments of the historical record, thus ignoring illuminating sources and Indigenous knowledge that might counter past historical narratives and biased interpretations. As a result, modern writers often perpetuate old falsehoods about Indigenous women. The role and place of Native American women in American society, past and present, requires a much more in-depth and nuanced analysis, which is the challenge for the next generation of scholars willing and unafraid to conduct community-based research among contemporary Native American women.

The present work offers short introductions to and biographical information about a select number of American Indian activists, all Indigenous women of the twentieth-century West or women that influenced the history of the West. The women selected for inclusion represent the world of politics and social justice. The women included in this work were or are people of action, accomplishment, organization, and energy. Some women included here were creators of movements and organizations. Others were activists primarily within Indian Country of the United States, but most served as political activists beyond the borders of reservations and Indian communities.

All of these women made a mark in the larger communities of the American West and the United States. Some of them influenced world history through their fight for social justice. All of them are prominent in their own right. Readers will come to know about each woman's life, elements of their activism, and their accomplishments. One purpose of this work is to bring forward the work of remarkable women and to ask readers to seek greater knowledge about these and other people and their contributions. Further, the editors hope contemporary and future scholars will research the lives of Indigenous women to write in much greater depth about them. We encourage future scholars to grow this research and share new knowledge about these women and many others who lived with character and distinction during the course of the twentieth century.

The lives and accomplishments of Native American women activists deserve greater examination and analysis. American Indian women and their activism, on and off reservations, and in numerous spheres of life deserve recognition. Indigenous women working on reservations and in urban areas have contributed to the well-being of their own people and others, regardless of race. All of the women presented in this volume are associated with the twentieth century, and the greater American West. The lives of some of these women sometimes overlapped with the nineteenth and twenty-first centuries. Thankfully, many of them are active today on local, state, and national scenes, continuing their contributions. They have given rise to many more young women who are contributing to the common welfare in the twenty-first century. No doubt, this trend will continue throughout the twenty-first century as activist Indigenous women are a growing and strong force on every level of politics and governments within the Western Hemisphere.

The early twentieth century brought a transitional period for Native Americans of the United States. The late nineteenth and early twentieth centuries corresponded with a time when settler colonialism and government policies destroyed American Indian economies and tribal organizations, and attempted to erase Native belief systems and languages. This era also marked a time when tribal people adjusted to wars, diseases, land theft, interventions, and anomie. The federal government attempted to confine all American Indians on reservations, sometimes forcefully removing people at gunpoint and forcing them to relocate to marginal lands. On reservations, the federal government hired non-Indian agents and Christian missionaries to regulate every aspect of Indigenous life from food to clothing, marriage to child rearing, and from ceremonies to Christian church service. Most of these agents sought to destroy Native American cultures, economies, languages, laws, religions—thus extinguishing every aspect of tribal life and replacing it with the institutions and values of the dominate society. In addition to the assimilationist programs brought by agents and missionaries to the reservation, federal agents and superintendents attempted to supplant the role of Native American women within tribes with the values and practices of the dominate society. Nowhere is this better seen than in the government's educational systems established by the United States.

Christian missionaries took the lead in establishing schools for Native American children during the colonial era and early nineteenth century. Missionaries schooled both boys and girls in mission schools. Baptists, Methodists, Catholics, and other denominations brought educational institutions to Indian Country. In 1879, Captain Richard Henry Pratt established the first federal off-reservation American Indian boarding school at Carlisle, Pennsylvania. Native American boys and girls attended this and the other off-reservation boarding schools during the late nineteenth and twentieth centuries. Assimilation became the central driving force at this school and all the federal Indian schools, where teachers and disciplinarians offered vocational education to Indigenous boys and girls with the objective of creating a national workforce of low-paid laborers. Reservation and non-reservation Indian schools taught basics in English, math, literature, history, and science, but more importantly, they also taught girls to be domestics, seamstresses, maids, babysitters, mothers, and nurses. Various churches allied with the federal government to establish and operate schools on reservations, especially the Catholic Church. At the Fort Yuma Agency of the Quechan Nation (Lower Colorado River), Catholic nuns established and ran the Fort Yuma Indian School, an on-reservation boarding school where children could see their homes in the valley located north of the huge hill where the school was located. Nuns trained girls to be subservient to God and men.

The Office of Indian Education incarcerated thousands of children for the purpose of cultural genocide, establishing a national project to destroy Indigenous cultures, languages, economies, religions, and traditions—including political traditions. At schools on and off reservations, educators tried to undermine the foundation of the Native Universe. Non-Indians purposely limited Indigenous horizons and opportunities for girls and women, training them in "domestic sciences" or home economics. Many girls used their education to better themselves and tried to help their families and their communities. At schools, they learned elements of public health, which helped them detect early symptoms of disease, such as tuberculosis, and actively had their families checked for the deadly disease. Some young women who had learned how to write English used their second language to provide the first written accounts by Native Americans to describe tribal lives and experiences. Through the written word, American Indian women writers, such as Mourning Dove and Zitkala-sa (Gertrude Bonnin), introduced readers to their Indigenous worlds, providing unique insights and interpretations about social, political, education, and economic issues from within American Indian communities of the American West. For the first time, Indigenous women provided accounts in writing, offering unique perspectives based on Indigenous knowledge. That tradition continues today. Women writers offer windows of understanding of Native American ways and cultures, works that we learn from today.

The twentieth century also witnessed a greater movement of Native Americans to urban areas where people sought job opportunities. The century saw the continued development of manufacturing in towns and cities of the West, offering new jobs for Native American men and women. The movement of Native Americans to urban areas sometimes was temporary, simply moving to a town or city to seek jobs and cash money. Sometimes the move to urban areas became permanent. Near Riverside, California, for example, Cahuilla Indians established Spring Rancheria, a small Indigenous community that housed American Indians who worked in the nearby town, farms, ranches, and citrus orchards for cash money. Once the Cahuilla could no longer survive from hunting, gathering, and farming in the deserts, mountains, and passes of the region, they went to work to earn minimum wages and eke out a living. Native American women worked on farms and ranches as well as managing their families. They cleaned houses, cared for children, cooked for other families, and did yard work to make ends meet. At the beginning of World War II, many Native American men and women served in the military of the United States, while other Indigenous women served the nation by working in the defense industry.

Native American women worked in defense plants during World War II. For example, Serrano-Cahuilla Martha Manuel Ormego (later, Martha Chacon) left her home on the San Manuel Indian Reservation near San Bernardino, California, to work in a defense factory in Los Angeles. Martha's mother watched her children during the week. Martha came home on weekends to be with her family. In this way, Martha earned money that helped her family survive during trying times. She is only one example of the many Indigenous women who worked away from their reservations to earn a living. After World War II, the federal government created American Indian relocation programs that encouraged Native Americans to leave their reservations and seek employment in the great cities of the United States, including New York, Chicago, Oklahoma City, Los Angeles, and Seattle. The movement of Native American women and men to cities did not sever their ties with their tribes, but it changed many lives and often expanded the loss of contact and immersion in their tribal communities. Women also entered cities temporarily for employment, but returned in the evening or on weekends to their homes on reservations.

The women addressed in this volume lived in a variety of places and influenced numerous spheres. They lived within reservations, Indigenous communities, or non-Indian communities. Many aspects of their lives, including their residences, changed dramatically over time. During the course of the early twentieth century, Native American clothing, tools, weapons, homes, and transportation systems changed. Most importantly, all Native American traditional economies failed as a result of white settlement, confinement to reservations, and destruction of species. Women changed with these new conditions, but women altered elements of their lives so that their families could survive. In their own way, every Indigenous woman served their people as activists by purposely changing elements of their daily lives in order to survive. At the same time, many women continued elements of their age-old tribal cultures and languages, passing on their heritage to those interested in knowing and learning. Women kept families together and engaged in their changed worlds. They earned money to feed and clothe their families. They also used their cultural foundations to lead their people in a rapidly changing political world on and off reservations. They adapted to changing times to advance their people by serving others, a cardinal tradition within Native American societies.

Many Native American women have kept Indigenous traditions alive through the oral tradition and the written word. They have used the English language to write about many subjects, including political activism. Through written and oral traditions, women recorded traditional Native American methods of solving conflicts, responsibilities, and commitment to preserving tribal sovereignty. All of these acts constitute activism. Women passed down past knowledge, which future generations used to perpetuate their cultures during the twentieth century. Other women used their cultures to provide innovations that reflected changing times and new innovations. Women served their communities as tribal council members, tribal chairs, and spokespeople.

They passed along memories, tribal laws, and activism that resulted in being Choctaw, Chickasaw, Wyandot, Delaware, Miami, Cherokee, Oto, Omaha, Lakota, Crow, Blackfeet, Nez Perce, Palouse, Lummi, Chinook, Modoc, Hupa, Ohlone, Mewuk, Navajo, Hopi, Tohono O'odham, Mojave, Chemehuevi, Cahuilla, Quechan, Serrano, Kumeyaay, etc. In other words, women taught younger generations how to be activist members of their particular tribe, band, village, and community. Women taught others about living a life of service.

For hundreds of years, women provided education for children and young people about ancient beliefs and commandments of life. Women taught children through practical experience, songs, and stories. Indigenous women have been activists since the time of each tribe's creation, and they have never stopped being activists, although most people know little about the activist roles of Native American women, especially in politics and government service. Women accomplished many activities of positive value to their families, communities, and tribes. Few people know the significant role Indigenous women have played in the modern world. It is our hope that this work introduces readers to a select few women who have made their mark through their activism in many politically oriented fields of endeavor. The authors of these vignettes hope the volume will encourage readers to dig deeper and learn more about the numerous accomplishments of Native American women who remain role models throughout Indian Country today.

In 1996, Clifford Trafzer and Donna Akers attended a meeting in Toronto—"The Meeting Place." They presented elements of their research at a meeting of the American Association for the History of Medicine. Wendat (Wyandot) scholars Eleonore Sioui and her son, Georges, of Wendake, Quebec, also attended the conference. Eleonore presented her research on Indigenous medicine ways and tribal sovereignty of her people. After the session, a group of participants enjoyed a meal together at a restaurant overlooking the wide expanse of Lake Ontario. During the meal, Dr. Sioui asked everyone sitting at the table for their attention. When the table went silent, Sioui pointed to a large picture window. From the table, everyone could see the beautiful shoreline of Lake Ontario. With a wave of her right hand, she explained, "our people used to cross Lake Ontario in a single voyage, never stopping." Men, women, and children set out across the wide lake, working their paddles hard and never stopping to make their journey across the waters before a storm swept them away. "Of course," she explained, "they had the help of *Aataentsic*. She watched over her children. She still does!"

Eleonore Sioui explained that she was a daughter of Aataentsic, just as every Iroquoian person was and is a child of the Woman that Fell From the Sky. Sioui said that Aataentsic was the ultimate mother and grandmother of the people, the spiritual matriarch of Iroquoian people who taught the people of their innate sovereignty. During Sioui's long life, the Wendat intellectual was an activist of her people and supported the sovereignty of all Indigenous people around the globe. She had worked in the eastern and western provinces of Canada as well as the American Southwest and Caribbean Islands. She shared her knowledge openly, explaining that if she did not explain the history and culture of her people, then others would likely misrepresent Wendat people. She explained that she had received her power, strength, energy, drive, dedication, and direction from Aataentsic, who played a major role in her life as a political activist, political advisor, and educator. She often served the First Nations people of Canada, United States, and Latin America. Sioui touched the lives of many people throughout North America from Canada to the Caribbean and from Quebec to California. She influenced the history of North America, working with Native Americans from many parts of the Canadian and American West.

Eleonore Sioui is but one of thousands of Native American women who contributed actively to a better understanding of Indigenous people of North America. Like so many American Indian activist women, she was best known for her work among Indigenous people, particularly the communities where she lived and worked. She was known as a generous and caring leader. She spent her life lifting up people and helping others along their paths. In that way, she was much like her contemporary, Lumbee activist and scholar Helen Maynor Scheirbeck. Like Sioui, Scheirbeck was from the eastern part of the United States, but her influence included many tribes and tribal people of the American West. She lived her life helping others, playing an important role in national American Indian Affairs, and allowing others to take the credit. Scheirbeck worked in Washington, DC, for many years—in the Senate of the United States, at the Department of Education, and at the Smithsonian's National Museum of the American Indian, where she directed public programming. In these capacities, Scheirbeck significantly influenced American Indian peoples of the American West.

Helen participated in a major gathering of Indians in Chicago in 1961, a political conference organized by Sol Tax. Helen joined a group of young Indians that included Vine Deloria Jr., that met with President John F. Kennedy to encourage the president to create a new and dynamic Native American agenda within the United States. Like many people who attended the Chicago Conference in 1961, Helen was a political, educational, and cultural activist. She supported American Indian self-determination and tribal sovereignty, enlisting the assistance of tribal leaders, presidents, cabinet members, senators, representatives, and various levels of governments. At every turn, Helen worked for the benefit of Native Americans, not her own ego. She worked for the Senate, Bureau of Indian Affairs, and Department of Education. Other women followed Helen's example, like Suzan Shown Harjo, who refused to advocate quietly behind the scenes but used the power of the pen, her razor-sharp mind, and her winning personality to fight for political, social, and cultural justice for American Indian people. In doing so, Harjo fought for the rights and liberties of all people, especially American Indians. Harjo has spent her life fighting misinformation, misunderstanding, and misrepresentations of Native Americans. She has long championed the fight against stereotypes exhibited by sports teams and school mascots. Suzan Shown Harjo has brought greater awareness of significant issues facing Native Americans, and she has made lasting changes to benefit Indian Country.

In recent years, people have come to know about the life and work of Wilma Mankiller. She was a Cherokee woman of distinction who served her people as the first female Principal Chief of the Cherokee Nation of Oklahoma. In 1969, Mankiller had participated in the Indian occupation of Alcatraz Island, and she turned her political activism into a desire to serve her people. Like so many American Indian women, she refused to allow ugly stereotypes about Native American women as backward, subservient, and shameless "squaws" to get in her way of personal and communal advancements of Cherokee and other Indigenous people, especially women. Like other American Indian women, Mankiller developed into a public servant. She demonstrated her activism in many areas, particularly political leadership. She became an effective writer and powerful speaker. She followed a trail of political activism led by Mohawk Molly Brant, Paiute Sarah Winnemucca, and Yankton Sioux Zitkala. Wilma Mankiller was one of many contemporary women activists.

The general public of North America may know of some Native American women, especially those working on a national level, but most people will have limited knowledge about these important women. People around the globe have virtually no understanding of contemporary American Indian women generally and less about activist Indigenous women of the American West. Thus, the present volume introduces a select group of Native American women to those interested in the lives and works of Indian America. Many contemporary people have heard of Pocahontas, Sacajawea, and Wilma Mankiller, but few people could name other inspiring Indigenous women such as Mary Ann Andreas, Cindi Alvitre, Lorene Sisquoc, Barbara Lyons, Celeste Townsend, Reba Fuller, Carol Ray, Lorena Dixon, Barbara Drake, Juana Mahjo, Georgiana Sanchez, Lynn Valbuena, Audrey Martinez, or Patricia Dixon. Yet, within every American Indian community of the twentieth century, women have taken leadership roles in a number of activities and fields. We would need multiple volumes to recognize the political activism of the thousands of activist Native American women of the American West.

Their contributions during the twentieth century have been highly significant to the history of the American West. In sum, they are too numerous to mention in one volume. As a result, we offer vignettes of women from many different tribes, worlds, and activities.

American Indian women of the American West expressed political activism through their written works. Lakota activist Beatrice Medicine from Standing Rock emerged as an accomplished anthropologist, but she was always a political activist and professional educator. Assiniboine activist, educator, and writer Kathryn Shanley continues her work in a variety of venues to advance Indian issues and people, just as Cheyenne scholar Henrietta Mann does from her position as a professor and director of American Indian Studies at the University of Montana. Cherokee Diane Glancy, Okanagan Jeannette Armstrong, Chickasaw Linda Hogan, and Spokane Gloria Bird have taught in several institutions and worked as educators for many years, but they are best known for their political activism through their writings in Native American Studies.

Winnemem Wintu Caleen Sisk-Franco continues to use spiritual medicine to help her people, at the same time, advocating politically and through various art forms to preserve Indigenous culture, language, medicine, religion, and landscapes. Flora Jones passed on the mantle of spiritual medicine to Sisk-Franco, who in turn used her personal and communal power to inform the public of political matters affecting her tribe and other Native Americans living in Northern California in the shadow of Mount Shasta. Echoing the words and actions of Sisk-Franco, women leaders throughout California and elsewhere extend their reach to the public through modern media, including documentary films. She used the rich oral traditions and accomplished oratory of her people to share political messages in opposition to raising Shasta Dam. Like other Native American leaders, Maria Pearson also used her gift of oratory and sharp wit to protect Native American human remains and material items found in graves disturbed by construction crews and archaeologists.

Born into the Yankton Sioux tribe, Maria Pearson or *Hai-Mecha-Eunka* (Running Moccasins) grew up under the influence of her grandmother, who taught Maria to stand up for others and fight the good fight for justice. While living in Iowa in 1971, she learned that construction crews improving U.S. Route 34 had excavated graves in an old cemetery, including those of Native Americans. While state archaeologist Marshall McKusich had most of the remains removed and reburied to another cemetery, he ordered a grave holding the remains of a mother and baby to be shipped to his office in Iowa City. This particular burial of mother and baby contained many items buried with the pair, including a profusion of beads and other items. When Maria learned of this action, she demanded the repatriation of the woman, child, and grave items. She took her activism to the state capital where she met Governor Robert Ray who agreed to help Pearson return the remains and goods to the earth. Not satisfied with the governor's promise, Pearson asked the Iowa State Legislature for help, which resulted in the politicians ordering McKusich to rebury the remains of the mother, baby, and grave items. Pearson's efforts led to the state passing the Iowa Burials Protection Act in 1976, which led Pearson into national politics. Working with Senators Ben Nighthorse Campbell and Daniel Inouye, she and others introduced and passed in 1991 the national Native American Graves and Repatriation Act (NAGPRA). Pearson is not well known today, but her life led to the protection of American Indian human remains and patrimony that continues to guide the nation today.

Many of the women presented in this volume learned from their elders and drew on the historical strength of their people and other American Indians to create new political directions for the benefit and delight of Native Americans and non-Indians alike. During the twentieth century, they worked through political activism, offering new visions, experiences, and promises to American Indians and peoples of all nations. They refused to allow others to stereotype them or keep them hemmed into a cultural box defined by non-Indians. Instead, they lived their lives to improve the lives of others. American Indian women used many methods to accomplish their goals. In the early 1990s, for example, Muscogee Creek Joy Harjo presented a lecture at Lund University in Sweden. Before engaging in her talk, she opened a large black case, exhibited her saxophone, strapped the instrument over her shoulder, and began to play a dramatic jazz tune. After finishing her musical number, she provided a moving lecture that emphasized tribal sovereignty and self-determination.

Like Joy Harjo, the women presented here did not and would not allow others to define them and their work. Native American women refused to be stereotyped by others. American Indian women have been thinkers and doers for thousands of years. The women represented in this volume provide only a small sample of Indigenous women of the West and their chosen forms of activism. The editors hope that students in the future will take a greater interest in the lives and works of Native American women and add to the growing scholarship about these remarkable women. The editors selected the women found in this volume as examples, knowing that many, many American Indian women activists of the American West would not be included. Whether or not particular American Indian women appear in this short work, Native American women throughout the West and within Indian Country in the twentieth century made a difference by preserving, changing, and innovating the art of politics.

Like the female characters found in creation narratives, Indigenous women throughout the United States and the Western Hemisphere have continued the process of creation through many forms of activism. Native American women of the American West contribute through their unique identities, deep knowledge, communal courage, and collective acts of political activism. Like the ancient female heroes found in the songs and stories, Native American women of the twentieth-century West acted like the old heroes. They acted out of concern for others, not their own egos. They acted for the benefit of others and the betterment of the Native Universe. They left a legacy that informed the contemporary political activism of Debra Anne Haaland, a member of Laguna Pueblo and the United States House of Representatives, and Sharice Davids, a member of the Ho-Chunk Nation and House of Representatives. In 2021, President Joe Biden appointed Laguna Indian Representative Debra Haaland Secretary of Interior, the first Native American to hold a cabinet position. Native American women of the twentieth-century West set the bar high, and they encouraged young tribal women to reach far beyond the accomplishments of the past, urging them to look to the future.

Chapter One

Red Power in the Northwest

Ramona Bennett
(b. 1938)

Vera Parham

The 1960s and 1970s were a dramatic and dynamic time for Native Americans of the Pacific Northwest. They were a time of revival, protest, and acknowledgment. They were a time when racism was still rampant, but the struggle against racism made a difference. It was a time when the youth took up the mantle of their parents in the struggle to retain Indian identity and tradition. It was a time when the terrible toll of Anglo American immigration, federal programming, poverty, and poor healthcare came to light through the press coverage of the Red Power Movement. Throughout these struggles of the late twentieth century, a handful of great leaders stand out as the builders of powerful movements, the elected representatives of their people, and the inspiration for many who would come after them. Ramona Bennett is one of these leaders. From the American Indian Women's Service League in Seattle, to the fish-ins of the Nisqually and Puyallup and the Survival of the American Indian Association, to election as chairwoman of her Puyallup tribe, to the Fort Lawton takeover of 1970, to the Seattle Bureau of Indian Affairs Office occupation of 1972, to engineering the Cushman Medical Hospital occupation in 1976, to co-founding the Indian Child Welfare Act Committee of the Pacific Northwest, Bennett's career in activism has been long, far-reaching, and successful.

Ramona Bennett was born in 1938 in Seattle, Washington, to a strong family. Her Puyallup grandfather had been an advocate for the tribe, working to protect the dwindling lands and resources of the reservation near Tacoma, Washington.[1] Her Puyallup mother was forced into boarding schools, away from her home, family, and heritage. Ramona watched her mother fight the discrimination surrounding her and Ramona, with her mother forced to use the woods as a bathroom instead of many restaurant restrooms around Tacoma due to policies and signs reading "no Indians or dogs." Ramona's white father was a hardworking union activist.[2] Bennett attended public schools in Seattle but always felt like an "odd duck" due to her differences from the dominant society.[3] After high school, she left Seattle for Olympia where she attended Evergreen State College gaining her bachelor in liberal arts. She then returned to the land of the Puyallups and the city of Tacoma to attend the University of Puget Sound where she gained her master's degree in education. During her years in college, Bennett also worked with various Native American groups attempting to improve the lives of urban Indians. In the 1950s Ramona Bennett began volunteer work at the Seattle American Indian Women's Service League. It was during this time that she realized her true life calling was to struggle for Indian rights and quality of life. In order to achieve this goal and be closer to her people, Bennett moved back to the Puyallup reservation.

Ramona came of age in the Puyallup tribe in a dire time. The tribe had little to no land remaining, the council had little power, and there were no services available for tribal members. Many tribal members lived in abject poverty and housing was substandard for those who managed to retain homes or lands on the shrinking reservation. The industrial town of Tacoma may have had jobs to offer, but the Puyallups faced racism and an economy that otherwise fluctuated heavily. Most of the Puyallups were isolated on their small remaining plots of land and abandoned by a government that offered few services to a tribe they assumed no longer existed.

In 1968 the people elected Ramona Bennett to the Puyallup Tribal Council. Ramona had driven her mother to a meeting and realized how her skills and determination could greatly benefit the tribe. During her years on the council, she worked hard to gain the support of congressmen and women for bills that would support the Puyallups with recognition and legal protections. She traveled to Washington, DC, incessantly, in one year making over thirty trips, and often hitchhiking to get there due to lack of funds. In 1971, she was elected chairwoman and served in that capacity until 1978, fighting through gender bias to become one of the first modern female chairwomen of a tribal council.[4]

One of the rights that Bennett worked hard to protect, due to its economic and spiritual importance for Puyallup fishermen and women, was the right to fish. In 1855, the Puyallups had been party to the Treaty of Point Elliott, which reserved for the tribe the right of "taking fish at usual and accustomed grounds and stations" and which "further secured to said Indians [that right] in common with all citizens of the Territory."[5] Throughout the twentieth century this right had been slowly chipped away through legal protections of fishing, mostly the enforcement of fishing licenses (which Native Americans were not legally required to have) as well as through environmental concerns and the encroachment of white fishermen onto Indian lands. The final stroke came when the state of Washington banned trap fishing, which was the Puyallup's main method of fishing. As enforcement officers from the Washington State Department of Fish and Game began to arrest and harass Indian fishers on the Puyallup River, a new method of resistance was born, that of the fish-in. At a fish-in, groups of Indian fishermen from all across the state would gather at locations where Indians had previously been arrested for fishing without licenses or for trap fishing, and which they considered usual and accustomed places, and there they would fish until they too were arrested. The fish-ins took their inspiration from the Civil Rights sit-ins occurring at the same time, but they were born out of a much earlier history as protection and retention of Native American rights and culture. Fishing, the protection of treaty rights, and opposition to state regulation and control of fishing were about more than the access to fish. They were about identity. Not only did the fish-ins reaffirm an older traditional American Indian identity based around fish, but they created a new identity of urban activists who utilized direct confrontation through the courts and the media to promote Native American rights on a national scale. Ramona Bennett reminded the press that her people did not fish to protest, "we fish as a way of life."[6] The harassment by the Department of Fish and Game was not only an attack on Indian economic rights and livelihood of Pacific Northwest Native Americans, it was an attack on their identity. And Ramona Bennett was fighting to protect both of those things.

In the early years of the fish-in protests, Ramona Bennett came together with Janet McCloud and others to help found the Survival of the American Indians Association (SAI) in 1964. The SAI worked to organize fish-in protests for the Nisqually and Puyallup. They also edited and distributed a newsletter that told the Indian side of the fish-ins story to the broader public. The SAI also helped raise funds to bail fishermen and women out of jail and provide them with legal council and defense in court.[7] The SAI represented the more militant stand against fishing encroachment and for the protection of treaty rights. However, SAI garnered more and more press each year. They may have been using tactics like fish-ins, that some found distasteful, but they were working for the preservation of tradition and a way of life. Eventually, Hank Adams, a Assiniboine Sioux and leader from the National Indian Youth Council, joined the SAI and helped steer the protests in a new direction.

In 1963 Bennett and Adams took a new action in support of the fish-ins, organizing a demonstration at the Washington State Capital in Olympia. In a stunning show of unity, two-thousand protesters showed up, as well as Charles Kuralt from CBS.[8] Bennett and Adams made huge strides in gaining the attention of the federal government, the press, and the public. They helped secure the financing to research and publish the American Friends Service Committee study, *Uncommon Controversy*, which garnered international support for the struggle, and they helped oversee the creation of three documentary films on the fishing rights struggle, and the importance of treaties for Indian rights and identity, including *As Long as the Rivers Run,* directed by Carol Burns, which was shown in Europe and the Soviet Union as well as on CBS in America. The SAI privately sold the film to help finance their activities.[9]

Throughout the 1960s, state and federal officials increased the number of arrests of Indian fishermen in Tacoma. In response, Bennett set up an armed camp on the banks of the Puyallup River. On September 9, 1970, police raided that fishing camp with tear gas and clubs. Law enforcement arrested almost sixty people from various Indian nations for fishing without permits and for resisting police. The police also destroyed the camp and fishing equipment there. In response, numerous white fishermen took their cue and began invading individual Indian fishing camps and destroying them.[10] The Puyallups moved back to their camp, to be forced out again by the theft and vandalism of many of their goods by white fishermen. Camp residents faced trial and long, tough sentences. But before they went to court, the Bureau of Indian Affairs recognized Puyallup lands with their original 1857 and 1873 boundaries and all those arrested, including Ramona Bennett, were discharged because the Indians were fishing on reservation lands and so under treaty rights.

Not only did the fish-ins and the Survival of the American Indian Association pressure the United States to recognize Puyallup lands, protesters forced the government to recognize the treaty rights of the tribe. The dramatic turn in events for Pacific Northwest Indian fishing rights came in 1974 with the decision of Judge George Boldt in *United States v State of Washington* (384 F. Supp. 312 [1974]). The case was initially brought against the state in an attempt to halt the arrests of Indian fishermen and women and to have the state acknowledge the treaty fishing rights of Pacific Northwest tribes. The case was brought by thirteen Western Washington tribes and the federal government. Judge Boldt's final decision was handed down on January 11, 1974.[11] In a surprise move, Judge Boldt used his decision to vindicate the Puyallup Tribe. He threw out claims by the Department of Game that the Puyallup tribe was no longer a legitimate entity and upheld the treaty status of the Puyallup. He ruled that any seizure of gear including boats and nets that had been taken during the fishing rights struggle was illegal and must be returned. But his biggest pronouncement came when he decided that the treaty phrase, "in common with" meant divided equally with. This meant not only that the licensing and arrests of Native American fishermen and women would have to stop, it also meant that the Departments of Fish and Game would have to regulate fishing to ensure 50 percent of the region's fish were able to spawn upriver at or near Indian fishing locations. Over the next years, Bennett continued the fight to ensure that the Puyallup were able to harvest as much of their fair share as possible as well as working with the tribal council to improve environmental conditions in the area and to clean up the waterways.

Ramona Bennett's efforts did not go unnoticed by outsiders. In 1972, during the *U.S. v Washington* proceedings, Harry Sachse, the Justice Department lawyer assigned to present the oral argument for the tribes in the Boldt case, traveled to Tacoma to meet the Puyallup and Nisqually tribes. He immediately felt a powerful presence in the region after meeting Ramona Bennett, and he described the Puyallups as a "tribe with hardly anything except a treaty, tradition of fishing, and a fighting spirit."[12] Bennett would take that fighting spirit that she had first developed at the University of Puget Sound, had honed through the fish-ins, and bring it to the struggle to win urban lands for a cultural and education center for urban Indians in Seattle, Washington.

Seattle had a large Indian population, but little to no services available for them. Issues with homelessness and joblessness also abounded in Seattle. In order to remedy this situation, Bernie Whitebear, a *Sin-Aikst* activist from the Colville reservation decided to follow the example of the 1969 Alcatraz occupation and take over and claim unclaimed federal lands. He did so in behalf of Indian people. The opportunity arose when the majority of Fort Lawton lands, just outside the city of Seattle, were declared surplus in 1968. The American Indian Women's Service League had also hoped for the land, but wished to continue pushing through the bureaucracy and not to become involved in a more militant protest. So, Bernie gathered the more supportive element, like Bob Satiacum, Joe De La Cruz, and other fish-in activists like Ramona Bennett, to himself and began planning their "re-occupation."

The day of the first attempt on Fort Lawton came in March of 1970. On that day Ramona Bennett drove as part of a caravan of protesters right up to the gates of Fort Lawton and helped supporters like Jane Fonda clamber onto fort lands. Once on the lands the protesters fanned out, hoping to find places to camp and occupy. However, they were quickly met by Military Police who rounded up the protesters and threw them into the stockades before expelling them from the fort. On April 2, 1970, the fort was again stormed and seventeen more persons were arrested by the Military Police and detained on the fort grounds. Those arrested included many well-known Native American activists including Grace Thorpe, Robert Satiacum, Bernie Whitebear, Leonard Peltier, Sid Mills, and Valerie and Allison Bridges.[13] Many of these activists, including Bennett, would become the core members of the United Indians of All Tribes, the incorporated foundation working to win the Fort Lawton lands. After numerous more attempts to occupy Fort Lawton, and further arrests, the protesters packed in the protest and moved on to lobbying congressmen and city council members to win the fort land. Eventually the tenacity of Ramona Bennett and Bernie Whitebear gained the attention of the mayor of Seattle and nineteen acres of land as well as funding for building a cultural and educational center known as Daybreak Star were granted to the United Indians of

All Tribes. Daybreak would go on to provide educational and career services as well as elder care to Native Americans across Washington State.

Not long after the fish-ins began to wind their way to the courtroom in the mid 1970s and negotiations on construction of Daybreak were being thrashed out, other protests were breaking out in Seattle. Ramona Bennett, by now the Chairwoman of the Puyallup Tribal Council, organized a protest on the Cushman medical grounds (Cascadia Juvenile Diagnostic and Treatment Center) in Tacoma to demand better health coverage and benefits for Native Americans. The Cushman hospital had originally been built in 1939 on lands sold by the Puyallup as an Indian hospital to service the local Native American community.[14] On Saturday August 11, 1973, the planned occupation looked as if it would fizzle with only a few demonstrators showing up. But Ramona Bennett and other leaders erected tents of occupation and spoke to the press about Indian health issues and needs. Soon they were joined by many other supporters and protesters. Finally in 1980, a federal judge ordered the United States to return the hospital and the property to the Puyallup tribe. Today the Puyallup run their own health clinic as well as an alcohol and drug treatment center and a mental health center.

Bennett was not just an activist. She was also a well-loved mother and mentor. Her own family grew over the years and included both biological and adopted children, reflecting her work in preserving Indian family life. In 2008, her house is open to all friends and relatives. Bennett supports her extended family in numerous ways. In 1972, Ramona Bennett co-founded the Local Indian Child Welfare Act Committee. By 1978, she translated the work of the committee into the National Indian Child Welfare Act, which was passed in 1978. The act helps keep Native American families together by placing orphaned and foster Native American children with families from their own or close tribes and by providing services for families struggling to stay together in times of need.

The 1980s ushered in a new era for Ramona Bennett who focused on Indian education. Bennett was concerned about providing Indian history and perspective to Native American students that offered American Indian voices and documents. She served as administrator for the Wa-He-Lut Indian School (a K–8 school created by the Nisqually community during the fish-ins) in Olympia. She also traveled on speaking tours to local public schools, educating students on Native American history. Bennett also worked to create programs on the reservation and for poor children in the area to provide after-school activities for them like sports, writing workshops, and art classes.

Ramona Bennett was also concerned about keeping Indian families together. In the 1980s, she founded the Rainbow Youth and Family Services nonprofit in Tacoma, which she is still the director of. The Rainbow Youth and Family Services works to place Native American foster and adoptee children in Native American homes, in order that they may retain their history and culture as well as connection with their people.

Today the Puyallup tribe hosts an enrollment of over one thousand members, and they have a thriving casino business and have worked hard to clean up the waterways around Tacoma to improve their fishing businesses. Ramona Bennett has been instrumental in building tribal capacity and has worked to provide health and education on the reservation. She has watched the tribe's budget grow from almost nothing to nine million dollars annually In addition, the tribe now has a workforce of over three-hundred people. She has helped grow reservation lands and worked for years for Puyallup rights.[15] Ramona Bennett made many of these gains possible. In 2003, the Native Action Network honored Bennett with the Enduring Spirit Award for her time spent creating and preserving Native culture and lifestyles. Her work and dedication to tribal rights lives today as does her voice: "it is a new day, with new opportunities. Despite all the things that have happened to my tribe, I believe there is hope. Our children are our bright and shining stars. With each child, the promise is reborn."[16]

NOTES

1. "Ramona Bennett," Gretchen M. Batailles, Laurie Lisa, eds. *Native American Women: A Biographical Dictionary* (New York: Routledge, 2001), 30.

2. Ramona Bennett, "Bennett: Working for Tomorrow," *Indian Country Today*, January 6, 2006.

3. "Bennett, Ramona," Liz Sonneborn, ed. *A-Z of Native American Women* (New York: Facts on File, 1998), 122.

4. "Bennett, Ramona," 122.

5. Charles J. Kappler, ed., *Indian Affairs: Laws and Treaties* 2 (Washington, DC: Government Printing Office, 1927), 669, Article 5, Treaty of Point Elliott. http://www.fws.gov/Pacific/ea/tribal/treaties/Dwamish_Suquamish.pdf.

6. *The Renegade*, June 1972.

7. Alvin M. Josephy Jr., *Now That the Buffalo's Gone: A Study of Today's American Indians* (Norman: University of Oklahoma Press, 1984), 193.

8. Charles Wilkinson, *Messages From Frank's Landing: A Story of Salmon, Treaties and the Indian Way* (Seattle: University of Washington Press, 2000), 44.

9. *The Renegade*, June 1972.

10. Native American Solidarity Committee, *To Fish in Common: Fishing Rights in the Northwest* (Olympia: Native American Solidarity Committee, 1978), 17.

11. *United States of America v. State of Washington*, February 12, 1974.

12. Charles Wilkinson, *Blood Struggle: The Rise of Modern Indian Nations* (New York: W.W. Norton and Co., 2005), 199.

13. Karen Smith, "United Indians of All Tribes Meets the Press: News Coverage of the 1970 Occupation of Fort Lawton," Seattle Civil Rights and Labor Project website.

14. Open letter from Ramona Bennett, Hank Adams Collection, Frederick T. Haley Papers, Box 81 Folder 5. Seattle: University of Washington Special Collections.

15. Bennett, "The Puyallup Tribe Rose from the Ashes" in Jane Katz, ed., *Messengers of the Wind* (New York: Ballantine Books, 1995), 160.

16. Bennett, "The Puyallup Tribe Rose from the Ashes," 160.

BIBLIOGRAPHY

Bennett, Ramona. "Bennett: Working for Tomorrow." *Indian Country Today*, January 6, 2006.

"Ramona Bennett." Gretchen M. Batailles, Laurie Lisa, eds. *Native American Women: A Biographical Dictionary*. New York: Routledge, 2001.

"Bennett, Ramona." Liz Sonneborn, ed. *A-Z of Native American Women*. New York: Facts on File, 1998.

Bennett, Ramona. "The Puyallup Tribe Rose from the Ashes." Jane Katz, ed., *Messengers of the Wind*. New York: Ballantine Books, 1995.

Josephy, Alvin Jr. *Now That the Buffalo's Gone: A Study of Today's American Indians*. Norman: University of Oklahoma Press, 1984.

Kappler, Charles J., ed. *Indian Affairs: Laws and Treaties*. Volume 2. Washington, DC: Government Printing Office, 1927. Treaty of Point Elliott.

Native American Solidarity Committee. *To Fish in Common: Fishing Rights in the Northwest*. Olympia: Native American Solidarity Committee, 1978.

Open letter from Ramona Bennett, Hank Adams Collection, Frederick T. Haley Papers, Box 81 Folder 5. Seattle: University of Washington Special Collections.

Smith, Karen. "United Indians of All Tribes Meets the Press: News Coverage of the 1970 Occupation of Fort Lawton." Seattle Civil Rights and Labor Project website.

The Renegade, June 1972.

Treaty of Point Elliott, Article 5, Charles J. Kappler, ed., Indian Affairs: Laws and Treaties 2 (*United States of America v. State of Washington*, February 12, 1974).

Wilkinson, Charles. *Blood Struggle: The Rise of Modern Indian Nations*. New York: W.W. Norton and Company, 2005.

Wilkinson, Charles. *Messages from Frank's Landing: A Story of Salmon, Treaties and the Indian Way*. Seattle: University of Washington Press, 2000.

FURTHER READINGS

Katz, Jane, ed. *Messenger of the Wind: Native American Women Tell Their Life Stories*. New York: Ballantine Books, 1995.

Thrush, Coll. *Native Seattle: Histories from the Crossing-Over Place*. Seattle: University of Washington Press, 2007.

Chapter Two

Being Mary Crow Dog: It Isn't Easy

Mary Crow Dog
(b. 1954–d. 2013)

Renae M. Bredin

"I am a woman of the Red Nation, a Sioux woman. That is not easy," Mary Crow Dog once proclaimed. Many would argue that the life and work of Mary Crow Dog, author of the as-told-to autobiography *Lakota Woman,* speaks to the heart of a woman's life as an activist and agent for social change. Others would take the opposite position, that Crow Dog/Lakota Woman speaks only to her own life, and that her most famous acts—giving birth at Wounded Knee and collaborating with Richard Erdoes to write her autobiography in two volumes—produced no social change. For some scholars and activists, her autobiography has harmed more than helped in representing Lakota cultural practices and the conditions of American Indians across the United States. Whatever position you take in reading Mary Crow Dog's life, her self-identified work as an activist[1] on behalf of Native American sovereignty, rights, and humanity make her story an important life's work.

    Mary Crow Dog is the coauthor of two as-told-to autobiographies, *Lakota Woman* and *Ohitika Woman*. Ted Turner and Jane Fonda made a movie from her book, also called *Lakota Woman*. She was an extra in Oliver Stone's movie *The Doors*. She was a member of the American Indian Movement in the 1970s, during which she participated in the Trail of Tears march on Washington in 1972 at sixteen years of age. She took part in AIM's occupation of Wounded Knee on the Pine Ridge Reservation. During that event, she gave birth to her first son, Pedro, and shortly after the occupation ended, she married Leonard Crow Dog, the spiritual leader of AIM. As the wife of a medicine man, she was deeply engaged in the traditional Lakota community, and during this time, she also became a member of the Native American church and a follower of the peyote way. She later married Rudi Olguin, a Chicano from New Mexico, and had two children with him.

These are the biographical bones of a life much richer and more deeply lived than is apparent on the surface, and a life lived through the stages of a journey that is reflected in the many different names by which Mary Crow Dog has been known. This essay is divided into sections reflecting the different aspects of her life story. It is through the stages of her naming that her activism emerges, recedes, and re-asserts its presence.

MARY MOORE

This is not a name that Mary Crow Dog takes up or claims in any of her autobiographical writings. It was her childhood name, the one she used up to and through her early years as an activist in the American Indian Movement. I use this name to frame the first section of this essay on her early life as a way of marking the first stage of the very heterogeneous nature of Brave Bird's life and work. She was born in 1953 on the Rosebud Reservation in South Dakota. Her mother, Emily Brave Bird, was married to Bill Moore, a mixed-blood Indian and white man, who absented himself from the family when Mary was a year old. She had three sisters, Kathie, Barbara, and Sandra, and a brother, Robert. In order to support her children and earn a living, Mary's mother left the children with her parents and went back to school to be trained as a nurse, then moved to Pierre, South Dakota, to work. It was the closest location for a job, but it was about hundred miles away. During this period, while living with her grandparents, Brave Bird began the process of living in multiple worlds. With her mother, who refused to teach her Lakota language and culture, she lived in a world governed by the desire to be successful, which meant living a middle-class white life.

With her grandparents, she lived in the world of the elders, the ones still connected to a way of life and culture with a worldview grounded in a very different idea of success, but also built in a world of few resources and a great deal of love, as recounted in *Lakota Woman*. The conflicts that would continue to plague Brave Bird throughout her life were born here, in the heart of a Lakota family that included a mixture of Indian and white blood, but a family that refused to teach her Lakota, because it would not serve her well in the white world. Simultaneously, Mary's great aunt was a 'turtle woman,' a medicine woman with a positive connection to traditional Lakota ways of thinking. Also, she was born into a family that was somewhere inbetween the extended, connected traditional *tipospaye* (those who live together, as in an extended family based on clan and kinship relations, but also includes all their relations) and the alienated conditions of the nuclear white family structure.

Her mother was remarried some eight years later to a man who was a wino. Family conditions deteriorated, and during this period, Brave Bird learned to drink and steal, living like a bum, at the same time attending school at the St. Francis Mission boarding school on the reservation. Mary's mother had attended the same school, and had experienced some of the same harsh treatment and abuse that Mary then encountered. The stories she relates in her books about St. Francis reverberate with anger and resistance. Her reflections on her boarding-school days offers a narrative common to Indigenous people forced to learn and behave in white ways that are antithetical to their own beliefs about the world. Her memories of St. Francis include attempts to assimilate her and destroy her cultural identity and personal Indigenous sovereignty. Following a series of incidents that exposed the hypocrisy and injustice of the Catholic Church and state education policies on the Rosebud Reservation, Crow Dog recounts the end of her tenure at St. Francis. After defending a young boy in her class against the priest's unfair correction of his English, she was held after class for a bit of arm-twisting.

> He [the priest] twisted my arm and pushed real hard. I turned around and hit him in the face, giving him a bloody nose. After that I ran out of the room, slamming the door behind me. He and I went to Sister Bernard's office. I told her, "Today I quit this school. I'm not taking any more of this, none of this shit anymore. None of this treatment. Better give me my diploma. I can't waste any more time on you people."[2]

As early as her school days on the reservation, Crow Dog actively defended her people against a *wasicu* (Lakota term for crazy white people) system of exploitation, abuse, and racism, a defense she began when she helped organize a student newspaper at the school, the *Red Panther*.

MARY BRAVE BIRD

Mary Moore became Mary Brave Bird, but not until much later. However, as this is the name she uses in her autobiography, it will be the name that is used for her for the rest of this essay. After leaving school, the hobo life of drinking, partying, fighting, and stealing became her only life. By her own account, she wandered aimlessly, until she encountered members of the American Indian Movement (AIM) at a "powwow held in 1971 at Crow Dog's place after the Sun Dance."[3] This was the second time that she encountered Leonard Crow Dog, the man who would later become her husband and guide into a more traditional way of living as a Lakota woman. AIM was in its nascent stages, organized by a group of young Indian men determined to take on and draw attention to the injustices committed by the U.S. government and the racism practiced and preached in the white community. AIM members occupied Alcatraz and Mount Rushmore, protested at Plymouth Rock, and confronted archeologists at dig sites of American Indian graves, asserting a very particular version of civil rights under conditions of what AIM saw as occupied land. At age sixteen, Brave Bird participated in many of these actions. Her narrative records her growing political awareness as she recalls her actions through the eyes of a more experienced activist. Finally, in 1972, AIM led a nationwide caravan of Indians young and old on an expedition to Washington, DC, ostensibly to meet with Bureau of Indian Affairs administrators. This event, known as The Trail of Broken Treaties, became a precursor to the even more crucial occupation of Wounded Knee. Brave Bird participated in both protests.

At the heart of Brave Bird's personal story is her participation at age seventeen in the occupation of Wounded Knee. In 1973, members of AIM, traditionalists from the Pine Ridge Reservation, and American Indians from tribes all across the North American continent came together and took over a small community on the Pine Ridge Reservation in South Dakota. The site was hallowed ground, the place where in 1890 the Seventh Cavalry had massacred three hundred unarmed Indian women, children, and elders. The Wounded Knee massacre stands in history both as a final moment of the Indian wars in the colonial expansion of U.S. territorial ambitions and one of the deepest wounds to date in the long genocidal history of Indigenous peoples of the Americas. The roots of AIM's occupation of Wounded Knee are located in several increasingly egregious racist incidents in the late 1960s and early 1970s in the area surrounding Pine Ridge, and in the corrupt BIA puppet regime of the notorious Dickie Wilson, Sioux Tribal Chairman of Pine Ridge Reservation at the time. Wilson was pro-BIA and accused of neglecting his people.

When the caravan of AIM members, elders, and Pine Ridge residents drove past the BIA offices and headed towards Wounded Knee, no one fully appreciated the historical significance of what would soon transpire. Mary Brave Bird was seventeen years old, pregnant, and prepared to do her part in resisting both Wilson's corrupt regime and the U.S. government's racist policies and practices. "Mary Brave Bird, a Lakota teenager present at Calico, described her emotions when she realized they were about to take over Wounded Knee. It was, she said, 'an excitement choking our throats.'"[4] The occupation lasted for seventy-one days, while FBI agents, Dickie Wilson's tribal GOON squad, and local sheriffs blocked access, set up barricades, and opened fire on the approximately three hundred protestors inside the perimeter. Wounded Knee II became a focal point for Indian resistance to U.S. government policies and one of the final moments in AIM's most active period of resistance. Two young Indian men were killed during the occupation by government bullets, and Mary Brave Bird gave birth to her first child, Pedro.

Some of the same women from Pine Ridge who had been instrumental in organizing the takeover of Wounded Knee attended Pedro's birth. They were deeply involved in organizing the daily support that made it possible for three hundred AIM occupiers to survive on limited resources. Women were integral to the decision to occupy Wounded Knee. At the meeting between chiefs, community activists, and AIM members, Ellen Moves Camp, Gladys Bissonette, Lou Bean, and others spoke forcefully for the community to bring AIM to Pine Ridge. However, Brave Bird spends little time in *Lakota Woman* on these women and their contributions to the movement or to the occupation, a pivotal event in her life story and in the resistance movement as well.

When government snipers killed Buddy Lamont, one of the AIM resisters, just a few days after the birth of Pedro, Brave Bird left Wounded Knee to help his family plan the funeral. Although the government and the protesters reached an agreement that no arrest would follow the occupation, police took Brave Bird into custody, leaving baby Pedro in the arms of Buddy Lamont's sister Cheyenne. The government held Mary for twenty-four hours before her release. She refused to answer their questions, telling U.S. marshals interrogating her, "I did not talk to pigs."[5]

Mary Brave Bird and Leonard Crow Dog met again during the occupation of Wounded Knee. He gave her newborn son his Lakota name. Within a year after the protesters had agreed to leave, Crow Dog and Brave Bird married, and she moved to Leonard Crow Dog's family allotment, called Crow Dog's Paradise on the Rosebud Indian Reservation. Mary become the wife of a traditional Sioux medicine man and mother to her son, three of Crow Dog's children, and eventually three more children of their own. Finally, the U.S. government agreed to the demands of the resisters at Wounded Knee and then, like all other treaties made between the government and the Indians, the agreements were never fulfilled.

MARY CROW DOG

In the year following the occupation of Wounded Knee, Mary Brave Bird married Leonard Crow Dog and became Mary Crow Dog, mother not only to her own child, Pedro, but also to Crow Dog's three children, Ina, Bernadette, and Richard. At age eighteen, she began to learn traditional Sioux ways for the first time. She didn't know how to cook, make coffee, or talk Indian, and yet she became the central caretaker to a never-ending stream of visitors As a Sioux medicine man, Leonard Crow Dog was the spiritual leader of AIM. Mary reported, "Leonard is a medicine man as well as a civil rights leader. This means that we have ten times more guests than the usual Sioux household. The whole place is like a free hotel for anyone who cares to come through." She cooked, cleaned, cared for the children, and confronted the problems of an outsider entering the close-knit *tipospaye*. Crow Dog's parents and siblings were not welcoming because she was a "half-blood, not traditionally raised," and Brave Bird's family felt she was "going back to the blanket," or returning to traditional Sioux ways that her mother had rejected. "Here my family had struggled so hard to be Christian, to make a proper red, white, and blue lady out of me."[6] Instead, Mary worked at becoming a traditional woman.

At the same time that Brave Bird was learning to make coffee, she was also taking a new journey into Native American spiritual practices. As the wife of a medicine man, she observed, assisted in, and participated in ceremonial life. Road trips to conduct rituals and ceremonies, often without any money for food or gas, were a regular occurrence. Mary participated in the Sun Dance and the Ghost Dance and became an active participant in the Native American church, a follower of the peyote way. Becoming Crow Dog's wife brought Brave Bird into deeper connection to her own spirituality.

Brave Bird and Crow Dog had three children together; Anwah, June Bug, and Jennifer, bringing the total number of children in the house to seven, including Pedro, and Crow Dog's three children. At the same time, Leonard Crow Dog's duties and commitments as activist, healer, and spiritual leader meant that the family constantly traveled all over the country to conduct ceremonies, intervene on behalf of Native prisoners, and engage in the struggle of Indigenous communities for tribal rights. Without money or resources, jammed into old cars that broke down constantly, sleeping sometimes in the mansions of sympathetic rich white people and sometimes on the ground next to the car, Mary tried to feed and care for her children, support her husband in his work, and participate in "the movement" in meaningful ways. It was overwhelming. She describes the exhaustion of this time period in *Lakota Woman*, and again in *Ohitika Woman*. "I broke down. I got sick. I was down to ninety pounds. My body just collapsed."[7]

LAKOTA WOMAN

In 1975, Brave Bird and Crow Dog experienced the full weight of the U.S. government's hostility. The Federal Bureau of Investigation (FBI) descended on Crow Dog's Paradise with 185 men, including marshals, agents, and SWAT teams, arresting Crow Dog and others in the house, including Anna Mae Pictou-Aquash. Later, it was learned that the FBI had mistakenly stormed Crow Dog's home based on a false tip from Crow Dog's brother-in-law that Leonard Peltier was hiding there. Peltier had been accused of killing two FBI agents early that year. He was not there, although he had been days earlier. Crow Dog was ultimately convicted of charges stemming from the occupation of Wounded Knee. Crow dog was sentenced to twenty-three years in prison. In *Lakota Woman*, Mary described the trials as "farce."[8] Crow Dog was certainly not alone. Means, Banks, Camp, Holder, and Peltier: all were AIM members and most had been at Wounded Knee for the occupation and were among the hundreds of Wounded Knee veterans who were dragged into court in the two years following the occupation. One scholar argued that the government used "trumped-up charges that were later dropped" against as many of the AIM leaders as possible. "Though 92 percent of cases that made it to trial were won by AIM, the costs in money, time, jail time while awaiting trial, and movement energy were devastating."[9] Crow Dog's case was one such case.

Crow Dog was incarcerated in several jails, finally landing in the federal penitentiary in Lewisburg, Pennsylvania. At the invitation of Richard Erdoes, her collaborator on both as-told-to autobiographies, Mary moved to New York City in the late 1970s in order to be close enough to visit Crow Dog in Pennsylvania. She coordinated with his defense lawyers and helped garner public support for his release. As the public voice for Crow Dog, Mary "composed leaflets, talked to lawyers, newspapermen, organization heads, made tapes, held speeches, and took care" of her baby.[10]

It was during this time that Mary Brave Bird became Lakota Woman. While living with Erdoes and his wife, Jean, Erdoes suggested that her life story as an activist and an Indian woman might be interesting. He had previously published an as-told-to autobiography of John Fire Lame Deer, and his publisher was interested in another book "in that vein."[11] The two worked together, taping the conversations about Brave Bird's life, and then Erdoes "put the manuscript together like a jigsaw puzzle out of a huge mountain of tapes."[12] Once the book was complete, the editor refused to publish it because it did not fit with the idea of the mystical Indian currently fashionable. "He told me [Erdoes]: 'This book is much too radical. The political climate has changed. This radical shit is out. Mysticism is in. Make her into a female Don Juan! Make her into a witch. Make her fly through the air!'"[13] The collaborators on the project refused, and the book was forgotten until 1989 when Grove Press picked it up and published the manuscript. It became a bestseller.

The publication of *Lakota Woman* created, as M. Annette Jaimes noted, a bit of gender balance in the previous histories published about AIM and Wounded Knee, all of which had been written by men and were primarily about the men in the movement. Jaimes argued that the book presented a positive account of the ways in which AIM brought many alienated, disaffected and deculturated Indian youth to a strong sense of self-worth—proudly, self-consciously, and often angrily *Indian* in the assertion of their collective existence."[14] Jaimes further asserted that "*Lakota Woman* is a much needed and unparalleled . . . articulation of the woman's experience in AIM.[15]

Others, like Lakota scholar and activist Elizabeth Cook-Lynn, were less positive about the book's portrayal of Indian women. Certainly, if you are reading Richard Erdoes' latest, *Lakota Woman*, you must prepare for uninformed political discussion, "dishonest cultural and historical interpretation, and the vision of a woman more deeply committed to the reputation of her husband as a Sioux medicine man than to history or self."[16]

Cook-Lynn goes on to argue that it is "treaty rights" not the "civil rights" that underpins Crow Dog's narrative that are really at the heart of Indian activism.[17]

> there is little or no information given in this woman's story which assists in the examination of the *REASONS* for the Indian resistance in the sixties and seventies called the American Indian Movement. . . . There is absolutely no mention in the entire text of the Federal Indian Policy of the fifties which brought about the "Termination and Relocation" laws passed by Congress which decimated Indian communities and reduced Indian land holdings all over the country, dislocating thousands of people in an urbanization policy still going on.[18]

Much later, in a keynote address to the fifth annual American Indian Studies Consortium in 2005, Cook-Lynn has even harsher words for the co-authors of *Lakota Woman*:

> he's [Erdoes] the European photographer who made a star out of a half-breed teenager named Mary Moore, aka, Mary Crow-Dog. And all the while Lakota and Dakota matrons were saying, "No, no, no, she's not a role model for our daughters; she's like a concubine for the AIM leadership." But she became a star, thanks to Erdoes.[19]

Many other women participated in the occupation at Wounded Knee and in AIM, and as Danyelle Means, the niece of Madonna Phillips, one of the women at Wounded Knee, noted, their stories were invisible in the larger history of the movement. "All of the women in my family . . . were involved from the start [of the Indian resistance movement]. I wanted to know why there isn't any attention given to their involvement. Why were their stories absent from the history books?"[20] It might be argued that Brave Bird's lack of attention to other women in the movement, aside from Anna Mae Pictou-Aquash, helped to perpetuate this invisibility in the histories of the occupation. However, in her sequel to *Lakota Woman*, Mary returns to Wounded

Knee and addresses what was missing from *Lakota Woman*. She lists the names and contributions of several of the women who were central to the occupation and celebrates their strength and power.

Notable in Cook-Lynn's later critique of the book is her dismissal of Brave Bird as a "concubine" for AIM men. This piece of the puzzle is perhaps the most difficult to address. There is a long history of conflict over the question of the relationship between Native America women and feminist movements. For many Native women, tribal survival and sovereignty are critical, and a white version of gender equality fails to address these concerns. Mary expresses this conflict in the book. Noting the sexism rampant in the movement, Mihesuah describes Brave Bird's responses to this sexism:

> There is a curious contradiction in Sioux society, wrote Mary Crow Dog. "The men pay great lip service to the status women hold in the tribe. Their rhetoric on the subject is beautiful. . . . they always stood up for our rights—against outsiders!" But the reality within the compound at Wounded Knee differed: "We did the shit work, scrubbing dishes or making sleeping bags out of old jackets." Crow Dog also lamented the chauvinism among the ranks of Lakota AIM men, including her one-time husband, medicine man Leonard Crow Dog. She expressed irritation at the Native and white female "groupies" who were willing to serve as "wives" to the AIM leadership—that is, in addition to providing sex, they cooked, cleaned, sewed, and braided the men's hair.[21]

However, rather than articulating a substantive analysis of the roots of this problem in the "imposition of Eurocentric outlooks" and the effects of colonization on men's self-image, Mihesuah argues that "nowhere in *Lakota Woman* does Crow Dog evaluate colonialism, and in only one sentence does she even hint at excusing men's behavior." In fact, Brave Bird responds to a white woman at Wounded Knee who criticized the women for doing the "shit work" as Brave Bird calls it, with "We told her that her kind of women's lib was a white, middle-class thing, and that at this critical stage we had other priorities. Once our men got their rights and their balls back, we might start arguing with them about who should do the dishes."[22]

Madonna Phillips offered a different perspective on gender relations at Wounded Knee.

> The women were equally involved, integral and respected just as they had been in traditional times. She emphasized that there was never a question of men vs. women or men's roles vs. women's roles but a common cause in which everyone had an equal role. She said, "We didn't have time to think about what was women's work and what was men's work. If there was a meeting Russ [Means] would call us and ask us to come and be there. He wanted quick thinkers, it

didn't matter if they were men or women. And when something was being planned we all got together to discuss it.[23]

Rather than doing the "shit" work, experienced women in the movement saw themselves as integral and equal. Valandra notes that this

> disparity in views on female participation between Mary Crow Dog and Madonna Philips boils down to *woksape*, or age-based wisdom. During the Wounded Knee II period, Philips was a mother in her thirties, while Mary Crow Dog was just twenty. Lakota norms value the former's life experiences. The valuing of age invariably allowed Philips access to Lakota decision-making processes, whereas Mary largely witnessed the processes' outcomes. Thus, for a youthful Mary Crow Dog, women as decision makers generally remained invisible, subject to misperception and, hence, misinterpretation when expressed in a Lakota context.[24]

The problem of positive, equitable traditional ideas of the relations between men and women and the uses of those ideas to make use of women as concubines by men without any connection to or understanding of traditional gender relations in Lakota culture are central to the contradictions of Brave Bird's narratives. These contradictions run through *Lakota Woman*, as Brave Bird cooks and cleans for hundreds of people at Crow Dog's Paradise, follows her husband back and forth across the country, and raises seven children. Crow Dog is represented as deeply connected to a very traditional way of living at Rosebud.

Mary's marriage to Leonard Crow Dog eventually ended, as chronicled in *Ohitika Woman*. After moving in with an unidentified man who hit her, she left and began moving from shelter to shelter, staying first in the women's shelter on the reservation, then moving to one in Marshall, Minnesota, then Omaha, Denver, and finally Tucson.[25] At one point, Crow Dog finds her through the computer system that tracks assistance payments, forcing her to leave Marshall. While she never accuses Crow Dog of any kind of abuse, she does critique the rampant domestic violence on the reservation, holding both men and women accountable for the physical abuse and resultant deaths. She celebrates the women's groups on several Sioux reservations that help women who are in abusive relationships, groups like the White Buffalo Woman Society and the Sacred Shawl Society.[26]

Returning again to Cook-Lynn's critique, another difficulty with Brave Bird's life story is its genre. The as-told-to autobiography that comprises a great deal of writing by and about Native Americans in the late twentieth century is deeply troubling, and this was not a problem only with *Lakota Woman* and *Ohitika Woman*. Several books coauthored by Richard Erdoes with Native Americans in this format were controversial. This as-told-to format follows a set of primarily Western literary conventions that reproduce a romanticized version of the "Indian" that reinstates colonialism's destructive ideal of the "noble savage" and "perpetuates colonialism-tainted misrepresentations."[27]

> The subjects and their biographers begin by issuing the expected lamentations about being Indian in America, ... They've made redundant statements of how the white man took over the land and how the Indians themselves, alas, fell to drinking great quantities of booze, committing debaucheries of various kinds, and emerging from such a hapless condition rhetorically at least, redeemed and at the edge of self-knowledge.[28]

Valandra notes that Richard Erdoes, the coauthor of both of Brave Bird's books, penned more than half of the seven popular as-told-to books published in the late twentieth century. The problem stems in part from the fact that these "auto"-biographies are in fact written by non-Native collaborators, and rather than acting as scribes, the white interviewers in fact frame the story, edit the words, and often insert their own interpretations. The voice of the subject is erased.[29] Substantive critiques of Erdoes' collaborations by Julian Rice, among others, makes clear that this particular format produces "wrong notions of Indians" and avoids the important issues of sovereignty, self-determination, genocide, and land rights. *Lakota Woman* and *Ohitika Woman* are in this vein, and while Brave Bird's activism is very much part of the narrative of her life, her primary concerns are very much personal rather than political. Brave Bird's story is a narrative of individual redemption, which for Cook-Lynn, fails to represent what the as-told-to claims to represent, history, culture, an "understanding of the times."[30]

MARY OLGUIN

Ohitika Woman, the sequel to *Lakota Woman*, opens with the story of Brave Bird's near death in a car accident on the reservation. She returned to Rosebud after a series of moves that took her through a Minnesota women's shelter, an attempted reconnection with her father, Bill Moore, and finally to a marginal neighborhood in Phoenix, Arizona, where she and Crow Dog make a final attempt to keep their marriage intact. The attempt failed, and Brave Bird divorced Crow Dog, returning not only to the reservation, but to her earlier, pre-AIM, pre-Crow-Dog's Paradise life of drinking and partying. Lakota Woman became Ohitika Woman and Mary Olguin.

The injuries from her accident were life threatening, and she acknowledged that they resulted from drinking. While the timing of the events of her life is at times opaque, the years that she covers in this book describe her life with Crow Dog, her spiritual awakening through the ceremonies of both the Native

American Church and traditional Lakota rituals. The voice of Brave Bird's second as-told-to autobiography with Erdoes takes a slightly different direction, moving between descriptions of her activist work with the resistance movement at Big Mountain on the Navajo reservation, descriptions of the Native American Church's peyote ceremony, the Lakota Sun Dance, and *yuwipi* (sweat lodge) and her personal odyssey with alcohol, leaving her marriage, and finding new love with Rudi Olguin. She also includes a critique of the conditions on the reservations in South Dakota, but as we have seen earlier in the critiques of Brave Bird's autobiographical story, there are contradictions implicit in all of these stories. Rather than participating in any work to help deal with the issues she represents, Mary Olguin's narrative simply describes the problems through a series of stories and lists.

Because the book is produced as an "update" to her life as Mary Olguin, she details the lives of her children, where they are, what their interests are, what she sees for the future. She also includes her newest arrival, Summer Rose. After her near-death injuries from the car accident, doctors removed one of her ovaries and told her she would never be able to have children again. She was pregnant again within six months, having married Rudi Olguin in the fall of 1991.

Brave Bird closes *Ohitika Woman* by asserting, "I will fight to the end of my days—for everything that lives." But in a 1998 interview with Christopher and Todd Wise, she says, "I used to fight a lot, and you get to a point, you look around and your fighting is using all your energy."[31]

MOORE/BRAVE BIRD/CROW DOG/BRAVE WOMAN/ OLGUIN/BRAVE BIRD

As noted at the start, this essay has been divided into sections reflecting the different aspects of Mary Brave Bird's life story. For instance, the first section, *Mary Moore*, indicates that this name is one that she does not use for herself in any of her writings. And yet, in the record of the occupation of Wounded Knee published by *Akwesasne Notes*, a Mohawk publishing house, two pictures use this name to identify her immediately after childbirth, and to identify her baby. This book was published in 1974, very soon after the occupation ended, and well before the publication of *Lakota Woman*.[32] In Leonard Crow Dog's 1996 as-told-to autobiography/history, he also calls her Mary Ellen Moore. But the question then must be asked, what does it mean to name, to categorize? As noted, the names reflect different moments in Brave Bird's life story, times during which she was an activist, a mother, a wife, a party girl, a teenage rebel. Is Mary Brave Bird an activist? Is an activist defined by the work they do or the life they lead? Does an activist have to be the leader of the group to be an activist, or is being there sufficient to qualify in the category? What we know about Mary Brave Bird's work comes to us not through her occupations, her leadership, her actions, but through her written story. Cook-Lynn argues that the need to assess "the life histories of Indians" is "in fact, a war for the future of Indian intentions. Art and literature and storytelling are at the epicenter of all that an individual or a nation intends to be."[33]

Sarah E. Turner argues that Native American women's autobiographical writing, which for her includes *Lakota Woman*, is a way of "Writing their own lives, telling their stories, [which] creates both the space and the identity for Native American women to establish their history and their subjectivity through an exploration of their unique and often overlooked cultural legacy."[34] The text becomes the life, and in turn becomes perhaps an act intended to work for social change, for the good of the community, whether or not its intentions succeed.

Given the widespread use of Brave Bird's narrative in college classrooms, and the popularity of her books, they clearly represent an active intervention. The critiques of the content, form, and genre of the books are correct in many ways, and yet, there are those both inside and outside of the Lakota and Native American communities who find that Brave Bird's work is important. Oklahoma Choctaw scholar Devon Abbott Mihesuah uses Brave Bird's life story to demonstrate her theory of the stages of identity formation modeled on Cross and Parham's life stages paradigm for African Americans in "Finding a Modern American Indigenous Female Identity." Mihesuah shows how Brave Bird moves from pre-encounter consciousness through encounter, then into immersion-emersion and finally comes to internalization, or becoming bicultural successfully, secure in her identity. While Brave Bird's narrative must be somewhat violated to fit into this model, in fact, her presence is as a bearer not of ancient history, or of the mythic Plains Indian of the nineteenth century, but of the contemporary struggles of Indigenous women in the United States in the late twentieth century. There is no question that her story is both compelling and a misrepresentation, but even as a troubled text, her life story offers an opportunity to engage in a conversation about why it is that, as Paul Chaat Smith's book title ironically read, *Everything You Know about Indians Is Wrong*.[35]

NOTES

1. Mary Brave Bird, *Ohitika Woman* (New York: HarperCollins, 1993), 241. In *Ohitika Woman*, Brave Bird describes herself near the end of the book as a "radical female Sioux activist."

2. Mary Crow Dog, *Lakota Woman* (New York: HarperCollins, 1990), 40.
3. Crow Dog, *Lakota Woman*, 74.
4. Paul Chatt Smith and Robert Allen Warrior, *Like a Hurricane: The Indian Movement from Alcatraz to Wounded Knee* (New York: New Press, 1996), 226.
5. Crow Dog, *Lakota Woman*, 166.
6. Crow Dog, *Lakota Woman*, 174–76.
7. Crow Dog, *Lakota Woman*, 183–84.
8. Crow Dog, *Lakota Woman*, 222; Smith and Warrior, *Like a Hurricane*, 272.
9. T. V. Reed, "Old Cowboys, New Indians," 87.
10. Crow Dog, *Lakota Woman*, 234.
11. Brave Bird, *Ohitika Woman*, xiii.
12. Brave Bird, *Ohitika Woman*, xiii.
13. Brave Bird, *Ohitika Woman*, xiii.
14. M. Annette Jaimes, Review of *"Lakota Woman." American Indian Culture and Research Journal* 15, No.1 (1991), 110–11.
15. Jaimes, Review of *Lakota Woman*, 110–12.
16. Elizabeth Cook-Lynn, Review of *"Lakota Woman." Studies in American Indian Literature* 3, No. 4 (Winter 1991), 78.
17. Cook-Lynn, Review of *"Lakota Woman,"* 80.
18. Cook-Lynn, Review of *"Lakota Woman,"* 79.
19. Elizabeth Cook-Lynn, "Keynote Address: Indian Studies—How It Looks Back at Us after Twenty Years." *Wicazo Sa Review* 20, No. 1 (2005), 179–80.
20. Danyelle Means, "From a Long Line of Strong Women," *Turtle Quarterly* 6, No. 1, 30–32.
21. Devon Abbott Mihesuah, *Indigenous American Women: Decolonization, Empowerment, Activism* (Lincoln: University of Nebraska Press, 2003), 164.
22. Mihesuah, *Indigenous American Women*, 166.
23. Means, "From a Long Line of Strong Women," 32.
24. Edward Valendra "The As-Told-To Native [Auto]biography, 118; Edward Valandra, "The As-Told-To Native [Auto]biography: Whose Voice Is Speaking?" *Wicazo Sa Review* 20, No. 2 (Fall 2005), 103–19.
25. Crow Dog, *Lakota Woman*, 135–36.
26. Brave Bird, *Ohitika Woman*, 179–92.
27. "Valandra, "The As-Told-To Native [Auto]biography: Whose Voice Is Speaking?", 103.
28. Elizabeth Cook-Lynn, Review Essay "Life and Death in the Mainstream of American Indian Biography," *Wicazo Sa Review* 11, No. 2 (Fall 1995), 90,
29. Kimberly Roppolo, "Samson Occom as Writing Instructor." Native Critics Collective, *Reasoning Together* (Norman: University of Oklahoma Press, 2008), 322. Roppolo provides a more positive reading of Brave Bird's narrative, and asserts that her voice is not erased or subsumed by Erdoes, but that because she is very much alive, she "would speak out if she felt erased in her 'own' text."
30. James Riding In and Chris Pexa, "Editors' Commentary," *Wicazo Sa Review* 20, No. 2 (Fall 2005), 5–13; Robin Ridington, "Voice, Representation, and Dialogue: The Poetics of Native American Spiritual Traditions," *American Indian Quarterly* 20,

Nos. 3 and 4 (Summer and Autumn, 1996), 467–88; Cook-Lynn, Review Essay "Life and Death in the Mainstream of American Indian Biography," 90.

31. Brave Bird, *Ohitika Woman*, 274.

32. Akwesasne Notes, *Voices from Wounded Knee*, 160–61.

33. Cook-Lynn, Review Essay "Life and Death in the Mainstream of American Indian Biography," 93.

34. Sarah E. Turner, "'Spider Woman's Granddaughter": Autobiographical Writings by Native American Women." *MELUS* 22, No. 4 (Winter 1997), 109.

35. Paul Chaat Smith, *Everything You Know about Indians Is Wrong* (Minneapolis: University of Minnesota Press, 2009), title page.

BIBLIOGRAPHY

Akwesasne Notes. *Voices from Wounded Knee, 1973: In the Words of the Participants*. Roosevelt, NY: Akwesasne, 1975.

Brave Bird, Mary. *Ohitika Woman*. New York: HarperCollins, 1993.

Cook-Lynn, Elizabeth. Review of "*Lakota Woman.*" *Studies in American Indian Literature* 3, No. 4 (Winter 1991), 77–79.

Cook-Lynn, Elizabeth. Review Essay "Life and Death in the Mainstream of American Indian Biography." *Wicazo Sa Review* 11, No. 2 (Fall 1995), 90–93.

Cook-Lynn, Elizabeth. "Keynote Address: Indian Studies—How It Looks Back at Us after Twenty Years." *Wicazo Sa Review* 20, No. 1 (2005), 179–80.

Crow Dog, Mary. *Lakota Woman*. New York: HarperCollins, 1990.

Crow Dog, Mary. *Not so official website*. http://www.marycrowdog.com.

Jaimes, M. Annette. Review of "*Lakota Woman.*" *American Indian Culture and Research Journal* 15:1 (1991), 110–11.

Means, Danyelle. "From a Long Line of Strong Women." *Turtle Quarterly* 6:1, 30–32.

Mihesuah, Devon Abbott. *Indigenous American Women: Decolonization, Empowerment, Activism*. Lincoln: University of Nebraska Press, 2003.

Native Critics Collective. *Reasoning Together*. Norman: University of Oklahoma Press, 2008.

Reed, T.V. "Old Cowboys, New Indians: Hollywood Frames the American Indian." *Wicazo Sa Review* 16, No. 2 (Fall 2001), 75–96.

Riding In, James and Chris Pexa. "Editors' Commentary." *Wicazo Sa Review* 20, No. 2 (Fall 2005), 5–13.

Ridington, Robin. "Voice, Representation, and Dialogue: The Poetics of Native American Spiritual Traditions." *American Indian Quarterly* 20, Nos. 3 and 4 (Summer and Autumn 1996), 467–88.

Roppolo, Kimberly. "Samson Occom as Writing Instructor." Native Critics Collective. *Reasoning Together*. Norman: University of Oklahoma Press, 2008.

Smith, Paul Chaat. *Everything You Know about Indians Is Wrong*. Minneapolis: University of Minnesota Press, 2009.

Smith, Paul Chatt and Robert Allen Warrior. *Like a Hurricane: The Indian Movement from Alcatraz to Wounded Knee*. New York: New Press, 1996.

Valandra, Edward. "The As-Told-To Native [Auto]biography: Whose Voice Is Speaking?" *Wicazo Sa Review* 20:2 (Fall 2005), 103–19.

FURTHER READINGS

Bataille, Gretchen M. and Laurie Lisa. *Native American Women: A Biographical Dictionary.* New York: Routledge, 2001.
Crow Dog, Leonard. *Crow Dog: Four Generations of Sioux Medicine Men.* New York: HarperCollins, 1995.
Rice, Julian. "A Ventriloquy of Anthros: Densmore, Dorsey, Lame Deer, and Erdoes." *American Indian Quarterly* 18:2 (Spring 1994), 169–96.
Smith, Andrea. "Native American Feminism, Sovereignty, and Social Change." *Feminist Studies* 31 (Spring 2005), 116–32.
Sonneborn, Liz. *A To Z of American Indian Women.* New York: Infobase Publishing, 2007.
Turner, Sarah E. "'Spider Woman's Granddaughter": Autobiographical Writings by Native American Women." *MELUS* 22:4 (Winter 1997), 109–32.
Udel, Lisa J. "Revision and Resistance: The Politics of Native Women's Motherwork." *Frontiers: A Journal of Women Studies* 22 (2001), 43–62.
Wise, Christopher and Todd R. Wise. "Mary Brave Bird Speaks: A Brief Interview." *Studies in American Indian Literature* 3, No. 4 (Winter 1991), 1–8.
Wise, Christopher and Todd R. Wise. "A Conversation With Mary Brave Bird." *American Indian Quarterly* 24, No. 3 (Summer 2000), 482–93.

Chapter Three

Power of Voice, Power in the Land
Ada Deer
(b. 1935)

Theodor Gordon and Michael Seager

Ada Deer was born August 7, 1935, on the Menominee Reservation in Wisconsin. She enjoyed a career as a champion for tribal sovereignty and human rights. She is best known for her fight for the restoration of Menominee's federal recognition and her nomination by President Clinton as the first American Indian woman Assistant Secretary of Indian Affairs. Formerly, Ada Deer led the movement to reverse the federal policy of termination and to restore tribal sovereignty. Through her activism and public service, she forged the political coalitions necessary to restore her tribe, the first to be restored from termination. She continued her fight for Indian rights as Assistant Secretary of Indian Affairs, where she reformed the Bureau of Indian Affairs (BIA). While the federal government's recognition of tribal authority shifted throughout the second half of the twentieth century, Deer consistently articulated a vision of sovereignty in which the federal government and tribal governments would have a government-to-government relationship. In 1993, she accepted the position of Assistant Secretary of the Interior, marking an important step in which American Indian men and women could initiate policies while working within the government. Deer has claimed that both her mother and the subjugation that her tribe experienced during the termination era motivated her. Through her activism, Deer responded to the urgent need to reform Indian policy in order to strengthen tribal sovereignty against the American government's attempts to regulate American Indian tribal property.

    Deer described her mother, Constance Wood Deer, as the single greatest influence in her life. Constance Deer deviated from her family's expectations and became a nurse. She worked at the Rosebud Reservation in South Dakota before she began working at the Menominee Reservation. Deer describes her mother as a "fierce crusader for Indian rights. She read Indian history and law and brooked no compromises. Many a tribal leader and lawyer would grow more than a little apprehensive upon her approach. Many would think 'here comes Connie Deer and it looks like she has something on her mind.'"[1]

Deer's father, Joseph Deer, was raised on the Menominee Reservation where he, like most of the reservation, had an eighth-grade education. Ada Deer spent her early childhood on the reservation with her family. She was the oldest of nine siblings, only four of whom survived infancy. During World War II, the U.S. Army drafted her father and many men from the Menominee Reservation. At six years of age, Deer and her family moved off of the reservation and into a working-class suburb of Milwaukee with the hope of finding better employment. Four years later the family returned to the reservation when one of Deer's brothers became ill.

Ada Deer went to the local public school, where the mostly white student body ostracized her. She attended Shawano High School, with the exception of a brief stay with a conservative Mormon family in Utah during her sophomore year. Deer joined the Wisconsin governor's Commission on Human Rights Youth Advisory Board during her senior year. After graduating from high school, Deer received a scholarship from her tribe and attended the University of Wisconsin, Madison, with the intention of continuing on to medical school. While at the university, she continued to pursue human rights activism. In the summer after her freshman year, Deer traveled to New York City in order to partake in the Encampment for Citizenship. Here she had the chance to meet Eleanor Roosevelt. Deer changed her major to social work and graduated in 1957. Later that year she began studying for a Master's of Science in Social Work at Columbia University. "I was drawn to social work," she explained, "for it embodies many Indian values and it is dedicated to social justice and the elimination of discrimination."[2]

While enrolled in the master's program, Deer worked for students at a predominantly African American high school in a Bedford-Styvesant housing project. In 1961, Deer received her master's degree and moved to Minneapolis, where she worked with urban Indians through the Waite Neighborhood House. While working in Minneapolis Deer maintained close contact with, and frequently visited, the Menominee Indian Reservation, as she was concerned about disastrous effects of the tribe's termination. In 1964, the Bureau of Indian Affairs (BIA) hired Deer to be a community services coordinator for the Minneapolis area. In 1966, while working for the BIA, Deer traveled to Indian communities throughout the United States to report on their economic and social problems. After her position as community service coordinator ended, Deer briefly worked for the University of Minnesota, then as a school social worker for the Minneapolis Board of Education. Shortly thereafter, she accepted an offer to direct the Upward Bound program at the University of Wisconsin at Stevens Point. In 1970, Deer joined the board of directors of Americans for Indian Opportunity.

Deer's motivation to fight for tribal restoration connects intimately to the historical injustices suffered by her tribe. In 1854, the Treaty of Wolf River created the Menominee Indian Reservation. Many Menominees earned their living through forest-products industry and sold the timber on their reservation, but in the early twentieth century, the BIA restricted their operation of their tribal sawmill. In 1905, the tribe sued the BIA for mismanaging the recovery of salvageable timber after a windstorm on the reservation felled forty million board feet of timber. Such problems motivated the Menominee to establish more power over their resources, as the BIA largely challenged and sidestepped such concerns. Fully expressing their concerns over land management, the utilization of Indian funds, and fair employment practices, tribal leaders happily integrated a more formal tribal structure. By the late 1920s, policies encouraged the Menominees to adopt their own constitution, complete with by-laws, an independent Advisory Council inclusive of ten adult members, and a General Council of all tribal members having veto power over the Advisory Council. Accordingly, members of the Advisory Council, who generally had more advanced educations than other tribal members, negotiated labor contracts for the mill and mediated between the BIA and the tribe.

While the BIA still managed the sawmill on reservation lands, the Menominee garnered more political sway over time and were thus able to sometimes fully reject proposed BIA measures. The Menominee came together to fight for their rights, especially against destructive programs like allotment. In the 1920s, Menominee people took a stand against the resumption of the allotment program and individualizing property holdings. The BIA attempted to undermine tribal cohesion. The government intended for Indians, including the Menominees, to exercise more personal autonomy without the government's support for an entire tribe. Prior to the allotment program, the Menominees had withstood critical attacks on their tribal unity. They had managed to hold together as an interdependent tribal entity, relying on, but also petitioning, the American legal system over the BIA's mismanagement of the timber business.

After World War II, income from the mill accelerated. At the same time, development increased on the Menominee Reservation, providing needed employment for many residents. The mill funded a significant portion of the tribe's utilities and a hospital. In 1946, Congress passed the Indian Claims Commission Act, enabling tribes to sue the government for treaty violations. In 1951, the tribe's 1905 lawsuit was settled for over $7.6 million. However, the compensatory payment required congressional approval. In 1953, the legislature attached a rider that allowed payment of the multimillion dollar settlement to individual tribe members provided the Menominees accept termination. The federal and state hoped to sever their financial obligations to the Indians. After World War II, many Americans believed that the federal government should not recognize or support tribal sovereignty. As a result, conservatives pushed for the termination of the Menominee and many other tribes, destroying the trust relationship of the United States with tribal nations. In sum, many in Congress and in the executive branch sought to "get out of the Indian business." This meant the United States could end all obligations to tribes provided for previously in treaties, executive orders, acts of the Bureau of Indian Affairs, decisions of the Supreme Court, and acts of Congress.

By the 1950s, the BIA officially set to task the breaking up of certain reservations as a means of desegregating and integrating Indian peoples into mainstream postwar American society. Beginning in 1954, the United States officially mandated a policy of "termination," dismantling particular reservations such as the Klamath Reservation in the Northwest and the Menominee Reservation in Wisconsin. By 1961, the BIA received congressional authority to eliminate tribes owning 3.2 percent of land and terminated reservations in California, Washington, Oklahoma, and Wisconsin. The new federal policy of termination aimed at opening reservation lands to private citizens, thereby destroying communal land ownership of Native Americans. Conservative policymakers also used termination as a tool of assimilation and destruction of tribal sovereignty. Termination also sought to disperse American Indians into the heart of American urban life as cheap laborers, which was another method of "civilizing" Indians. As a part of a nationwide federal effort to terminate tribal sovereignty, the federal government officially terminated the Menominee tribe in 1958.

Many members of Congress and policymakers believed the Menominee were substantially well-off and would easily conform to non-reservation life. Senator Arthur Watkins, the originator of termination policy, believed the Menominees' position was one of high acculturation, due to their involvement with and allocation of profits from the timber industry. The Menominee Indian Reservation became a county of Wisconsin after the government enforced termination. For the Menominee, their spiritual and economic life centered on their intimate relationship to their ancestral lands. The people had used the land for generations as a means of their livelihood and had long sustained a lucrative tribal business intimately connected to the lumber industry. Ada Deer and her family had an association with this way of life, and Ada watched as federal policymakers deconstructed her reservation.

In 1957, and after graduating with a bachelor of science in social work, Ada Deer's sister informed her of the government's termination policies and its target of terminating the Menominee Indian Reservation. The BIA removed instillations and services it had once managed, including the hospital and governance over legal services, road maintenance, as well as labor contracts for the sawmill. The government sold the electrical plant that served the reservation. The government ended its support of Menominee education, health, and employment in the reservations. Indeed, the federal government intended to use termination as a means of assimilating the reservation with surrounding communities, rather than working with tribes to improve deplorable conditions. The Menominees, in effect, had to contract out for and pay for all public services, formerly under federal supervision, a result of their treaty. Termination significantly taxed the resources of Shawano County, causing greater racism and resentment of Indians. At the same time, an unforeseen wave of tuberculosis spread throughout the Menominee community, which created another deadly form of termination.

The tribe's funds and the sawmill became the Menominee Enterprise Inc. (MEI), a private, for-profit corporation. Each tribal member received equal shares of MEI, and the First Wisconsin Trust Company of Milwaukee held shares that belonged to minors and physiologically incompetent members. However, many Menominee people in need of income sold their shares in MEI, which led to non-Menominee individuals increasingly controlling the profitable timber and sawmill. Deer explained that "my tribe literally went from being prosperous to being Wisconsin's newest, smallest and poorest county."[3] Short on cash, MEI began taking steps to sell lakefront property on the former reservation land to outsiders.

Seeking to restore the Menominee tribe, in 1963 Constance Deer established the Citizens' Association for the Advancement of the Menominee People (CAAMP). Connie, a shareholder in MEI, attended a shareholders meeting in 1969 and asked to review the corporation's plans to sell lakefront property. When MEI denied her request, Ada Deer contacted a state legal services agency to help her and her family receive the MEI documents as shareholders. MEI subsequently opened its records to its shareholders. Deer and many of her family and friends mobilized the Menominee in Milwaukee to gain control of MEI. Deer worked with Nancy Lurie, an anthropologist at the University of Wisconsin at Milwaukee, who published articles about the termination of the Menominees.

By 1970, Ada and the Menominees facilitated significant change. Ada's community experience outside the reservation allowed her to bring together a broad range of groups. Befriended by Oklahoma Senator Fred Harris, and his wife Comanche Indian LaDonna, who founded Americans for Indian Opportunity (AIO), Ada served on the board of directors. These two significant and powerful women advanced critical issues concerning American Indian poverty and economic dislocation. The political tide began to turn in the favor of Indian tribes in July of 1970, when President Richard Nixon called for an

American Indian Self-Determination Act and for an end to the termination. Nixon championed tribal sovereignty.

By the 1970s, Jim White, Ada Deer, and others organized the Determination of the Rights and Unity of Menominee Shareholders (DRUMS). As its first president, White united the Menominee with public demonstrations at MEI headquarters and land development offices, while Deer appealed to the larger public. Both leaders protested property development on the reservation and moved toward ending MEI's rule. Between 1970 and 1972, DRUMS used two major tactics against MEI. In the first instance, Ada, Jim White, and others staged highly visible marches while allying their forces to vote MEI out of existence. The marches garnered the support of Wisconsin legislators. However, their efforts suffered a setback while trying to obtain the necessary amount of votes to discontinue the trust. Every ten years, shareholders of the MEI could vote on the continuance of the trust itself, and although DRUMS managed to collect a large number of proxy votes, many of whom were Menominees residing off the reservation, they failed to obtain a majority.

Undeterred, Menominee activists committed to a seat change in November 1971, electing prominent DRUMS leaders into the MEI voting trust that eventually included Ada Deer as its chair. DRUMS effectively controlled the trust, and Deer set off to Washington, DC, to further align DRUMS' objective with the growing discontent in Congress over the policy of termination. Ada petitioned congressional leaders, working up contacts she made in earlier years, advancing DRUMS's new position to congressional legislators. Making great strides, her testimony to Congress rallied media attention. Ada's leadership made her the iconic visage of Menominee rights and the personification of American Indian leadership restoring tribal property.

Indeed, in 1973 Ada became chair of the Menominee Restoration Committee and actively engaged in multiple efforts to promote tribal sovereignty. Meanwhile, associated with DRUMS, she lobbied various influential congressional lawmakers to fully restore Menominee lands under the Menominee Restoration Act of 1973. President Nixon willingly and eagerly signed the act into law in December of the same year. The success in reconciling the Menominee as legal holders of their lands and business served only one facet of Ada's accomplishments. In 1976, Deer stepped down from the Menominee Restoration Committee, believing that Menominee restoration, including new tribal laws, had achieved their DRUMS's goals.

Despite her role in the effort to restore the tribe, many Menominee members criticized Ada Deer and others in the new tribal government. Clara Sue Kidwell noted that "because her efforts had been carried out in Congress rather than on the reservation," tribal members accused her and others "of being aloof and operating too much on their own initiative, similar to the charges that earlier had been leveled against the governing board of MEI." While head of the new tribal government, Deer faced opposition from a new grassroots organization, the Warrior Society, a coalition of former DRUMS supporters, members of the American Indian Movement, and radical white activists. In December 1974, the Warrior Society seized control of the Alexian Brother's facilities, a Catholic medical station. The Warrior Society aimed to give the facility to the reservation so that the Menominee would have a hospital again. After the governor deployed the Wisconsin National Guard to the Warrior Society, and following Deer's rejection of the facilities, the occupation ended.

In 1975, President Ford signed into law a bill creating the American Indian Policy Review Commission. The commission appointed Deer to serve as an Indian representative. The commission was divided over the issue of the federal government's responsibilities to tribes and whether the BIA should even exist. The central challenge was to transform the BIA into a more effective tool for Indian sovereignty than an overseer of their affairs. After two years, Ada and the commission concluded that a restructuring of the BIA should include, as its role, a decentralized partnership with Indians. The commission also argued that the BIA should become independent of the Interior Department. Such a rationalization depended on ending, once and for all, the paternalistic relationship the BIA held over Native peoples. The American Indian Self-Determination Act of 1975 enabled a tribe, such as the Menominee, to receive funding directly from the government and thereby determine the course of social services by establishing contracts with the BIA. The new system has improved reservation life for some tribes, a true watershed in Indian history, but some of the essential features of tribal autonomy remain hotly debated today.

After stepping down from her role as commissioner in 1977, and having listened to and documented the numerous grievances among Native people across the United States, Ada decided to run for office in her home state. She vied for the office of Secretary of State of Wisconsin. Although she lost her bid for secretary in 1978 and again in 1982, she was a key player in the Democratic National Convention and Walter Mondale's unsuccessful bid for the presidency in 1984. From 1977 to 1997, Ada taught intermittently at the School of Social Work, University of Wisconsin. Earlier, Deer had been an effective member of the Native American Rights Fund (NARF), an effective nonprofit organization that provided legal advice to DRUMS during the period of restoration. Ada continued to work with this nonprofit for three years until 1981, taking a brief leave of absence from the University of Wisconsin, working as a contact between members of Congress and NARF. Later, she served as chair of NARF's National Support Committee and chair of the board of directors until 1990.

Ada Deer also took on more direct positions in the political arena, where she once again showed her full determination. Deer ran for Congress in 1992, and although unsuccessful in the primary election, she accepted, a year later, the position of Assistant Secretary of Indian Affairs under the Clinton administration. As the first woman to control the BIA, Deer used her authority under the Self-Determination Act of 1975 for the benefit of Indian people. Working directly under the Secretary of the Interior, Ada once again reconciled old wrongs between the government and Indian groups. Calling for accuracy over the relationship between the Alaskan Native Villages, Ada recognized all 226 groups in the state, reversing the earlier Alaska Native Claims Settlement Act of 1971, which erroneously named only 211. Federal funds earmarked for "official" tribes were vitally important to Alaskan Indians, as it was for the Menominee. The severity of being completely left out was unimaginable. Equally important during Deer's tenure in office, 180 tribes began to contract for their own services as the Menominee had done. Ada also settled the long-standing dispute between the Crow tribe and the federal government over mineral rights, recompensing the Crows for their loss of potential revenues.

By the early 1990s, Ada had become the consummate political voice for tribal autonomy especially where land was of primary importance. Ultimately, Deer's goals and achievements garnered national attention. Her efforts bridged local and national issues to beget real change. Ada found her work "rewarding, and sometimes, frustrating." Journalist Dave Zweifel revealed that Deer "hasn't slowed" down a bit. "In fact," Zweifel claimed, "she's taken up a new cause: Wisconsin's overburdened prison system." Deer lamented that "The United States has the highest number of people in prisons of any other industrialized society." In response, she teamed up with AmeriCorps facilitating the readjustment of former convicts into the American mainstream. Looking to the past, Deer noted that "my mother always told me . . . I was put on this Earth for a purpose," and that "along the way I found social work." With an eye on the economics of Wisconsin's prison system and a penchant for observing the larger sociological patterns involved, Deer continually lives up to her mother's wisdom: "If you want to change things, there's only one place to start—by speaking out."[4]

NOTES

1. Ada Deer. Statement of Ada E. Deer before the Senate Committee of Indian Affairs July 15, 1993. *Wicazo Sa Review* 9, No. 2 (Autumn 1993), 105.

2. Statement, *Wicazo Sa Review*, 106.

3. Statement, *Wicazo Sa Review*, 106.

4. Dave Swelfel, "Ada Deer's New Cause: State's Ballooning Prisons," *Madison Capital Times*, March 26, 2008.

BIBLIOGRAPHY

Deer, Ada. Statement of Ada E. Deer before the Senate Committee of Indian Affairs July 15, 1993. *Wicazo Sa Review*, Vol. 9, No. 2. Autumn 1993.

Deer, Ada with R. E. Simon Jr. *Speaking Out*. Chicago: Children's Press Open Door Books, 1970.

Swelfel, Dave. "Ada Deer's New Cause: State's Ballooning Prisons," *Madison Capital Times*, March 26, 2008.

FURTHER READINGS

Ames, David W. and Burton R. Fisher, "The Menominee Termination Crisis: Barrier in the Way of a Rapid Cultural Transition," *Human Organization* 18. Fall 1959.

Beck, David R. M. *The Struggle for Self-Determination: History of Menominee Indians since 1854*. Lincoln: University of Nebraska Press, 2007.

Hertzberg, Steven J. "The Menominee Indians: From Treaty to Termination," *Wisconsin Magazine of History* 60 (Summer 1977), 267–29.

Kidwell, Clara Sue. "Ada Deer: Menominee." R. David Edmunds, ed., *The New Warriors: Native American Leaders Since 1900*. Lincoln: University of Nebraska Press, 2001.

Lurie, Nancy Oestereich. *Wisconsin Indians*. Madison: State Historical Society of Wisconsin, 1980.

Ourada, Patricia K. *The Menominee Indians: A History*. Norman: University of Oklahoma Press, 1979.

Peroff, Nicholas C. *Menominee Drums: Tribal Termination and Restoration, 1954–1974*. Norman: University of Oklahoma Press, 1982.

Shames, Deborah, ed. *Freedom with Reservation: The Menominee Struggle to Save Their Land and People*. Madison: National Committee to Save the Menominee People and Forests, 1972.

Chapter Four

Cheyenne and Hodulgee Muscogee Activist

Suzan Shown Harjo
(b. 1945)

Michelle Lorimer

Activist, advocate, writer, and poet, Suzan Shown Harjo has fought for cultural and religious freedom, land rights, sovereignty, and the protection of Native Nations. She is the President of the Morning Star Institute and has worked as the News Director for the American Indian Press Association and Executive Director of the National Congress of American Indians. In 2014, Harjo received the highest civilian honor—the Presidential Medal of Freedom—from President Barack Obama. Born in Cheyenne treaty territory in El Reno, Oklahoma, on June 2, 1945, Harjo's family is tied to leadership and advocacy. From her family's farm outside of Tulsa, Oklahoma, twelve-year-old Harjo moved to Naples, Italy, when her father, a World War II veteran and career servicemember in the U.S. Army, was stationed at a NATO base in the country. After returning to the United States for her senior year of high school, Harjo visited Washington, DC, with Cheyenne leadership—first exposing her to federal advocacy work. Throughout her decades of activism, Harjo has fought to end stereotypical and derogatory depictions of Native peoples. Her legal advocacy against the name of the Washington, DC, National Football League team and leadership in founding the National Museum of the American Indian are but two examples of her distinguished career.

Harjo has worked to protect sacred places and recover more than one million acres of sacred lands. In a statement before the U.S. Senate Committee on Indian Affairs in 2003, Harjo articulated the struggles that Native peoples encounter when trying to protect their sacred spaces:

> Federal actions and inactions caused or allowed most of the damage and destruction of Native sacred places when the U.S. policy was to eradicate our traditional religions and keep us from the places where we pray. Now that the U.S. policy is to preserve and protect our traditional religions, the federal

government has an affirmative obligation to do that and to take remedial action on our behalf, including returning and restoring those places that still have life.[1]

Harjo served as a founding trustee of the National Museum of the American Indian (NMAI), and a trustee of the Museum of the American Indian, Heye Foundation. As co-curator of the NMAI's exhibition "Nation to Nation: Treaties Between the United States and American Indian Nations," (2014–2021), Harjo promoted the national telling of treaty relationships between Native Nations and the U.S. government. As a policy advocate, she has labored to secure repatriations, and to protect Native art, culture, and ancestry.

Museum displays of disturbing representation of Native peoples sparked Harjo's activism in constitutional law, religious freedom, and reparations in the mid-1960s. Urged by her mother after viewing sacred objects and burial clothes on display at the Museum of the American Indian in New York, Harjo met with Cheyenne elders to plan reform and action. This first alliance—the Sacred Places, Sacred Lands Coalition—served as a means to bring Native people together across the United States in the late 1960s. From this advocacy work, Harjo developed relationships with members of the House of Representatives and Senate senators, including Daniel Inouye, Charlie Rangel, Barry Goldwater, Ted Kennedy, and Ben Nighthorse Campbell. These relationships proved important for the passage of the American Indian Religious Freedom Act (1978).

With the administration of President Jimmy Carter in 1978, Harjo employed her policy activism as Special Assistant for Indian Legislation and Liaison. Moreover, as the principal author of the President's Report to Congress on American Indian Religious Freedom, Harjo worked across government agencies to implement the American Indian Religious Freedom Act.

In 1984, as Executive Director of the NCAI, Harjo met with the Secretary of the Smithsonian, Robert McCormick Adams, to discuss reforming Native American exhibitions at the Smithsonian museums and issues with the collections. As a result, staff at the Smithsonian completed an inventory of their Native American collections that included thousands of sacred objects and human remains. Together with Vine Deloria Jr. as trustees to the Museum of the American Indian, Heye Foundation, Harjo lobbied for the establishment of the NMAI in Washington, DC, on the National Mall in the late 1980s. At the same time, Harjo positioned for repatriation of sacred objects and remains. With the congressional passage of the National Museum of the American Indian Act (1989), Harjo's work led to the creation of the National Museum of the American Indian and the inclusion of reparation policies that established a process to return human remains, sacred and funeral objects, as well as other culturally significant items in museum collections to affiliated tribes. This work paved the way for the passage of the Native American

Graves Protection and Repatriation Act (NAGPRA) the following year. Harjo continued her political lobbying and advocacy for many decades—serving on presidential candidate Barack Obama's Native American Policy Committee in 2008.

Harjo took to heart the words of Clyde Warrior, a Native American activist, who spoke out against the derogatory and demeaning depiction of Native peoples as mascots in 1962. He tied the use of Native caricatures and mascots to the historic oppression and marginalization of Native peoples. Working in the 1970s and 1980s, Harjo and others successfully pushed on many organizations to retire the use of Native mascots. As a journalist, Harjo has brought popular attention to the lasting legacy of violence and discrimination against Native people in the United States. Tying the name of the Washington football team to the brutality and traumas inflicted on Native Americans across generations, Harjo continued to combat the racist depiction of Native peoples. For decades she advocated against the name of Washington, DC's National Football League (NFL) team—and filed lawsuits including *Harjo et al v. Pro-Football Inc.* (1992) that challenged the name of the team. In this case, Harjo and her co-petitioners pushed for the U.S. Patent and Trademark Office (USPTO) to cancel the trademark for Washington's NFL team name as a disparaging term used against Native Americans for generations. She similarly organized the case *Blackhorse v. Pro-Football, Inc.* (2014) that sought to have the term "Redskin" labeled as an offensive racial slur that could not maintain its U.S. trademark protection. In July 2020, under pressure from its major financial sponsors, the Washington NFL team officially announced that it would change its name to the "Washington Football Team" while it explores options for a new name.

As a journalist, poet, scholar, and curator, Harjo has advanced the public representation of Native people on the national stage for decades. In the 1970s, she served as News Director for the American Indian Press Association in Washington, DC. She produced *Seeing Red* on New York's WBAI-FM Radio—the first Native news radio program in the United States. As curator, her exhibition "Visions from Native America" (1992) was the first Native art exhibition displayed in the rotundas of the Senate and House. The exhibitions that Harjo has curated at the NMAI bridge Harjo's artistic and activist work. In recognition of her longtime advocacy and association with the Institute of American Indian Arts, the school honored Harjo with an honorary doctorate of humanities degree in 2011.

Harjo's ancestors served as delegates of the Muscogee during the Treaty of New York (1790) with the United States. Moreover, Harjo's maternal great-grandfather, Chief Bull Bear, was a signer of the Medicine Lodge Treaty (1867) between the United States and the Arapaho Nation. He was also the leader of the Dog Men Society. As with many treaties with Native Nations, the U.S. government failed to uphold its obligations situated in Medicine Lodge Treaty. Among other things, the treaty created reservation boundaries in western Indian Territory, established the roles of the Indian Agent, and provided for annuity goods (clothing and farming implements). Native Nations who signed this treaty failed to receive annuity goods and rations—leaving people deprived and starving. In turn, tribes raided outside of the reservation. The political fallout from this treaty led to the end of federal treaty-making with Native Nations in 1871. Harjo's ancestral connection to treaty-making is reflected in her work to protect and recover control of sacred lands. Her work as a founding member of the National Museum of the American Indian and guest curator on "Nation to Nation" bridges this work into the present.

NOTES

1. U.S. Congress, Senate, *Statement of Suzan Shown Harjo, President, The Morning Star Institute, Washington, DC.* Hearing Before the Committee on Indian Affairs, United States Senate, One Hundred Eighth Congress, First Session, June 18, 2003, 54.

BIBLIOGRAPHY

U.S. Congress, Senate, *Statement of Suzan Shown Harjo, President, The Morning Star Institute, Washington, DC.* Hearing Before the Committee on Indian Affairs, United States Senate, One Hundred Eighth Congress, First Session, June 18, 2003.

FURTHER READINGS

Champagne, Duane, ed. *Native North American Almanac.* Detroit: Gale Research, 1994.
Discussion with Poetry by Suzan Shown Harjo, "Reflections on Repatriation in Light of the French Judicial Decision on Hopi Sacred Objects and Cultural Patrimony," August 15, 2013 10:30 am through 11:30 am. indianartsandculture.org
Harjo, Suzan Shown. "Cultural Heritage, Art, & Living Beings: Justice Lost in Translation," *First American Art Magazine*, No. 1, Fall 2013.
Malinowski, Sharon, ed. *Notable Native Americans.* Detroit: Gale Publishers, 1995.
Philips, Patsy. "Suzan Shown Harjo: The grace of water and the focus of rock," *Indian Country Today*, June 16, 2019. https://indiancountrytoday.com/culture/suzan-shown-harjo-the-grace-of-water-and-the-focus-of-rock-5i2NqYjdXkK2BITYmW9Ecg.

Preucel, Robert W. "An archaeology of NAGPRA: Conversations with Suzan Shown Harjo," *Journal of Social Archaeology* 11(2), 130–43. https://doi.org/10.1177/1469605311402567.

Romero, Mateo and Suzan Shown Harjo. *Painting the Underworld Sky: Cultural Expression and Subversion in Art.* Santa Fe, NM: SAR Press, 2006.

Zotigh, Dennis. "Fulfilling Her Promise: Museums Honor Native Rights Advocate Suzan Harjo," *Smithsonian Magazine*, September 18, 2019. https://www.smithsonianmag.com/blogs/national-museum-american-indian/2019/09/19/suzan-harjo-promise-fulfilled/.

Chapter Five

Strikes with *Puha*—Power!
Comanche Activist, LaDonna Harris (b. 1931)

Clifford E. Trafzer

LaDonna Harris has a powerful presence. She has *puha* or power.[1] When she enters a room, those assembled sense her magnetic personality and special presence. Her dark eyes sparkle as they visit those present, providing a warm greetings to everyone present. She wears a genuine and friendly smile, as if she knows everyone or is eager to meet them. She addresses everyone as if she has known them for years. She unarms people with her striking presence, dancing eyes, and visual embrace. This Comanche woman sees through others and seems to know the depth of people and willingness to help others. Within seconds of meeting others, LaDonna knows whether or not the person understands her Native American past and her interest in improving the lot of others. LaDonna Harris is always involved in some significant cause intended to benefit humanity, especially to Native Americans.

LaDonna Harris possesses a mind as sharp as a razor, which she has used to build partnerships, programs, and coalitions. She is as smart as she is personable. She exudes confidence, kindness, and experience. Her eyes reach out to others, asking those near and far to join her in some new initiative that she has already organized in her mind. She is charismatic and astute. She is wise and knows the value of relationships, one of the hallmarks of her success. She uses politics in a progressive way, not for crass political purposes but for the benefit of others, especially Indigenous people of North America and beyond. Harris is reminiscent of characters found in ancient Comanche stories, narratives about cultural heroes who lived their lives as an adventure and quest to serve others. Her purpose in life has been one of service. Like the Buffalo, Coyote, Wolf, Eagle, Osprey, Blue Jay, and other characters found in those old oral stories of Comanche people, Harris has lived a life of service, dedicated to working with and for others.

LaDonna Harris is not about her own ego. She is a vessel of service, following the teachings of her grandparents and traveling a productive path through community-based initiatives and organization. She has always been, and remains a master at crafting partnerships and building bonds. Since 1965, she has brought people together for common causes, including the preservation of tribal lands, growing Native economies, fighting discrimination, furthering Indian education, and increasing the franchise among Native Americans. This was her goal in calling a meeting of American Indian leaders in her home state, the result of which was the creation of Oklahomans for Indian Opportunity (OIO). Since the 1960s, LaDonna Harris has been a political force in the United States and the world. She has wielded political power in a positive way on local, state, federal, and international stages. Harris is infused with *puha*, the Comanche word for power, which she uses for the common good. She strikes with power and has accomplished much during the past fifty years, and she has not stopped yet but continues to help and nurture others. This has been her destiny from her birth and growing up in rural Oklahoma.

On February 26, 1931, Lily Tabbytite gave birth to a little girl. Lily and her husband, Donald Crawford, named the girl child LaDonna who was born to and for the *Numunuu*, Comanche people. Shortly after her birth, LaDonna's father, a man of Irish American descent, left the family for California. LaDonna was born in Temple, Oklahoma, about thirty-five miles south of present-day Lawton in the southwestern part of Oklahoma. She was born into a rural environment of open fields, rolling hills, and clumps of trees growing along Cache Creek. After the Red River Wars in which Comanche people fought the United States for their sovereignty and freedom, the government designated this part of Indian Territory to be shared with a few tribes, including Comanches. LaDonna's maternal grandparents raised her on a farm near other Comanche families. Her grandfather was a former Indian scout who had served the U.S. Army at nearby Fort Sill. He was a traditional medicine man, a healer who called on the eagle for his special power. Her grandmother was a Christian who taught LaDonna Christian charity and kindness.

Although her grandparents held different religious beliefs, they had a loving, cooperative relationship that served as model for young LaDonna, who grew up on a farm where her family barely made ends meet during the Great Depression. However, living on a farm in rural Oklahoma ensured that the family had food to eat. Hard times and love bound the small family together into a cohesive relationship of mutual cooperation and trust. In addition to farm produce, the family ate game animals and natural plant foods they hunted and gathered in farm fields and the woods along Cache Creek. Most important of all, LaDonna grew up in a caring family with kin relations and family friends throughout the nearby Kiowa, Apache, and Comanche communities. She grew up in a loving family and modeled her life after giving and caring folks who raised her.

Life in Southwestern Oklahoma was not always idyllic. LaDonna Tabbytite grew up in an era of racism and segregation against American Indians. Although Oklahoma boasted of its Native American past, Comanche, Caddo, Kiowa, Cheyenne, Arapaho, and Apaches knew the sting of discrimination against American Indians whether or not they were Christians. LaDonna grew up speaking *Numu tekwapu* or the language of Comanche people—not English. The young Comanche girl witnessed and experienced racism, which hurt her deeply when it was directed at her grandparents, Indian friends, or herself. Once LaDonna entered public school at the age of six, she experienced racial hatred in serious ways. Still, LaDonna refused to allow racism against her, her loved ones, and her people to define her. She would not allow racism to damage her personality, her inner self, her confidence, or her opinion of the good people she knew from many diverse family, ethnic, and religious backgrounds. In fact, she learned from experiencing racism and later in life could easily related to the racism known to African Americans, Asian Americans, Latinx, and others found around the globe.

Even as a young person, LaDonna knew there were good and bad people among all peoples of this earth. When meeting other people, she made a conscious effort to bring out the good in everyone and kept her distance from those devoted to hate, anger, and destructive words and acts. At an early age, she learned to navigate negative personalities. She learned to turn the power, taking that negative and mean-spirited actions of others and turning them into something positive to benefit her people. She used her education, words, patience, and knowledge to teach others about Native Americans and even created a course of action she labeled "Indian 101," which taught others about basic elements of Native American history, culture, and diversity.[2] By teaching others about the first peoples of North America, she developed deeper relationships and enlisted the support of others for her causes.

LaDonna used her *puha* to convince others to assist Native Americans of North America and Indigenous people around the world. That was and is part of her magic, which she developed as LaDonna Tabbytite, long before she met her high school sweetheart and future husband, Fred Harris. Before falling in love, LaDonna Tabbytite, the Comanche girl, had developed her own unique personality based on the teachings of her family and tribe. She was born of Comanche people and learned the Comanche Way. She had begun to walk a path of caring and service to others prior to meeting Fred. As a young person, she learned that others were drawn to her magnetic personality. This included a handsome young man from Walters, Oklahoma, with dark hair and features. Like LaDonna, Fred had also grown up in poverty, the son of a sharecropper in rural Oklahoma. His days working on the farm taught him the value of hard work, a lesson he applied to his work as a public servant. Growing up near numerous American Indians, Fred understood some of the challenges of Native American people. He learned more from his wife, friend, and partner. Like many young men, Fred Harris was attracted to the beautiful and vivacious young woman he first knew as LaDonna Tabbytite.

After completing high school in 1949, LaDonna and Fred married. Fred was an ambitious fellow who wanted to attend college and law school. LaDonna agreed to help Fred attain his goals of an education and a political career. The couple moved to Norman, Oklahoma, where Fred attended the University of Oklahoma. He earned his bachelor's and law degree and left the university in good standing. With LaDonna, the couple organized their efforts to get Fred elected to public office. With his mind fixed on politics, LaDonna helped Fred win a seat in the Oklahoma state senate. The couple set their sights higher, and soon Fred ran for the U.S. Senate. In a narrow election in 1964, Fred defeated famed football coach, Bud Wilkinson, for the Senate seat vacated by Robert S. Kerr. In 1965, LaDonna, Fred, and their three children—Kathryn, Bryon, and Laura—moved to Washington, DC, where Fred began his career in the U.S. Senate.

Although LaDonna supported Fred and the development of his career, she also executed plans of her own. In 1965, she organized a meeting of sixty tribes that came together to form Oklahomans for Indian Opportunity. Like many of the organizations LaDonna originated or embraced, the OIO sought to improve the lives of Native Americans, end discrimination against Indians, and improve the educational and economic standing of Indigenous people. She also furthered Indian rights generally, which began a new era in Oklahoma's history. LaDonna Harris brought together the first modern Native American organization in the state of Oklahoma, a remarkable and lasting contribution. Her experience with the OIO served her well, as she continued to form relationships that resulted in the formation of many organizations devoted in improving the lives of others.

LaDonna's work among Indian people received the attention of President Lyndon B. Johnson who invited her to join the National Council for Indian Opportunity, which she joined. She was eager to engage in developing programs supportive of Native people, and she remained on the council after the election of Richard Nixon. However, Nixon placed the council under the direct control of Vice President Spiro Agnew, who ultimately disgraced himself through political corruption. Agnew had little or no interest in the National Council for Indian Opportunity, which became, like Agnew, a do-nothing office. In frustration, LaDonna Harris resigned from the council but in typical fashion, she turned the power. She used her energy and zeal for accomplishment to form Americans for Indian Opportunity (AIO), an organization LaDonna has guided from its inception in 1970. During the early years of existence, the organization focused on issues of culture, politics, education, and economic development of Native Americans of the United States. However, over the years, and the more LaDonna traveled in Latin America, Africa, Europe, the former Soviet Union, and other countries, she grew more interested in Indigenous peoples around the world. LaDonna Harris became the first Executive Director of Americans for Indian Opportunity, a position she still holds over fifty years later.

After the formation of Americans for Indian Opportunity, new opportunities opened for LaDonna. She was living in Washington, DC, during the late 1960s when African Americans actively sought new civil rights legislation related to economic development, housing, voting rights, and the elimination of segregation in the United States. She related to all the civil rights issues relating to African Americans because they applied to Native Americans living in new reservation boarding towns where non-Indians frequently discriminated against the first Americans. LaDonna became interested in all of these issues as well as those associated with women's rights. Naturally, LaDonna was a feminist who championed the causes of women. She also became involved with President Johnson's War on Poverty, which led to the president appointing LaDonna to chair the National Women's Advisory Council of the War on Poverty. While in the nation's capital, LaDonna Harris also held positions on the National Association of Mental Health, National Committee Against Discrimination in Housing, and the National Steering Committee on the Urban Coalition. To cap off her efforts, she became a founding member of the National Women's Political Caucus. LaDonna was the first wife of a senator to offer oral testimony to Congress. She spoke of racism as a cause of devastating mental health problems for children of color, and she advocated for more funds to be spent on mental health initiatives for children of color. LaDonna supported several causes as a senator's wife, but she always returned to issues involving Native Americans.

During the administration of Richard Nixon, LaDonna Harris supported two significant American Indian causes, including the return of Blue Lake to the people of Taos Pueblo. In 1906, the U.S. Forest Service stole Blue Lake and the surrounding watershed of the Pueblo River from the Indian people of Taos Pueblo. Since the beginning of known time, creative forces gave the people of Taos Pueblo their Blue Lake. The sacred body of water was the alpha and omega of these Pueblo people. As one member of the tribe explained, "The story of my people and the story of this place are one single story. No man can think of us without also thinking of this place. We are always joined together."[3] For those who have visited Taos Pueblo, the river flowing out of the mountains snakes its way through the village and continues its journey through New Mexico. When LaDonna Harris learned about the theft of the holy Blue Lake, she joined the Taos people in their quest to have the sacred place returned to its ancient owners.

Not long after the Forest Service claimed Blue Lake in the early twentieth century, the people of Taos Pueblo launched a sixty-four-year fight for their sacred place. Blue Lake had long served Indian people as a place of worship, and for the people of Taos Pueblo, the most sacred place on earth. In 1924, Taos tribal member Jesus Romero told the public that the theft of Blue Lake threatened the very being of Taos and other Pueblo people. Losing the sacred place was tantamount to ending the life of the people. For Romero, without Blue Lake, the people of Taos would lose their community, identity, and their spiritual place within the cosmos. According to tribal member Paul Bernal, "Our tradition and our religion require people to adapt their lives and activities to our natural surroundings so that man and nature support the common life of both." He explained that Native Americans live with nature and do not feel compelled to conquer or tame the landscape, but to live in and with the environment. Bernal continued, saying, "The idea that man must subdue nature and bend its processes to his purpose is repugnant to our people."[4]

When LaDonna learned of Blue Lake, she worked with tribal people and politicians to support the return of the lake and its surrounding environment to the pueblo. She reported that when the Taos elders entered the Senate office of her husband, Fred Harris, she was impressed by their powerful presence and charisma, which made her think of her Comanche grandfather, the powerful but quiet man who raised her. They had a powerful presence, and after meeting these men who were seeking the help of senators to support their request for the return of their land and lake, LaDonna and Fred became committed to the Taos cause. While Fred became the strongest advocate in the Senate supporting a bill to return Blue Lake to the people of Taos, LaDonna targeted the White House to seek the support of President Richard M. Nixon. In that regard, she found a friend and advocate in a dynamic woman and White House staffer, Bobbie Green Kilberg.

Bobbie Kilberg listened to LaDonna about the Taos issue and decided to put her considerable energies and intelligence to work in support of the effort. From her position as a key staff member of the Domestic Policy Council in the White House, Kilberg had access to President Nixon. With information provided by LaDonna Harris and her own research, she learned that in 1906, President Theodore Roosevelt had signed legislation creating the Carson National Forest, securing for the U.S. Forest Service thousands of acres of mountainous forest lands of northern New Mexico. Kilberg learned that these mountains included Blue Lake and that the people of Taos Pueblos believed the entire landscape, but especially Blue Lake, was sacred to them, a gift from their creators. Harris and Kilberg formed a partnership in the effort to return the lake and a portion of the mountains to Taos Pueblo. Both women understood that the issue before them was a matter of religious freedom for the Taos people who sought the return of their holy lake and landscape so they could practice their religion at *Ba Whyea*, Blue Lake.

In 1924, the U.S. government offered the people of Taos money for the lands the government had stolen in 1906, but the people refused money. In the 1940s and 1950s, the Indian Claims Commission offered Taos Pueblo money for Blue Lake and lands surrounding the lake. The Taos leadership categorically refused the money, saying that money could never buy their sacred lake or lands. As Jim O'Donnel points out in his recent, insightful, and moving essay in *El Palacio*, the magazine of the Museum of New Mexico, a Taos elder explained, "What did we want with money? We wanted our land. But mostly we wanted the mountains. We wanted the mountains, our mother, between whose breast lies the blue eye of faith. The deep turquoise lake of life. Our lake, our church. Where we make our pilgrimages, hold our ceremonies."[5] LaDonna Harris understood the deep and abiding connection between Native Americans and their sacred cultural landscapes. So she committed herself to lobby on behalf of Taos people and their just cause.

LaDonna Harris quietly worked among members of the legislative and executive branches of government as well as influential women in Washington, DC, to advance the Taos agenda to return the lake. She used her winning personality and influence to educate non-Indians in Washington, DC, through her personal course of Indian 101. LaDonna Harris became skilled at informing people about the spiritual connection of Native Americans to their homelands. In 1969, House Bill 471 was introduced in the House of Representatives, calling for the return of Blue Lake to Taos people. The bill went through many iterations and ultimately emerged as Public Law 91-550. Fred Harris became the leading champion of the bill, overcoming objections of two powerful lawmakers, Senators Henry M. Jackson and Clinton Anderson. Harris used his influence and political prowess to move the bill through both houses of Congress. He was a powerful influence when the Senate Subcommittee on Indian Affairs held hearings about Blue Lake. The committee heard from numerous people, including Taos people who gave important testimony. When the Senate voted to return Blue Lake and surrounding lands to Taos, the chamber burst into applause. Reportedly, LaDonna Harris and Bobbie Kilberg cried at the emotional moment when a bipartisan Senate stood up for religious rights of Indian people.

Both houses of Congress voted to return Blue Lake and 48,000 acres surrounding the lake. In addition, the bill provides that the United States would recognize the exclusive use of 1,640 acres around Blue Lake as a way of keeping other people away from the sacred site. In this way, the people of Taos could worship in their outdoor church without interference from tourist and curiosity seekers. The new law, PL 91-550, forbid people from invading the sacred space and ceremonies associated with the lake and surrounding landscape. As a result of the legislation, the area is visited and used only by tribal citizens of Taos Pueblo. LaDonna and Fred Harris were only two of the many people who had supported the bill, but their influence proved key to opening a new era in American history. Many Republican and Democratic law makers, and thousands of Americans joined hands with the Taos people to support the return of Blue Lake because it was the right thing to do. Together, the Indian nation and the country came together to reaffirm religious freedom as prescribed by the Constitution and Bill of Rights.

On December 15, 1970, LaDonna and Fred Harris joined a select group of distinguished visitors to the White House, including leaders from Taos Pueblo, as President Nixon signed PL 91-550 into law. Representatives from Taos Pueblo attended the signing as did others who the president had invited to the signing celebration. LaDonna sat in the front row of seats facing the desk where President Nixon inscribed his signature on the document conveying Blue Lake to Taos people. The president spoke from his heart because of his own commitment to Indian rights. "This is a bill that represents justice, because in 1906 an injustice was done in which land involved in this bill, 48,000 acres, was taken from the Indians involved, the Taos Pueblo Indians. The Congress of the United States now returns that land to whom it belongs." To emphasize the importance of the day, the president stated, "I can't think of anything more appropriate or any action that could make me prouder as President of the United States."[6]

On the same day of the month that Nixon signed PL 91-550 but eighty years before, Chief Sitting Bull was shot and killed on the Standing Rock Reservation. In 1970, President Nixon righted a wrong committed by the federal government against American Indian people, and in so doing, inaugurated the era of American Indian self-determination. The change that occurred on December 15, 1970, was not lost on LaDonna Harris, who saw the signing of PL 91-550 as a watershed in Native American and American history. Concepts of Indian self-determination and Native American sovereignty became an important element of the nation's consciousness. LaDonna believed the time had arrived when the nation could and would support Indigenous rights. She wanted to capitalize on the momentum achieved with the signing of PL 91-550, the return to Blue Lake. She felt the time was right to push new political agendas to benefit the first peoples of the United States. Thus, LaDonna Harris continued her work to further Indian rights.

Like her efforts on behalf of the Taos people, Harris became committed to the effort to restore federal recognition to the Menominee tribe of Wisconsin. She joined the political movement led by Menominee tribal members Ada Deer and Jim White to support actions designed to restore federal recognition to their tribe. Since 1954 when Congress passed the Menominee Termination Act, Menominee people had worked diligently through the national political system to have the termination of their tribe reversed. Although they staved off full termination during the 1950s, the bill went into effect on April 30, 1961. During the early 1960s, Menominee people continued to lobby congressmen and senators to restore their tribe's status through federal recognition. Ada Deer, the dynamic and effective leader of the Menominee cause, found a powerful ally in LaDonna Harris. Previously, the Menominee had created their own political organization to fight for recognition, calling it Determination of Rights and Unity for Menominee Stockholders or DRUMS. Following the victory to restore Blue Lake, Harris turned her energies into restoring recognition for her Menominee friends. She lobbied members of the House of Representatives and Senate on behalf of the Menominee, and she enlisted the help of friends she had made in the White House. Her efforts and those of Menominee people led to the Menominee Restoration Act of 1973 that President Nixon signed into law on December 22, 1973.

LaDonna Harris also joined in the effort to complete the Alaskan Native Claims Settlement and Indian Education Act of 1975, and the creation of the Council of Energy Resources Tribes (CERT) the same year. CERT emerged as an organization dedicated to tribal sovereignty over Indian resources. Tribes demanded tribal control of natural resources found on Indian reservations, including uranium, gas, coal, oil, water, timber, and others. In the past, the Bureau of Indian Affairs had negotiated business deals and long-term contracts with major companies at low prices to curry favor with big business and corporations. The Indian Office gave lucrative contracts to Mobile, Exxon, and other oil companies. Commissioners of Indian Affairs allowed coal and uranium companies to rape Indian lands and leave behind poisonous and cancer-causing waste byproducts. The Bureau of Indian Affairs (BIA) allowed companies to pollute Indian water supplies. CERT sought to change this by asserting greater authority over contracts and policies affecting Indian people. LaDonna Harris worked in the world of environmental responsibility and joined in CERT's effort to hold companies responsible for the destruction, ill health, and violation of the earth resulting from the companies. CERT was part of the larger initiative of American Indian self-determination, allowing tribal government to make their own contracts with businesses interested in obtaining natural resources on reservations.

For many years, at least since her high school days, LaDonna Harris had advocated for the assertion of tribal sovereignty and self-determination. She believed that Indian tribes did not need the Bureau of Indian Affairs. Instead, she felt that Indian people she knew, including her grandfather and grandmother, did not need non-Indian federal agents, superintendents, and district officers of the Bureau of Indian Affairs telling Indians what to do or think or how to act. Indians, she felt, were more than capable of handling their own affairs in terms of economic development, tribal governance, education, health, resources management, judicial systems, etc. Indians, she felt, could and would do a better job than the Indian Office, so LaDonna was an early advocate for self-determination and tribal sovereignty. As a result of her robust contacts in Washington, DC, LaDonna helped pass the Indian Self-Determination and Educational Assistance Act of 1975. Public Law 93-638 gave tribes the opportunity of taking over many aspects of tribal life and to seek federal funding through contracts for many aspects of tribal life, including health care, education, resources management, fire departments, police protection, and many other elements of tribal life.

In addition to her work on Indian initiatives, LaDonna Harris contributed in many other ways to the birth, growth, and development of organizations. During the administration of Jimmy Carter, Secretary of State Cyrus Vance appointed LaDonna to serve on the Board of Directors of the United Nations Education, Scientific, and Cultural Organization (UNESCO), which took Harris in many diverse countries around the world where she often witnessed Indigenous people struggling as her own people had struggled through racism, ill-health, poverty, inadequate housing, water and air pollution, and malnutrition. As a result of her experiences, LaDonna became more international in her work, which influences her work today. While she continued to advise tribal leaders, governments, and organizations, she has remained in contact with groups in Latin America, Africa, Pacific Islands, and Asia. In years past, LaDonna worked as a feminist with the National Organization of Women (NOW), Save the Children, and the National Urban League. She continues to serve on boards for Think New Mexico, National Institute for Colored Women, Advancement of Maori Opportunity, and the Institute for Twenty-First Century Agoras.

La Donna Harris also served on the Board of Directors for the National Museum of the American Indians, supporting the museum programs throughout Indian Country as well as the museums on the mall of Washington, DC, and in New York City at the old Custom's House. Harris also contributed to the Richard Nixon Presidential Library and Museum. On April 24–25, 2015, LaDonna joined some alumni of the Nixon administration in Yorba Linda, California, the birthplace of President Nixon. LaDonna reunited with her friend and colleague, Bobbie Kilberg, who provided the opening keynote of the conference, "Self-Determination and Tribal Sovereignty: The Lasting Impact of the Nixon Administration."[7] Harris joined Kilberg on a panel that included Wally Johnson, Reid Chambers, and Bradley Patterson, all of whom had worked closely with the president in framing American Indian policies relating to Blue Lake, Alcatraz Island, Wounded Knee of 1973, the Trail of Broken Treaties, the end of termination and assimilation, and the beginning of an era of self-determination. Although LaDonna knew about all these issues, she shared intimate details about the return of Blue Lake to Taos people and the importance of the Nixon years as a springboard into the era of tribal sovereignty.

LaDonna Harris has been involved in many other organizations and political movements but those addressed here provide some understanding of her vibrant personality and commitment to making life better for other people and the country she dearly loves. During her discussions of Indian 101, Harris carefully navigated the tragic and destructive elements of past Indian policies, but she also enlightened others about the beauty, tenacity, talents, and strengths of American Indian people. Native Americans, she often pointed out, were survivors and people of action, not victims. Through individual and communal strengths, Native Americans from the North Pole to the South Pole and from the Atlantic to the Pacific Oceans survived many changes that resulted from the invasion of America. She sought to teach others about the determination of American Indian people to look forward but keep one foot in their cultures, languages, and ways of being. LaDonna Harris, her family, and Comanche people are examples of Native American resilience. LaDonna has always looked forward to the next challenge, the new opportunity to uplift and support others in their quests to improve the human condition.

LaDonna Harris has lived her life in the service of others, especially Indian people. She has never wavered from positive action, and she never sought to harm or hurt others. She has lived a heroic life to build up, promote, and partner with others for the common good. She has approached life in a constructive manner that led to results. Her aim has always been one of accomplishment, not to nourish her ego but to work in the service of others. Although she has received many awards, accolades, and praise, she has not sought out publicity or money for herself. Like the cultural heroes found in ancient Comanche stories, she followed the hero's path. In spite of adversity and setbacks, she faced challenges wisely and courageously. Harris has always fought bravely on behalf of others. She had learned as much from her grandparents and tribal elders. As a young girl growing up in rural Oklahoma, LaDonna learned from her grandmother and grandfather to walk humbly and fearlessly as she made her journey in pursuit of a better life for all her brothers and sisters on earth.

NOTES

1. Clifford E. Trafzer and Matthew Hanks Leivas, *Where Puha Sits: Salt Songs, Power, and the Oasis of Mara* (Riverside: University of California, Riverside, Rupert Costo Endowment, 2018), 4–5.
2. LaDonna Harris, *Indian 101*, Documentary Film, www.wmm.com.
3. Taos Blue Lake, Sacred Lands Film Project, Sacredland.org.
4. Taos Blue Lake, Sacred Lands Film Project, Sacredland.org.
5. Jim O'Donnell, "Land Back," *El Palacio* (Fall 2020), Elpalacio.org.
6. "Return of Blue Lake," Taospueblo.com.
7. Flyer, "Self-Determination and Tribal Sovereignty: The Lasting Impact of the Nixon Administration," April 24, 2015, Author's Collection.

BIBLIOGRAPHY

LaDonna Harris: Indian 101, Documentary Film.
O'Donnel, Jim. "Land Back," *El Palacio*, Fall 2020. Elpalacio.org.
"Taos Pueblo Lake." Sacred Lands Film Project. Sacredlands.org.
"The Return of Blue Lake." Taospueblo.com.
Trafzer, Clifford E. and Matthew Hanks Leivas. *Where Puha Sits: Salt Songs, Power, and the Oasis of Mara.* Riverside: University of California, Riverside. Rupert Costo Endowment, 2015.

FURTHER READINGS

Americans for Indian Opportunity, "LaDonna Harris," AIO@AIO.org.
Champagne, Duane, editor, *The Native North American Almanac.* Detroit: Gale Research Inc., 1994.
Chavez, Aliyah. "LaDonna Harris 'Stumbled' into a Legacy," *Indian Country Today*, August 18, 2019.
Fluharty, Sterline. "Harris, LaDonna Vita Tabbytite," *Encyclopedia of Oklahoma History*, www.okhistory.org.
Kasee, Cynthia R., "LaDonna Harris," in Sharon Malinowski, editor, *Notable Native Americans*. Detroit: Gale Research Inc., 1995, 183–185.
LaDonna Harris, *LaDonna Harris: A Comanche Life.* Lincoln: University of Nebraska Press, 2000, edited by H. Henrietta Stockel.
New Mexico Business Journal, January 1997.
Trafzer, Clifford E., editor, *American Indians, American Presidents.* New York and Washington, DC: Smithsonian National Museum of the American Indian and Harper Collins, 2009.

Chapter Six

Tribal Community and National Activist
Wilma Mankiller
(b. 1945–d. 2010)

Jeffrey Allen Smith

Wilma Pearl Mankiller was the first female Principal Chief of the Cherokee Nation of Oklahoma, and the first woman to head a large Native American tribe. From 1985 to 1995 she served as the Principal Chief of the Cherokee Nation, headquartered in Tahlequah, Oklahoma, the largest of the three federally recognized Cherokee tribes in the United States. The recipient of many awards and honors, Mankiller served as an inspiration and leader to her people and women across the Native Universe.

Wilma Pearl Mankiller was born November 18, 1945, in W. W. Hastings Indian Hospital in Tahlequah, Oklahoma. Her parents were Charley Mankiller, a full-blooded Cherokee, and Clara Irene Sitton, her mother of Dutch and Irish decent. Wilma was short for Wilhelmina, the name of her fraternal uncle's wife, and Pearl came from her maternal grandmother. The name Mankiller traces back to Wilma's great-great-great-grandfather, whose name was written *Ah-nee-ska-yah-di-hi*, which translated into English meaning "Menkiller." Mankiller's ancestors came from the lands near Tellico in present-day eastern Tennessee. Wilma Mankiller's recollections involved growing up with her parents and eight of ten of her brothers and sisters on her family's home and allotment land in Mankiller Flats near Rocky Mountain, Oklahoma.

Residing among the hills and trees the Mankiller family used its allotment to grow strawberries and other produce. It was a rural setting where Mankiller and her brothers and sisters had to carry water a quarter mile due to a lack of indoor plumbing. Mankiller recalled that her family "bartered with neighbors and ate what we grew."[1] However, Mankiller viewed this period as formative. "Those days," she explained, "helped me so much. I was raised with a sense of community that extended beyond my years."[2] During this period, Mankiller listened to Cherokee elders and relatives speak of their ancestry, including the federal government's policy of Indian removal, which resulted in the forced removal and the Trail of Tears of the Five Civilized Tribes. Mankiller characterized this event as the Cherokees' Holocaust.

Already in place to a greater or lesser extent, the federal policy finally reached Mankiller Flats in the 1950s. Mankiller, like many Native peoples, believed, "The government wanted to break up tribal communities and 'mainstream' Indians, so it relocated rural families to urban areas."[3] While voluntary, the Bureau of Indian Affairs strongly advocated and encouraged the resettlement of rural Native peoples and families to larger cities under the pretense of helping Indians find better lives and jobs through increased financial opportunities and stability. At the age of ten, Mankiller moved with her family from their ancestral farmlands in Oklahoma to San Francisco, California. Mankiller described the harsh transition of the federal Relocation Program as a "culture shock." While her father and oldest brother began working in a rope factory, Mankiller understandably struggled "to deal with the mysteries of television, neon lights, and elevators" in a very large city.[4]

To cope with her foreign surroundings and orient herself in a non-Native world, Mankiller utilized her memories of Cherokee stories from Oklahoma. Mankiller likened herself to the "clever rabbit . . . who found herself surrounded by wolves."[5] However, while the animal could escape its predators by hiding in a hollow stump, Mankiller had to seek refuge elsewhere. Through her father's participation in the San Francisco Indian Center, Mankiller maintained a sense of herself and her Native American heritage during her formative adolescence. In addition to the center, Mankiller sought solace and wisdom from her "opinionated, outspoken, tough, and very independent" maternal grandmother, Pearl Halady Sitton, who lived in the Sacramento Valley.[6] Later in her life, Mankiller would draw inspiration from the time she spent with her grandmother, for she explained it aided in the formation of her "adolescent thinking."[7]

In the tumultuous summer of 1963, at the age of seventeen, Mankiller met an Ecuadorian man from an "old money" family named Hector Hugo Olaya de Bardi. After a whirlwind courtship, the two married on November 13, 1963, only five days shy of Mankiller's eighteenth birthday. The couple had two daughters together, Felicia in 1964 and Gina in 1966. Mankiller described herself during this period of her life as "a typical housewife at that time."[8] Events in November 1969 profoundly affected Mankiller and her family life. The Native American "invasion" of Alcatraz Island in San Francisco Bay inspired and invigorated many Indians, including Mankiller.[9] When the occupation of "Alcatraz occurred, I became aware of what needed to be done to let the rest of the world know that Indians had rights too. Alcatraz articulated my own feelings about being an Indian. It was a benchmark. After that, I became involved."[10] She developed a new sense of independence.

Mankiller began taking sociology classes at San Francisco State College and immersed herself in Native American causes. Her activism manifested itself in volunteer work with Native communities. She worked on issues pertaining to treaty rights, legal defense, and reclaiming ancestral lands for the Pit River tribe in California. Mankiller also gave of her time in Native preschools and adult education programs.

Mankiller's newfound activism came at a price. "Once I began to become more independent," she recalled, "more active with school and in the community, it became increasingly difficult to keep my marriage together."[11] In 1974, Mankiller divorced her husband of eleven years, becoming a single parent and head of the household. Her "stronger desire to do things in the community than at home" led her back to Oklahoma with her daughters two years later.[12] Mankiller "was delighted to be back on [her] ancestral homelands."[13] Over the next three years, she was instrumental in developing grants and desperately needed rural services and programs for her tribe, in addition to commuting to the University of Arkansas, Fayetteville, for graduate classes.

In the fall of 1979, Mankiller returned home from one of her university classes and became involved in a horrific automobile accident. Rounding a blind curve, Mankiller approached a slow-moving vehicle, when another oncoming car swerved into her lane to pass. She tried, unsuccessfully, to avoid the car. Mankiller's station wagon and the other car struck almost head on. Critically injured, the collision crushed Mankiller's face and broke her ribs and legs. Many thought she might not survive, as the driver at fault in the oncoming car did not. Incredibly, the other driver was Sherry Morris, Mankiller's best friend. The accident took a heavy physiological and physical toll. Mankiller believed the accident in 1979 forever changed her life. She struggled to avoid the amputation of her right leg, while enduring seventeen surgeries, which left her bedridden for months. Mankiller felt she "came very close to death, felt its presence and the alluring call to complete the circle of life."[14] Mankiller credited her positive outlook throughout her entire ordeal on the Cherokee philosophy of being of "good mind."[15] However, she was soon tested again.

Shortly after her horrific accident, November 1980, Mankiller was diagnosed with myasthenia gravis, a chronic neuromuscular disease. Proactive, Mankiller quickly began a treatment that included prolonged drug therapy and an operation to remove her thymus gland. Her resilience, upbeat attitude, and "good mind" again proved effective, and Mankiller returned to work only one month later. The combination of her overcoming a potentially fatal car accident and a debilitating neuromuscular disease provided Mankiller with a new perspective. She understood "The reality of how precious life is," which enabled her "to begin projects [she] couldn't have otherwise tackled."[16]

In 1981, Mankiller headed a project that would revitalize the Cherokee community, increase her standing in the tribe, and gain national publicity and recognition. The Bell Community Revitalization Project combined hundreds of thousands of federal and private dollars with the labor of Native peoples to completely rebuild the Cherokee community of Bell in eastern Oklahoma. The program rehabilitated distressed homes, built modern ones, and brought running water to many residents of Bell for the first time through a sixteen-mile pipeline. The project rightfully garnered national attention from the media and other tribes interested in Indian self-reliance. In addition, the success of the program also brought Mankiller to the attention of the Principal Chief of the Cherokee Nation of Oklahoma, Ross Swimmer.

In 1983, Swimmer asked Mankiller to run with him as his Deputy Chief in the upcoming election. Mankiller accepted the invitation. The Cherokee Nation elected Swimmer and Mankiller, with the duo taking office on August 14, 1983. A little over two years later, on December 5, 1985, Swimmer resigned from his office to head the Bureau of Indian Affairs in Washington, DC, and Mankiller took over as Principal Chief. Although this made Mankiller the first Principal Chief of the Cherokee Nation of Oklahoma, she did not feel she truly possessed a mandate from the Cherokee people until she won reelection on her own in 1987. She held this position until 1995, when she chose not to run again mainly because of health issues.

During her terms in office, Mankiller achieved numerous successes for the Cherokee Nation. Under her leadership, tribal revenue increased, while new businesses and health clinics developed, resulting from more than $20 million in construction projects. Mankiller also sought a new tribal tax commission, an energy-consulting firm, and a pilot self-government program with the federal government. However, like all administrations, Mankiller suffered through controversies, the majority of which stemmed from issues over tribal membership and jurisdiction matters with the nearby federally recognized Cherokee tribe, United Keetoowah Band of Cherokee Indians, headquartered in Tahlequah, Oklahoma. Nevertheless, Mankiller's time as the first female Principal Chief of the Cherokee Nation was a rousing success and inspiration to "young Cherokee girls [who] would never have thought that they might grow up and become chief."[17]

Mankiller later married her old friend Charlie Lee Soap, a Cherokee man she had met in October 1986. A Native community leader himself, Soap paired naturally with Mankiller. She relished how Soap was "supportive of women, of women's causes, and of me and my work."[18] Each named the other on their list of personal heroes. Mankiller also listed her brother, Donald Louis Mankiller, as another, because in 1990 he donated one of his kidneys to Mankiller so she could live, rather than succumbing to the same kidney problems that took their father's life in 1971.

Over the course of her life, Wilma Mankiller's actions and spirit have transcended the lands of her people and gained her praise, admiration, and recognition across the United States. Mankiller has won several awards and honors including *Ms. Magazine*'s Woman of the Year in 1987, the John W. Gardner Leadership Award in 1988, the Elizabeth Blackwell Award in 1996, and the Presidential Medal of Freedom in 1998. In addition, Mankiller was inducted into the Oklahoma Women's Hall of Fame in 1986, the National Women's Hall of Fame in 1993, and the Woman's Hall of Fame in New York City in 1994. Although significant in her life, Mankiller is best known for her political activism among Cherokee people who continue to remember her contributions to the people. Wilma Mankiller died in 2010 but her legacy among women around the world will forever remain intact.

NOTES

1. Wilma Pearl Mankiller and Michael Wallis, *Mankiller: A Chief and Her People* (New York: St. Martin's Press, 1993), xx.
2. Mankiller, *Mankiller*, xx.
3. Cornelia Hughes Dayton, Jane Sherron De Hart, Judy Tzu-Chun Wu, and Linda K. Kerber, *Women's America: Refocusing the Past* (New York: Oxford University Press, 2016), 788.
4. Robert L. Dorman, *Hell of a Vision: Regionalism and the Modern American West* (Tucson: University of Arizona Press, 2012), 145.
5. Mankiller, *Mankiller*, 76.
6. Melissa Schwarz and W. David Baird, *Wilma Mankiller: Principal Chief of the Cherokees* (New York: Chelsea House, 1994), 44.
7. Schwartz and Baird, *Wilma*, 44.
8. Michael Wallis, *Way Down Yonder in the Indian Nation: Writings from America's Heartland* (Norman: University of Oklahoma Press, 2007), 223.
9. Sharon Malinowski and George H. J. Abrams, *Notable Native Americans* (New York: Gale Research, 1995), 257.
10. Wallis, *Way*, 223.
11. Mankiller, *Mankiller*, 158.
12. Mankiller, *Mankiller*, xxi.
13. Mankiller, *Mankiller*, xxi.
14. Wallis, *Way*, 224.
15. Wallis, *Way*, 224.
16. Mankiller, *Mankiller*, xxii.
17. Dean Chavers, *Modern American Indian Leaders: Their Lives and Their Work* (Lewiston: Edwin Mellon Press, 2007), 146.
18. Mankiller, *Mankiller*, xxiii.

BIBLIOGRAPHY

Dell, Pamela. *Wilma Mankiller: Chief of the Cherokee Nation.* New York: Compass Point Books, 2006.
Chavers, Dean. *Modern American Indian Leaders: Their Lives and Their Work.* Lewiston, NY: Edwin Mellon Press, 2007.
Dayton, Cornelia Hughes, Jane Sherron De Hart, Judy Tzu-Chun Wu, and Linda K. Kerber. *Women's America: Refocusing the Past.* New York: Oxford University Press, 2016.
Dorman, Robert L. *Hell of a Vision: Regionalism and the Modern American West.* Tucson: University of Arizona Press, 2012.
Janda, Sarah Eppler. *Beloved Women: The Political Lives of Ladonna Harris and Wilma Mankiller.* DeKalb: Northern Illinois University Press, 2007.
Lowery, Linda. *Wilma Mankiller.* Minneapolis, MN: Carolrhoda Books, 1996.
Malinowski, Sharon. *Notable Native Americans.* Detroit: Gale Research, 1995.
Mankiller, Wilma and Michael Wallis. *Mankiller: A Chief and Her People.* New York: St. Martin's Press, 1993.
Schwarz, Melissa and W. David Baird. *Wilma Mankiller: Principal Chief of the Cherokees.* New York: Chelsea House, 1994.
Wallis, Michael. *Way Down Yonder in the Indian Nation: Writings from America's Heartland.* Norman: University of Oklahoma Press, 2007.

FURTHER READING

McMaster, Gerald and Clifford E. Trafzer. *Native Universe: Voices of Indian America.* Washington, DC: Smithsonian Institution, 2004.

Chapter Seven

Numakshi Mihe: The Lead Woman of the Three Affiliated Tribes

Alyce Spotted Bear (b. 1945–d. 2013)

Daniel Archuleta

In April of 1950, a delegation of Indians from the Fort Berthold Reservation in North Dakota arrived in Billings, Montana. The group included Ben Youngbird, Nathan Little Soldier, Mark Mahto, and the then Tribal Councilman Carl Whitmer. The delegation's business was urgent; the U.S. government selected to drown their homeland on April 1, 1953. The Garrison Dam's construction had already begun, and the group of Indians thought they would be consulted by an appraisal board to discuss reimbursement for the flooding. Instead, a locked door greeted the delegation. The flooding of the Three Affiliated Tribe's reservation, composed of the Hidatsa, Mandan, and Arikara Nations, had been a significant turning point for the tribe.

The Garrison Dam destroyed 152,360 acres from the Three Affiliated Tribes' reservation, 94 percent of agricultural lands subsumed by water, and 325 families relocated. Alyce Spotted Bear spent her life defending water rights and fighting for flood compensation for the Missouri River Tribes. Spotted Bear earned the *Nu'eta* (Mandan) title *Numakshi Mihe*, or "Lead Women," for her stalwart defense of culture, which she viewed as inherently intertwined with tribal sovereignty. As Tribal Chairwomen Spotted Bear brought the buffalo back to her people, she also supported language reclamation and educating tribal youth. Alyce Spotted Bear was only five years old when her tribal delegation met that locked door. Spotted Bear dedicated her life, making sure that the door would never be locked again. Her political and educational work ensured that Indians would always have a seat at the table and doors would be opened.

Alyce Spotted Bear was born on December 17, 1945, in the now-submerged town of Elbowoods, North Dakota, on the Fort Berthold Indian Reservation. Spotted Bear was one in a family of thirteen children. Education had always been a priority for Spotted Bear. She earned a bachelor's degree in secondary education from Dickinson State University in 1970. Alyce Spotted Bear went on to Pennsylvania State University and earned a master's in education, and at the time of her death, she was completing coursework for a PhD in education administration at Cornell University.

Alyce Spotted Bear was elected Tribal Chairwoman in 1982 and served until 1987. As a political leader, Spotted Bear put her blend of tribal knowledge and western education to work in her administration. Once elected, Alyce Spotted Bear's top priority involved finding work for the estimated 70 percent unemployed on the Fort Berthold Reservation. In 1983 Spotted Bear arranged to create a buffalo herd on the reservation. She acquired thirty-two cows and twenty-four bulls from the Theodore Roosevelt National Park rangers. In bringing the buffalo back to her community, she mended the severed spiritual ties between the Three Affiliated Tribes and the buffalo. For these and other people of the Great Plains, the buffalo was a holy animal and give of creators. Buffalo were a mainstay within Plains Indian culture and significant to the survival of the people. This move to acquire the herd was personal for Spotted Bear. Earlier that year, elders held the buffalo calling ceremony, performed for the first time since the nineteenth century. Spotted Bear attended the ceremony where she fasted and danced. She said, "the experience inspired me, and I ended up having a personal commitment to them [the buffalo]."[1]

Numakshi Mihe was politically savvy and realized the buffalo fueled a cultural and spiritual rebirth and had the potential to fuel an economic rebirth. Alyce Spotted Bear leveraged the herd and reinvigorated the economy and culture of the Three Affiliated Tribes. After slaughtering a buffalo, the meat was butchered and sold, local medicine men took the skulls, and the people used the hides to make high-end coats, purses, and gloves. In doing so, tribal people followed their traditions, just as their ancestors had done but not for commercial purposes. As Spotted Bear had predicted, the buffalo herd provided food and new jobs in the community. By 1998 the small herd acquired by Spotted Bear had turned into 235 buffalo on thirteen thousand acres of land. Before the overhunting of settlers, there were an estimated fifty-million buffalo in North America; by 1890, there were less than five hundred in the wild. Destruction of the buffalo herds and the flooding of the land took its toll on the tribe. As Spotted Bear said, "We belong with the buffalo," the buffalo's return aided in the healing of the Three Affiliated Tribes.[2]

Along with the buffalo's reintroduction, Spotted Bear employed the Tribe's Cultural Concerns Committee to jump-start cultural revival further. The committee fought to preserve the clan system and encouraged the youth to join elders in annual fasting. The Cultural Concerns Committee, while Spotted Bear was Chairwoman, continued its fight over sovereignty. The

Southwest Pipeline Project threatened the Three Affiliated Tribes' ancestral sites, including eagle-trapping pits and the graves of ancestors. Spotted Bear viewed the work of the Cultural Concerns Committee as necessary to maintaining tribal sovereignty.

Numakshi Mihe thought it necessary she convey the cultural differences between her people and the general public. In 1986, while talking to reporters, Spotted Bear said, "[a]s long as the cultural differences continue to show, we will be better able to make people understand our unique status as Americans. But if we lose our culture, we're on the road to losing our sovereignty."[3] During her time as Tribal Chairwoman, Alyce Spotted Bear felt the tension between preserving tradition and fighting for progress. *Numakshi Mihe* viewed progress as assimilation-educated tribal youth. The federal government viewed progress as an assimilation of the Indian population, which included flooding Indian lands. Spotted Bear felt that the government's progress threatened views of tribal sovereignty and left Indian leaders with the problem of "attempting to progress and maintain our culture at the same time."[4] This tension between progress and culture was not a new problem for Native Americans. Spotted Bear struggled to balance the two choices. Eventually, she came to believe her people had to protect their culture, language, and spiritual beliefs if they were to progress in the Indian way.

Numakshi Mihe realized that for healing to occur, the Three Affiliated Tribes needed reconciliation for the historical injustices the people had experienced. Spotted Bear's next goal as Chairwomen was to seek compensation for the Missouri River's flooding onto reservation lands. In 1986, Spotted Bear started the drive that led to the Joint Tribal Advisory Committee (JTAC) report. At the time, Secretary of the Interior Donald Hodel charged JTAC with reporting on the Missouri River's damming effects on the Three Affiliated Tribes and Standing Rock reservations. The JTAC members reported that the Fort Berthold Reservation suffered somewhere between $178 million and $412 million in damages, and the Standing Rock Reservation lost between $181 million and $350 million in damages. The report stated its recommendations attempt "to replace what was destroyed by the creation of the two dams, so that the tribes may attain economic independence." And "[w]e feel that . . . in view of the benefits downstream, that it's only fair that Indian tribes that suffered substantial portion of the damages in North Dakota be compensated."[5]

After the release of JTAC recommendations, Spotted Bear reported being pleased but emphasized that it could never make up for what the tribe had lost. The September 1, 1986, issue of The Washington Time's magazine *Insight*, called the Fort Berthold people "refugees on their own land."[6] The floodwaters drowned whole social and economic systems, JTAC reported, but Spotted Bear recognized that money could help stimulate economic growth on the reservation. Although *Numakshi Mihe* was pleased with the report's findings, others were less optimistic that the federal government would take any action. Charles Murphy, Chairmen of the Standing Rock Tribe at the time, thought the odds the recommendations would get implemented was about 50 percent.

Alyce Spotted Bear remained resolute, and even after her term ended, she encouraged tribal leaders to pressure the federal government to fulfill its obligations to the tribal nations. In 1992, six years after the Spotted Bear administration started the drive toward compensation, President George H.W. Bush signed legislation providing $149.2 million to the Three Affiliated Tribes and $90.6 million to the Standing Rock Tribe. A bittersweet victory this was, it could never replace what was lost, but *Numakshi Mihe* was hopeful that the money could fund Fort Berthold Community College in New Town, programs for elders, and rehabilitation services to fight alcohol and drug abuse on the reservation. The funds also allowed the tribe to increase its employees and acquire land to lease to tribal members for farms, ranches, and homes. Spotted Bear felt that in the end, "the more people in the community, the better off that community is. New Town will benefit in that."[7] *Numakshi Mihe*, although no longer Chairwoman and away in New York attending Cornell University, she remained concerned about her culture and community.

After leaving office in 1987, Alyce Spotted Bear continued her education. She earned a master's degree in education from Pennsylvania State University. She then moved on to Cornell University where she continued work on her PhD. in education administration. Although often away from her Fort Berthold Reservation, *Numakshi Mihe* remained committed to her community and stayed active in tribal politics and education. Spotted Bear was a lifelong student, but also a lifelong teacher. Alyce Spotted Bear worked at all levels of education from preschool to college. She taught high school and worked as a school administrator and superintendent. Spotted Bear founded and was vice president of the Native American Studies and the Tribal Relations Program at the Fort Berthold Community College in New Town, North Dakota. Alyce Spotted Bear also served as a visiting faculty member in the Native American Studies Program at Dartmouth College in Hanover, New Hampshire. In 1990, while at Cornell, Spotted Bear contributed to a journal article on the effectiveness of consolidating smaller schools into larger schools.

The paper argued that the advantage of school consolidation only benefited a small number of students while the adverse effects of consolidation, such as alienation, indiscipline, and parental disengagement, were largely ignored. In 2003, Spotted Bear utilized her consolidation knowledge to speak out against several North Dakota consolidation bills. Alyce Spotted Bear argued that "the school is the hub of the community," and small-town schools are "the place that the community revolves around."[8] For Spotted Bear, local schools were not just a place of learning, but they also served as a communal space where the community shares knowledge and builds strong ties. Spotted Bear understood that knowledge creation and community-building go hand in hand, which can be seen by her decision to invite Ivy League schools like Cornell to tribal powwows to recruit Native students. Her actions were guided by her motivation to protect her people's spiritual and material condition.

In 2009 Spotted Bear worked with tribal elder Edwin Benson to preserve the *Nu'eta* (Mandan) language. The Mandan, Arikara, and Hidatsa languages were all taught at Fort Berthold Community College. While vice president of the community college, *Numakshi Mihe*, obtained a Documenting Endangered Languages grant from the National Science Foundation. She was the principal investigator, and in this capacity, worked to establish an endowment and a foundation for the *Nu'eta*. Spotted Bear's work with the community college showed that education and Mandan, Hidatsa, and Arikara tradition could go hand in hand. She showed that culture and language could move forward together with progress. As Spotted Bear said, "At our college, we have been able to assist our students in meeting rigorous academic goals within a cultural context."[9] Spotted Bear's success in education propelled her back onto the political scene.

In 2010, President Barack Obama appointed Alyce Spotted Bear to the National Advisory Council on Indian Education (NACIE). She was the first member of the Three Affiliated Tribes to serve. The NACIE advises the secretary of education on the funding and administration of Native American programs. At the federal level, Spotted Bear now influenced all education policies aimed at Native Americans. While on National Advisory Council on Indian Education, she worked with various tribes and fifteen corporate, educational, and tribal council representatives. Sadly, Alyce Spotted Bear's time on the council was short-lived.

On July 25, 2013, Spotted Bear's doctors told her they suspected she had cancer of the liver. Not long afterwards, on August 13, 2013, *Numakshi Mihe* passed away. Although gone, her memory lives in all those touched by her work, not just with the Mandan, Arikara, and Hidatsa Nation, but for all Indian Country. On October 14, 2016, President Barack Obama signed into law bill S.246; the "Alyce Spotted Bear and Walter Soboleff Commission on Native Children Act." This act created the Alyce Spotted Bear and Walter Soboleff Commission on Native Children. In a statement issued by President Obama's Office of the Press Secretary: "The Commission is tasked with the important work of undertaking a comprehensive study of Federal, State, local, and tribal programs that serve Native children, and making recommendations on how those programs could be improved."[10] The bill utilized $2 million in funding to establish an eleven-member commission, delivering its recommendations within three years. After three years, the commission gets disbanded, and the federal, state, and tribal leaders would follow through with the commission's recommendations. Writing in the *American Indian Law Review*, T. Michael Andrews argued the bill offered a comprehensive approach in evaluating the "barriers to the development of sustainable, multidisciplinary programs designed to assist high-risk Native children and their families."[11] The bill would also study the effects of poverty on reservations in South Dakota and North Dakota.

It was appropriate to name the bill after Alyce Spotted Bear since she dedicated her life to the betterment of Native American children. Spotted Bear's fight for flood compensation and her programs that promoted job creation improved children's material conditions on the reservation—while her cultural programs in language reclamation and the reintroduction of the buffalo improved children's spiritual condition on the reservation. In 2013, when Senator Lisa Murkowski and Senator Heidi Heitkamp first introduced the bill creating the Native Children Act to the Chairmen of the Three Affiliated Tribes, Tex Hall thought the bill's naming appropriate, because Spotted Bear dedicated her life to the caring for children. "In our culture, children are sacred . . . they are the future leaders of tribes and the future parents and grandparents who will help carry on our traditions."[12]

Before her death in 2013, *Numakshi Mihe* spoke at the Mandan, Hidatsa, Arikara Tribal Tourism Grand Opening. Spotted Bear offered her comments while speaking in a traditional earthen lodge, and she echoed the words of Tex Hall when she said, "Children are our future leaders" and that, "to speak in front of your people is an honor."[13] Spotted Bear's commitment to her Nation is what guided her through life. She respected the past but always looked towards the future. During this speech, Spotted Bear applauded the new tourism industry the tribe was promoting. She envisioned a future where the Three Affiliated Tribes would once again be a hub for all people to come together, learn and trade with one another like in the past when the Mandan, Hidatsa, and Arikara land was the site of a vibrant trading center for all of the entire Great Plains region.

Spotted Bear thought that people would learn about Indians, and rid themselves of the outdated images and stereotypes of Native Americans perpetuated by the U.S. government and other non-Native agencies, through tourism. Spotted Bear argued that this negative imagery justified the United States' ongoing dispossession of Indigenous lands. Spotted Bear said, "having us imaged as being almost non-human made it easier for them to take our resources and take our lands."[14] The pain behind these words is audible, as if saying them summoned images of the flood that sixty years before took so much from her people.

The Mandan, Hidatsa, and Arikara Nations originally had 12.5 million acres. The U.S. government subsequently stripped their land base down to 643,000 acres. After the Garrison flood, only 490,640 acres remained for a tribal homeland.

In May 2009, the *Missoulian* interviewed Mandan elder Edwin Benson. During his interview, he admitted that when reminded of the flood, "I still cry every time I go back down to that area . . . It's kinda hard. I can't help but cry now."[15] One can imagine the cottonwood trees used to make traditional earthen lodges inundated with water. The trees slowly drowned over the next decades. However, some dismissed the Missouri River's damming and the subsequent flooding that accompanied it by arguing that the water project represented progress. Carl Whitman, the Tribal Council chairmen and part of the delegation sent to Billings, Montana, in 1950, said, "[w]e did everything we could to stop the building of the Garrison dam . . . we didn't want it and we don't pay for any part of it."[16] Whitman later admitted "[w]e don't want to stand in the way of progress, but we are wondering just what progress is."[17]

Spotted Bear earned her title *Numakshi Mihe* because she was a steadfast leader who understood that progress for Native Americans was and is rooted in their culture. Native American culture and progress includes communal permission and consensus, which has guided and will continue to guide the Indigenous people of this land for generations to come. Alyce Spotted Bear was an influential politician and educator because she realized progress and tradition were not at odds with each other, but complimentary and Tribal sovereignty itself depended on the continued transmission of these cultural values.

NOTES

1. "Fort Berthold Reservation Tribal Group to use Buffalo Herd as Economic Resource," *Star Tribune*, December 9, 1985.

2. Jodi Rave, "Tribes Ignite Comeback," *Rapid City Journal*, September 27, 1998.

3. Frederic Smith, "'Refugee' Label Tags Fort Berhtold," *The Bismarck Tribune*, August 30, 1986.

4. Smith, "'Refugee' Label," *The Bismarck Tribune*, August 30, 1986.

5. "Tribal Chairmen Want Compensation for Losses," *Argus-Leader*, July 9, 1986.

6. Frederic Smith, "'Refugee' Label Tags Fort Berthold," *The Bismarck Tribune*, August 30, 1986.

7. "Ex-Tribal Leader's Effort Succeeds in Settlement," *The Bismarck Tribune*, November 5, 1992.

8. Sheena Dooley, "Fighting for the Schools," *The Bismarck Tribune*, January 26, 2003.

9. Jodi Rave, "Tribal Colleges Meet to Plan Students' Future," the *Missoulian*, March 29, 2009.

10. The White House Office of the Press Secretary, Statement by the President—S. 246, October 14, 2016, https://obamawhitehouse.archives.gov/the-press-office/2016/10/14/statement-president-s-246.

11. T. Michael Andrews, "Continuing to Work for Indian Country in the 115th Congress." *American Indian Law Review* 41 (2017), 362.

12. Dirk Lammers, "Bill Aims to Protect Indian Children," *The Bismarck Tribune*, October 31, 2013.

13. Alyce Spotted Bear, "MHA Tribal Elder: Alyce Spotted Bear," MHA Culture Channel, March 19, 2014, video, 9:11, https://www.youtube.com/watch?v=xVjdIatctQk.

14. Spotted Bear, "MHA Tribal Elder: Alyce Spotted Bear," MHA Culture Channel, March 19, 2014, video, 9:11, https://www.youtube.com/watch?v=xVjdIatctQk.

15. Jodi Rave, "The Last Speaker," *The Missoulian*, May 11, 2009.

16. "Indians Don't Get Voice in Confab on Land-Flooding," *The Bismarck Tribune*, April 13, 1950.

17. "Indians Don't Get Voice in Confab on Land-Flooding," *The Bismarck Tribune*, April 13, 1950.

BIBLIOGRAPHY

Andrews, T. Michael. "Continuing to Work for Indian Country in the 115th Congress." *American Indian Law Review* 41 (2017), 361–65.

Dooley, Sheena. "Fighting for the Schools." *The Bismarck Tribune*, January 26, 2003.

"Ex-Tribal Leader's Effort Succeeds in Settlement," *The Bismarck Tribune*, November 5, 1992.

"Fort Berthold Reservation Tribal Group to use Buffalo Herd as Economic Resource." *Star Tribune*, December 9, 1985.

"Tribal Chairmen Want Compensation for Losses." *Argus Leader*, July 9, 1986.

"Indians Don't Get Voice in Confab in Land-Flooding." *The Bismarck Tribune*, April 13, 1950.

Lammers, Dirk. 2013. "Bill Aims to Protect Indian Children." *The Bismarck Tribune*, October 31, 2013.

Rave, Jodi. "Tribes Ignite Comeback." *Rapid City Journal*, September 27, 1998.

Rave, Jodi. "The Last Speaker." *The Missoulian*, May 11, 2009.

Smith, Frederic. "'Refugee' Label Tags Fort Berthold." *The Bismarck Tribune*, August 30, 1986.

FURTHER READINGS

Estes, Nick. *Our History Is the Future*. Brooklyn: Verso, 2019.
Rapid City Journal. 1989. "Ivy League Recruiters Come to Tribes." *Rapid City Journal*, September 10, 1989.
Johnson, Hannah."Spotted Bear Dies." *The Bismarck Tribune*, August 17, 2013.
"School Size and Program Comprehensiveness: Evidence From High School and Beyond." *Educational Evaluation and Poly Analysis* 12 (1990), 109–20.
"Tribal Delegation Wants Pipeline Intake Relocated." *The Bismarck Tribune*, December 7, 1982.

Chapter Eight

Navajo Judge, Ramah and Crownpoint Districts

Irene Toledo
(b. 1953)

Thomas Long

Irene M. Toledo, now retired, was a District and Family Court Judge for the Ramah and Crownpoint Districts of the Navajo Nation. The 27,000 square miles of the Navajo Indian Nation in the southwestern United States straddles the borders of the states of New Mexico, Arizona, and Utah. The Navajo Nation controls the largest Indian reservation in the United States with a land base larger than ten states. The Navajo are one of the most populous Indian nations within the United States.

Judge Toledo was first appointed to the bench in 1989. Prior to her tenure as a jurist, Toledo served as a court advocate for the Navajo People's Legal Services in the areas of administrative, criminal, civil, and family law for a decade. During her lengthy career as a court advocate, Toledo first made a name for herself in the legal arena as a woman of exceptional intelligence, sage judgment, and fortitude of character who tirelessly strove to improve the lives of the Navajo. Within three years of her ascension to the Navajo District Court, Judge Toledo's reputation spread well beyond the Navajo Reservation, leading to becoming in 1992 a member of the advisory board of Education Development Center, Inc. (EDC) in Massachusetts. In this capacity, Judge Irene Toledo assisted in the development of the new protocols and training curriculum aimed at improving the rights of victims. This cutting-edge project prefigured contemporary anti-hate crime initiatives that have become common across the entire United States.[1]

After gaining national attention for her successful activist role in formulating her EDC project, President Bill Clinton, through the U.S. Department of Justice (DOJ), tapped Irene Toledo in 1997 as a consultant. For the DOJ, Judge Toledo led a task force that studied the impact of crime upon victims for the development of a presidential initiative to assist victims. Toledo presented her findings and recommendations regarding how the judicial system could function more compassionately toward victims, both in the courtroom and throughout the entire legal process. Due to the adversarial nature of the U.S. legal process, during the cross-examination, the accuser must often endure an intense line of questioning that can border on combative. Toledo's findings illuminated the negative effects of such a system, which not only push the rights of the accuser to the fringes of the law, but forces him or her to face a hostile defense attorney. This leads many victims to remain silent and not report crimes committed against them.[2]

Ultimately, Toledo's task force produced an official report that argued for new directions in dealing with victims' rights and looked to the next century through a foundation of Navajo culture. Judge Toledo stated that when criminals arrive in court, the contemporary courtroom protocol demands that they, the accused, be immediately and fully advised of their legal rights, while the defendants and/or victims receive no such counsel. Toledo argued that in order to fully serve justice, this archaic component of the historical adversarial system should be brought up to date with the current trend in the United States to equally serve the rights of all participants in a case. In no small measure, Toledo's vast knowledge of and experience within the Navajo legal system has influenced this intellectual response to an outmoded, punitive form of law. The influences for Judge Toledo's breakthrough efforts clearly trace back to the Navajo legal system, in particular the Navajo system of peacemaking.[3]

The structure of the Navajo courts closely resembled the federal judicial system of the United States. The Navajo Nation has a Supreme Court and a system of eleven District Courts. However, one role within the Navajo system has no parallel within the courts of the United States. Navajo people have a position known as Peacemakers. These powerful individuals, central to Navajo society since the beginning of time, have legal standing and judicial authority, giving them tremendous power within the legal system. After decades of forced assimilation by the Bureau of Indian Affairs, the Navajos suspended the Peacemaker system but ultimately restored the sacred tradition in 1982. For over twenty-five years, the offices of the Peacemakers have resided in each Navajo District Court. The Peacemaker form of conflict resolution does not follow an adversarial pattern. Outsiders often mistakenly perceive the Peacemaker effort as a form of mediation or arbitration. It is a collective effort that incorporates Navajo culture and spiritual beliefs. Peacemakers attempt to bring about a harmonizing process that ends the conflict. According to Navajo Supreme Court Chief Justice Herb Yazzie, the Harmonization Project provided Navajo people a new method for tribal courts based on *Diné bi beenahaz'áanii* or traditional Navajo cultural beliefs.[4]

Toledo has played an ongoing central role in the Peacemaker initiative. This restorative system of laws positions all participants as equal parties, and not in the context of one as the accused and the other the victim. In this manner, the Navajos seek to restore harmony, as opposed to meting out punishment or retribution. In 2002, the Navajo Nation legislated that this ancient component of their culture be included in all criminal and civil cases. This overarching concept strongly protects the rights of all, as well as the equality of all participants in a conflict. This mentality informed Judge Toledo in her study for the Department of Justice.

Irene Toledo has drawn worldwide attention as an expert in the area of family law, with a specialty in conflict resolution. Drawing on her practice of eliminating the concept of the accused, thus removing the need for either party to enter a defense in her courtroom, Toledo has facilitated exceptional results. The Family Violence Prevention Program of San Francisco became aware of Toledo's remarkable success, and they tapped her expertise in family law and conflict resolution to assist the city with its growing problem of domestic violence and neglect. Toledo's collaboration with the San Francisco organization in 1994 concluded with a landmark judicial bench book, *Domestic Violence and the Consideration of Cultural Factors in Criminal and Civil Court Cases.*

After witnessing the expansion of domestic violence that plagued families with veterans of the Vietnam War, Toledo theorized that a connection existed between those suffering from post-traumatic stress disorder (PTSD) and the abuse of their younger relatives. She commissioned her probation officer to research the existence of PTSD among Navajo veterans resulting from the conflict in Vietnam. The results of her study bore out Toledo's suspicion. A significant percentage of the veterans who suffered from PTSD not only committed violent offenses, but the study overwhelmingly demonstrated that the children of the veterans or the veteran's younger siblings or extended relatives had in effect learned the violent PTSD behavior patterns. After establishing these facts, Toledo moved to eradicate this pattern of violence through the Navajo peacemaking process, and within a year, the shift away from the violence associated with PTSD had become noticeable. The process of dismantling this unfortunate aftereffect of the Vietnam War continues.

The persistence of domestic violence on the Navajo Reservation, even in the wake of the restored process of peacemaking, led Judge Toledo and her colleague, Judge Angela Keahanie-Sanford, to co-appoint James W. Zion to research the domestic violence cases in Crownpoint, and to analyze when peacemaking worked and when it failed. Toledo and Keahanie-Sanford envisioned a synthesis of traditional Navajo peacemaking with Anglo-American judicial procedures, which they hoped would produce a more effective method of coping with domestic violence issues and developing a system of preventative methodology.[5]

Zion's study concluded that peacemaking usually succeeded when the process took place completely outside of the court and when more relatives of each party played a role in the outcome. Instances of severe violence, the area of greatest concern for Toledo and Keahanie-Sanford, enjoyed the lowest success rate under the peacemaking process. Although cases of severe violence were the rarest form of conflict on the Navajo Reservation, they arguably have the greatest negative impact upon the Navajo people. However, Zion's study also revealed that in the cases of severe violence, peacemaking rehabilitated and restored amicable relations. These improvements probably would not have resulted from Western legal proceedings. Zion concluded that while no consensus existed indicating that peacemaking worked without failure, overall it had a success rate that warranted its continuation and that other legal systems might benefit from studying the process.

Although Toledo made her most significant mark in the areas of family law and victims' rights, she garnered national attention in a landmark case, *Navajo Nation v Russell Means*, while serving as Justice-designate on the Navajo Supreme Court in the late 1990s. Longtime American Indian activist and Hollywood actor Russell Means, a Lakota man, had lived in the Navajo Nation for nearly a decade with his former wife, Gloria Grant, a Navajo. In December 1997, while still married to Grant and living on Navajo land, Means fell into an argument with his father-in-law, which escalated into a fistfight and assault charges leveled against Means. The case was slated to go before the Navajo District Court of Chinle, Arizona, but before the case opened, Means sued the Navajo Nation on the grounds that it had no legal jurisdiction over him. According to Means, even though he lived on Navajo land, his non-Navajo ancestry precluded him from being a subject to the Navajo Nation's courts. He insisted that only a federal court of the United States had any legal authority in this matter.[6]

Given Means' celebrity status, his lawsuit against the Navajo Nation gained instant and widespread attention. Native American issues in general had become more visible since the development of Indian casinos and resorts following the *Cabazon v California* decision of 1987, which opened the door for Native American economic self-reliance. Resultantly, by the late 1990s, Native American legal issues captured the attention of the greater legal system of the United States. Law schools around the nation actively developed programs that focused on Native American outreach, law, and legal issues.

When the largest Indian nation became involved in a lawsuit with one of the most well-known, high-profile Native American activists, Harvard Law School, the most heralded institution of its kind in the entire United States, reached out to the Navajo Supreme Court and offered the use of their facilities in Massachusetts. Over the years, many Supreme Court justices have sat in the Harvard Law School Ames Moot Courtroom and heard cases. However, when Judge Irene Toledo and her fellow Navajo Supreme Court justices heard *Navajo Nation v Russell Means*, it became the first nonfictional court case ever tried at Harvard Law School. Understandably, the unprecedented nature of this high-profile dispute only added to the pre-trial publicity, which placed added pressure on both sides in the case.[7]

The core components of the case dealt with Navajo common law, congressional authority to control the lives of Indians, equal protection legal rights afforded by the Constitution of the United States, the jurisdiction of the Navajo courts over non-Navajos within reservation borders, and ultimately the sovereign status of the Navajo Nation to self-govern on its land. The last issue, sovereignty, was by far the most significant aspect of the case, transcending the context of *Navajo Nation v Russell Means*. Rather, this momentous court case applied to American Indians across the United States.

Russell Means' attorney, John Trebon, opened his argument by claiming the Treaty of 1868 between the Navajo Nation and the United States stipulated that the Navajo government and courts did not have any jurisdiction over nonmember Indians. Trebon also argued that, when Congress legislated in 1991 that Indian tribes could prosecute nonmember Indians who resided on their reservations, although non-Indians remained beyond the legal reach of Native American court systems, it had implemented a racist law that was illegal under the national Constitution's Equal Protection clause.

The chief prosecutor of the Navajo Nation, Donovan Brown, argued that since Russell Means lived on Navajo land, married a Navajo woman, and conducted business that benefited from the Navajo Nation, Means "consented to the jurisdiction of the Navajo." He further posited that the Treaty of 1868 actually conceded that the Navajo Nation did have legal authority over all nonmember Indians who lived on Navajo land. In the end, the Navajo Supreme Court voted 3–0 against Russell Means. Not willing to accept the Navajo decision, Means petitioned the U.S. Supreme Court, which declined to hear his case. The Navajo decision held, and the U.S. Supreme Court recognized the sovereign status of the Navajo Supreme Court. For Judge Toledo and her colleagues, it was a significant victory that strengthened the sovereignty of the Navajo Nation. The decision represented perhaps Toledo's greatest contribution to the sovereignty of all Native Nations within the United States.[8]

Irene Toledo has been a legal activist championing tribal sovereignty for the *Diné* (Navajo People) and all Indigenous people. Her work as a Peacemaker touched the lives of Navajos and people off the reservation who learned about methods of conflict resolution. Many people have never heard of Judge Toledo or her methods but her contributions have had significant implications to tribal sovereignty and the sovereignty of Indigenous people everywhere.

NOTES

1. Irene Toledo, Judge, www.ballotpedia.org.
2. Nancy Waring, "The Law of Their Land," *Harvard Law Today* (Summer 1999), today.law.harvard.edu; James W. Zion and Elsie B. Zion, "Hozho' Sokee'—Stay Together Nicely: Domestic Violence Under Navajo Common Law," *Arizona Law Journal* 25, No. 2 (Summer 1993), 407–10.
3. Robert Yazzie, "Life Comes from It: Navajo Justice Concepts," *New Mexico Law Review* 24 (Spring 1994), 175–76.
4. Yazzie, "Life Comes from It," 175–76, 180–82.
5. Yazzie, "Life Comes from It," 180–84; Barbara Gray and Pat Lauderdale, "The Web of Justice: Restorative Justice Has Presented Only One Part of the Story," *Wizcazo Sa Review* 21, No. 1 (Spring 2006), 29–35.
6. Supreme Court of the Navajo Nation. Original Petition of Russell Means, No. SC—CV—61-98, May 11, 1999, www.tribal-institute.org.
7. Waring, "The Law of Their Land," today.law.harvard.edu.
8. Jason M. Goins, "Navajo Nation Case Could Redefine Scope of Tribal Courts," *The Harvard Crimson* (February 1999).

BIBLIOGRAPHY

Goins, Jason M. "Navajo Nation Case Could Redefine Scope of Tribal Courts." *The Harvard Crimson* (February 1999). www.thecrimson.com.

Gray, Barbara and Pat Lauderdale, "The Web of Justice: Restorative Justice Has Presented Only One Part of the Story," *Wizcazo Sa Review* 21, No. 1 (Spring 2006), 29–35.

Supreme Court of the Navajo Nation. Original Petition of Russell Means, No. SC—CV—61-98, May 11, 1999, www.tribal-institute.org.

Toledo, Irene. Judge, www.ballotpedia.org.

Waring, Nancy, "The Law of Their Land," *Harvard Law Today* (Summer 1999), today.law.harvard.edu.

Yazzie, Robert. "Life Comes from It: Navajo Justice Concepts." *New Mexico Law Review* 24 (Spring 1994).

Zion, James W. and Elsie B. Zion, "Hozho 'Sokee'—Stay Together Nicely: Domestic Violence Under Navajo Common Law," *Arizona Law Journal* 25, No. 2 (Summer 1993).

FURTHER READINGS

Danis, Fran. "New Directions from the Field: Victims' Rights and Services for the 21st Century." United States Department of Justice, Office of Justice Programs, Office for Victims of Crime. Washington, DC, 2006.

Holm, Tom. *Strong Hearts, Wounded Souls: Native American Veterans of the Vietnam War.* Austin: University of Texas Press, 1996.

Navajo Nation v Russell Means, February 6, 1999.

Nelson, Marianne and James Zion, eds. *Navajo Nation Peacemaking.* Tucson: University of Arizona Press, 2005.

Witmer, Sharon. *Tribal College Journal of Indian American Higher Education* 7, No. 1 (July 31, 1996), 24.

Yazzie, Herb. "Strategic Plan of the Navajo Nation Judicial Branch." Window Rock, Arizona, Navajo Nation (October 16, 2007).

Chapter Nine

"In Unity There Is Strength," Writer and Activist

Marie Potts
(b. 1895–d. 1978)

Daniel Stahl-Kovell

Marie Mason Potts—*Chankutpan* (One With Sharp Eyes)—was a California Indian activist, journalist, and scholar, most famous for her role as editor of the nationally renowned newsletter of the Federated Indians of California, *Smoke Signal*. Potts (Northern Maidu) devoted her life to fighting for social and economic justice for California Indians, and her service extended well-beyond her work with *Smoke Signal*. She played a fundamental role in the foundation of the Federated Indians of California, helped found the American Indian Press Association, and published on Maidu cultural heritage and history. Potts was integral to the movement for Native self-determination in California both as a leader and for establishing a precedent for unity among California Indians during the twentieth century.

Potts was born in 1895 at Big Meadows in northwestern Plumas County, California, a picturesque mountain valley cradled between the Sierra Nevada Mountains to the south and Lassen Peak and its dramatic lava fields to the northwest. Her father, whom she had never known, was a white prospector who had violated her mother and left her to raise Marie and the other children, herself. Despite the living memory of her violent conception, Potts reflected on her youth in *The Northern Maidu* with fondness, recalling her early childhood spent in a cedar bark house with her family and listening to the "orchestra of the Great Spirit" while lying awake at night, only to wake to the smell of the pines and the songs of the birds.[1] The onslaught of white settlement in the years following the discovery of gold in Northern California had dramatically altered Maidu life and left an indelible mark on the landscape. War, violence, competition for resources, disease, and environmental destruction forced the Maidu people to adapt to ensure the survival of their culture, language, and religion. Even in the face of genocide and the real threat of extermination, they endured. In 1914, the Great Western Power

Company completed construction of the hydroelectric Canyon Dam project, effectively damming the North Fork of the Feather River and flooding Big Meadows, forming Lake Almanor, now a popular recreational lake. The dam and lake destroyed former village sites, cultural resources, and Indian burials. The lake forcibly displaced Maidu from their ancestral homelands.

Potts spent much of her adolescence from 1900 to 1912 at Greenville Indian Boarding School, not far from Big Meadows. Two of her older siblings had already attended Greenville, and at Greenville school officials gave Potts the surname Mason. At Greenville, Potts learned to speak English and her teachers forced her to suppress her culture, language, and religion. The government later sent Potts to Carlisle Indian Industrial School to complete her education in Pennsylvania, and she graduated with the Carlisle class of 1915. She contended that it was her own decision to go to Carlisle after facing such complete assimilation at Greenville and the destruction of her homeland by Lake Almanor at Big Meadows. No less, after graduating from Carlisle, Potts moved back home to marry Hensley Potts, whom she had known from Greenville, and the two made a home in Plumas County, raising five daughters and operating a fishing and hunting camp on the banks of Lake Almanor.

In 1947, at the age of fifty-two, Marie Potts first became closely involved with the Federated Indians of California (FIC). At the time, Potts was living with her daughter, Pansy, in Sacramento. Pansy was working as a secretary for the FIC, and the two offered office space at their house to the fledgling organization. The FIC was established in opposition to the disappointments of the California Indians Jurisdictional Act (CIJA) of 1928, which established a court of claims to determine compensation for the eighteen unratified treaties with California Indians and representation by corrupt private attorneys under the leadership of Frederic G. Collett and the exploitative Indian Board of Co-operation. When CIJA finally yielded a settlement in 1950, California Indians received a meager five million dollars ($150 per capita) for the theft of nearly seven and a half million acres of land. Therefore, in 1946, when the Federal Indian Claims Commission began its hearings, California Indians, many of whom had been members of Collett's organization, sought to create an organization to advocate on behalf of California Indians and win a just settlement for the millions of acres that the United States and state of California had stolen from California's first people. Marie Potts and her daughters, Kitty Flores and Pansy Marine, served as early founders of the Federated Indians of California.

Potts and her daughter, Flores, quickly involved themselves on the FIC board and in publishing the FIC newsletter, *Smoke Signal*. The newspaper appeared bi-monthly or sometimes monthly, relaying the FIC's most recent meetings, conveying the organization's political message, and disseminating important news concerning land claims, social advocacy, and political action. *Smoke Signal* was written, edited, and printed out of the home of Marie Potts, and following the death of Flores in a tragic automobile accident in 1951, Potts took over as the newsletter's principal editor. The paper was almost always a collective endeavor by FIC members passing through the office. Each issue of the paper had to be painstakingly typed on mimeograph stencil paper, and any illustrations or large headings had to be carved into the stencil by hand. After Marie and her associates created a master copy, someone could run copies. They created the newsletter by hand, on a mimeograph machine. No less, it was Kitty Flores's hard work and determination that had brought *Smoke Signal* to reality. However, for nearly thirty years, *Smoke Signal* was characterized by Marie Potts's tenacity for social and political justice and her drive to unite Native Californians under a shared collective experience. This was firmly reflected in the *Smoke Signal* motto: "In unity there is strength."

The paper largely focused on fostering a sense of California Indian identity, unity, and community. Issues followed legislative efforts impacting California Indians and included advertisements for educational and social events, an occasional Indian joke, links to other Native organizations around the state, and later on, letters from the editor offering Potts's own opinion on Indian issues. *Smoke Signal* developed alongside Potts's own intellectual growth with each passing decade, and by the 1970s, the paper spoke with the authoritative voice of experience. Nevertheless, Potts's political involvement was not limited to her work with *Smoke Signal* as she became increasingly involved in Native organizing and activism at the national level. In 1961, Potts actively began working with the National Congress of the American Indian (NCAI) in the planning phases of the American Indian Chicago Conference, working as a guest editor with NCAI *Bulletin* editor Helen Peterson.

Potts's political involvement at the national level widened as time passed. She became the NCAI's western regional vice president and regularly offered detailed coverage of national Indian affairs in *Smoke Signal*. Likewise, *Smoke Signal* became regionally and nationally influential to other Native American news outlets as an authoritative voice on land claims issues and for relaying important events. Further, Potts generated an audience for Indian affairs in California, paving the way for later organizations to distribute information concerning education, culture, and social justice. In the 1960s and 1970s, Potts extended coverage of *Smoke Signal* to the burgeoning Red Power protest movement, visiting Alcatraz Island during the occupation in late 1969 and reporting on developments surrounding the creation of D-Q University, the incipient off-reservation tribal college outside of Davis, California. Potts felt that the Red Power protest groups had a role to play in garnering the attention of policymakers and the non-Indian public to promote change.

In 1970, Potts and a select group of Native American journalists from the United States led by Charles Trimble (Oglala Sioux) met to consider creating a national association of Native journalists devoted to promoting Native print journalism and shifting popular misconceptions of Native people in the media by bridging the gap between Native and non-Native press. In 1971, they founded the American Indian Press Association (AIPA). The AIPA drew more attention to Native American journalism. However, the organization's success was checked by extreme financial difficulty. Despite the AIPA's determination and vision of promoting Native media, the organization disbanded in 1975.

Nevertheless, the impact of the AIPA in galvanizing Native journalists left a lasting impact on Native media. With more than two decades of experience with the FIC, *Smoke Signal*, and national Indian affairs, Potts was a venerated and accomplished cofounder of the AIPA. Rupert Costo recognized her in the *Indian Historian* as an Honored Indian Historian, and AIPA honored her by naming an award after her. The Marie Potts Achievement Award celebrated exceptional journalistic excellence at the annual meetings of the AIPA. Potts was even recognized by the state of California when the second floor of the State Office Building Number One was named after her. The California Native American Heritage Commission also honored her as a remarkable woman, placing her photograph in the Jessie Unruh Building on the Capitol Circle in Sacramento. Today, the commission is located at 1550 Harbor Boulevard, Suite 100, West Sacramento.

In the 1970s, Potts began work on *The Northern Maidu*, a rich account of Maidu history and culture, which was published in 1977, just one year before her passing. The work also served as a personal reflection of Potts's own early life at Big Meadows—her life before her boarding school education at Greenville and Carlisle. In *The Northern Maidu*, Potts grieves for a past torn by westward expansion that resulted in genocide. In her book, she conveys a deep sense of gratitude for the endurance of her people and hope for the future. This is most clear in her description of the Bear Dance (*Wahdom Buyam*), a ceremony which gives thanks for surviving the winter and appeases the bear and rattlesnake for the coming year. Potts was both active in reviving and continuing this tradition. As the bear, a symbol for life, endures the winter, so do the people. The Bear Dance brings people together to reassert community, share food, and preserve Maidu cultural and religious heritage. It offers a message of friendship and unity in each coming year, marking a new beginning and celebrating the endurance of the tribe.

Marie Potts passed away in the spring of 1978 in a Susanville hospital while attending a Bear Dance. Like the bear, Potts's life represented the strength of Native American culture and perseverance. Having been born less than forty miles away, Potts had endured many winters and found her calling in political activism, the FIC, and editing/writing *Smoke Signal*. During this time, Potts had been a founding member of the Federated Indians of California and the American Indian Press Association. She had edited and wrote for *Smoke Signal* and other leading Native American newspapers, furthering the cause of American Indian affairs. She had worked for state and national issues as an advocate for California Indian affairs. She actively sought to retain and revive Maidu knowledge, culture, and identity.

Marie Potts's life and career exemplify the Maidu and other California Indians' capacity to survive through generations of colonialism and disenfranchisement and to resist oppression and reassert their cultural heritage. Marie Potts had faced adversity and stood for American Indian self-determination and Native American sovereignty to enhance the lives of millions of Indigenous children.

NOTE

1. Marie Potts, "Childhood Games," in *The Way We Lived: California Indian Stories, Songs, and Reminiscences*, ed. Malcolm Margolin (Berkeley, CA: Heyday Books, 1981), 16.

BIBLIOGRAPHY

Potts, Marie. "Childhood Games." In *The Way We Lived: California Indian Stories, Songs, and Reminiscences*, edited by Malcolm Margolin, 15. Berkeley, CA: Heyday Books, 1981.

FURTHER READINGS

Castaneda, Terri A. "California Indian Land Claims Activism and Urban Indian Place-Making." *Proceedings of the Southwestern Anthropological Association* (2010): 1–7.

Castaneda, Terri A. "Making News: Marie Potts and the *Smoke Signals* of the Federated Indians of California." James P. Danky and Wayne A. Wiegand, eds. *Women in Print: Essays on the Print Culture of American Women from the Nineteenth and Twentieth Centuries*, Madison: University of Wisconsin Press, 2006, 77–125.

Forbes, Jack. *Native Americans of California and Nevada*. Happy Camp, CA: Naturegraph Publishers, 1982.

La Potin, Armand S. *Native American Voluntary Organizations*. New York: Greenwood Press, 1987.

Margolin, Malcolm, ed. *The Way We Lived: California Indian Stories, Songs, and Reminiscences*. Berkeley, CA: Heyday Books, 1981.
Murphy, James E., and Sharon M. Murphy. *Let My People Know: American Indian Journalism, 1828–1978*. Norman: University of Oklahoma Press, 1981.
Potts, Marie. *The Northern Maidu*. Happy Camp, CA: Naturegraph Publishers, 1977.

Chapter Ten

Cultural Activist
Zitkala-Ša, *Gertrude Simmons Bonnin* (b. 1876–d. 1938)

Benjamin Jenkins

Zitkala-Ša, better known as Gertrude Simmons Bonnin, a Yankton Dakota woman, refused to let others define her. Through her eloquent writing and linguistic talents, Gertrude actively shaped the record of her life as an activist. "Loosely clad in a slip of brown buckskin," she once wrote, "and light-footed with a pair of soft moccasins on my feet, I was as free as the wind that blew my hair, and no less spirited than a bounding deer. These were my mother's pride,–my wild freedom and overflowing spirits."[1] Gertrude's femininity and her freedom shaped the course of her life and influenced her decision to share her heritage in as many ways as possible. Women have traditionally acted as the guarantors of Dakota culture, a responsibility Bonnin took very seriously. For decades, Gertrude used these talents to help all Native peoples in the United States, writing books and giving speeches in favor of Native rights and living a life that balanced her white and Native heritages equally.

Born onto the Yankton Reservation in South Dakota, Gertrude Simmons Bonnin claimed February 22, 1876, as her birthday.[2] Significantly, this was the same year Sitting Bill led Lakota and Cheyenne warriors to defeat Colonel George A. Custer and the Seventh Cavalry of the U.S. Army at Little Bighorn. Gertrude's mother was Ellen Simmons, or *Tate I Yohin Win*, a Yankton/Dakota woman who raised her daughter to cherish her Native traditions. Ellen claimed that a white trader called Felker had been Gertrude's father, but he abandoned the family before Gertrude's birth, never to return. Gertrude spent almost the first decade of her life very close to her mother and her brother, David. As an enrolled member of Yankton Indian Nation, she received land under Dawes Act in 1916. Through these links, Gertrude retained ties to her Dakota roots for her entire life. However, as she grew up, she also learned to respect white culture and to integrate it into her worldview.

Assimilationist educational practices inform the direction Gertrude's life took, as well as the zeal for educating Native children that she championed in the twentieth century. At eight years of age, in 1884, Gertrude left her home to attend a Quaker school for Native Americans in Indiana. This institution followed Carlisle Industrial Training School's dictum to "kill the Indian in him and save the man." The model education pioneered at Carlisle stressed acculturation, or the abandonment of Native customs and beliefs for western culture and Christianity. For the rest of her life, Gertrude retained bitter memories of how white educators attempted to uproot her Yankton traditions, best exemplified when they cut her hair to fit Anglo-American norms. "I cried aloud," Gertrude later wrote, "shaking my head all the while until I felt the cold blades of the scissors against my neck, and heard them gnaw off one of my thick braids. Then I lost my spirit."[3] Because of her distance from the Yankton Reservation, Gertrude grew culturally distant from her mother and brother, David.

However, Gertrude also developed new talents during her education, which she used to promote the value of Native cultures. From 1895 to 1897, she attended Earlham College in Indiana. She trained to become a teacher during her matriculation, but never finished her degree due to illness. However, she did hone writing and oratorical skills, realizing she could use these tools to promote Indigenous values she had learned on Yankton Reservation as a child.[4] Gertrude practiced violin, and grew skilled enough to enter the New England Conservatory of Music at Boston, where she studied from 1899 to 1901. In Boston, Gertrude worked closely with the journalist Joseph Edgar Chamberlin, who connected her to a number of venues that would later publish her work. Gertrude's fame prompted her to play with the Carlisle Indian School Band at the Paris Exhibition of 1900, where she soloed and received praise for her musical talent. Along with her writing and speaking talents, Gertrude used her musical skill to craft a legacy of cultural activism.

One episode from her youth particularly demonstrates Gertrude's aptitude as a speaker. She participated in the Indiana State Oratorical Conference, delivering a speech titled "Side by Side." Gertrude focused on Native repression during the conference, as well as her desire to learn from and live in harmony with whites. She decried assimilation, which she believed whites used to eliminate native cultures. Audience members shouted epithets and raised a banner demeaning Bonnin as a "squaw," but none of this interrupted Gertrude, and she won second place in the competition.

The final years of the nineteenth century marked a period of transition for Gertrude Simmons. After her departure from Earlham College, Gertrude taught at Carlisle Indian School from 1897 to 1900. She voiced strong opposition to the school's tenet of assimilation, and believed that Native peoples should have opportunities to attend college, not just institutions that specialized in technical training. For a brief period, Gertrude was engaged to a Yavapai doctor and activist, Carlos Montezuma, but she broke the engagement because of their conflicting stances on assimilation. Gertrude opposed assimilation.

In the first decade of the twentieth century, Gertrude's star began to rise. She gained national attention for her ability to share Dakota stories, and she led Americans who empathized with the struggle of North America's first peoples. Her writing skills also flourished, and she published prolifically. Stories of her life and Native folklore she adapted from oral traditions appeared in nationally renowned periodicals such as *The Atlantic Monthly* and *Harper's Magazine*. Gertrude later collected these stories into books, *Old Indian Legends* in 1901 and *American Indian Stories* in 1921.

In 1901, Frederic Remington, a master painter of the American West, illustrated one of Gertrude's first articles in *Harper's Magazine* in 1901. Her articles and essays demonstrated the struggles of a Native girl who had been cut off from her culture and forced to behave completely differently through education. Gertrude used her writing to reach out to non-Native audiences to highlight the difficulties Native peoples faced in the United States. In *American Indian Stories*, for instance, she explained the importance of oral beliefs and cultural traditions to Native peoples. Her Dakota roots shaped much of her early writing. In one letter to a friend, Gertrude wrote from the Yankton Reservation, "This place is full of material for stories," and she expressed "hope [that] I may soon find a good writing mood—to do justice to the abandoned material around me."[5] The recovery of Dakota stories, many of which she published, formed one of the core aspects of Gertrude's mission as a cultural ambassador.

Gertrude wrote under a Lakota name she adopted: *Zitkala-Ša*, or Red Bird. For public matters, she used the surname of Simmons after her mother's second husband, which her brother, David, also used. By adulthood she spoke Nakota, Dakota, and Lakota in addition to English, making her an ideal activist to share Native American cultural beliefs with white audiences and to reinterpret the role of Indians in American society. For instance, Gertrude saw Sitting Bull as a hero, a patriot fighting to preserve Indigenous culture in the face of invasion. Gertrude called him "grandfather," not because of any biological relationship, but because she saw herself carrying on his mission, albeit through cultural exchange, not warfare.

Through her stories, Gertrude loquaciously summarized the history of exploitation of Indigenous peoples by European colonists and, later, American settlers. She juxtaposed the respect of Native peoples for multiculturalism with white Eurocentrism. "The hospitality of the American aborigine,"

Gertrude once explained, "saved the early settlers" of Spain, England, and France "from starvation during the first bleak winters." In return, "the old world snatched away the fee in the land of the new" and "the aborigines were dispossessed of their country." Even after centuries to learn from each other and practice tolerance, Native and Euro-American societies diverged. American Indians remained "as wards" of the United States "and not as citizens of their own freedom loving land," Gertrude lamented.[6] However, rather than promoting revenge or warfare against the United States, Gertrude espoused a belief that Natives and Euro-Americans had passed through their conflicting adolescence and could live in harmony during the twentieth century. She devoted the remainder of her life to realizing this belief.

Gertrude started her own family after she completed school. In 1902, she returned to the Yankton Agency and married Raymond Talesfase Bonnin, who worked for the Bureau of Indian Affairs. The year after this marriage, Gertrude gave birth to a son, *Ohiya*. The couple worked with Ute people in Utah on the Uintah and Ouray Reservation from 1903 to 1916. Here Gertrude taught children and instructed them in music, and helped women on the reservation. During this period, Gertrude adopted Christianity, flirting with Roman Catholicism before joining the Church of Jesus Christ of Latter-day Saints.

Despite her many duties on the Uintah and Ouray Reservation, Gertrude continued to share Native cultures with readers across the United States. In 1913, she co-wrote a Native American musical titled *The Sun Dance Opera* with William F. Hanson, a fellow music teacher. The two composed the opera to share traditions of Ute peoples. Gertrude played tribal songs on violin and Hanson transcribed them. The plot of the play focused on two Ute lovers, and it served mainly as a mechanism for Native players to perform the Ute Sun Dance. Although ostensibly focused on part of culture that whites had tried to erase, the play still often cast white actors, and it was written by two non-Utes. *The Sun Dance Opera* was staged across Utah for white and Native audiences. Many critics praised the piece for its unprecedented glimpse into a Native culture, a form of exposure many Americans had not been able to enjoy prior to Gertrude's efforts.

By the second decade of the twentieth century, Gertrude's successes in the realms of publishing and storytelling, paired with her oratorical ability, made her an ideal proponent for Native American rights at the national level. Gertrude joined the Society of American Indians, moving to Washington, DC, in 1916 to work for the organization, where she served as Secretary. She lectured audiences on the importance of securing Native rights and corresponded with the Bureau of Indian Affairs to improve the status of Indians across the United States. From 1917 to 1919, she edited *The American Indian Magazine*, the society's periodical, where she often wrote articles of her own.⁷ Gertrude resigned editorship of the magazine in 1920, and it ceased publication later that year. However, Gertrude used other opportunities to promote Indigenous causes.

Gertrude confronted a number of serious social and political issues through her writing. She composed an essay on corruption among Oklahoma Indian agents titled *Oklahoma's Poor Rich Indians: An Orgy of Graft and Exploitation of the Five Civilized Tribes, Legalized Robbery*, with coauthors Matthew K. Sniffen and Charles H. Fabens. The essay unveiled how the government of Oklahoma stole lands that the Dawes Severalty Act had allotted to Native peoples in 1887. The Bureau of Indian Affairs and Department of the Interior had no choice but to respond to Gertrude's accusations, holding hearings looking into graft. From her lofty national perch at the Society of American Indians, she tried to sway Native peoples to send their children to school. She championed a number of human rights issues. For instance, Gertrude wanted to stem the use of peyote by Utes because of its alleged detrimental health effects. She also worked within the General Federation of Women's Clubs to connect the movements with Native American and women's rights.

Gertrude once remarked that Native peoples were just as worthy of the name "American" as whites. This notion exemplified her entire career: she consistently portrayed Indians and whites as equals, and attempted to undo their previous relationship as enemies. She championed the cause of Indian self-determination and publicly spoke out against the Bureau of Indian Affairs for its attempts to quash Native sovereignty. Gertrude sternly remarked that "I hope someone will rise up in Congress to trim the long tentacles of the Bureau, until it starves to death."⁸ She regularly wrote to politicians, identifying herself as Zitkala-Ša, rather than Gertrude Bonnin. She had contacts with Republicans in Washington, DC, and convinced wealthy families such as Rockefellers and DuPonts to support her cause. She promoted pan-Indianism, minimizing the distinctions among Native nations.

Even in her final years, Gertrude's efforts to promote Native rights never waned. In 1926, at age fifty, she founded the National Council of American Indians, Incorporated, in Washington, DC.⁹ This entity hoped to facilitate "a constructive effort to better the Red Race and make its members better citizens of the United States." Gertrude led this organization as president until the 1930s. It fought for Indian education and citizenship, again under the umbrella of pan-Indianism. The National Council of American Indians published the *Indian Newsletter* to uphold this cause. The organization died in the 1930s.

Gertrude Bonnin died in 1938 and was buried at Arlington Cemetery.¹⁰ Even in death, her example influenced generations of Native activists. Publishers continue to reprint *Old Indian Legends* and *American Indian Stories*.

To this day, scholars write essays interpreting the influence of Gertrude's body of work. By giving voice to the Yankton Dakota traditions that had shaped her childhood, Gertrude showed the Native peoples of North America that a female Indian voice could overcome generations of animosity to create a more inclusive worldview. Her work and lifestyle showed that a Native woman's writing could make a difference.

NOTES

1. Zitkala-Sa, *American Indian Stories* (Washington: Haysworth Publishing House, 1921), 8.
2. P. Jane Hafen, "'Help Indians Help Themselves': Gertrude Bonnin, the SAI, and the NCAI," *Studies in American Indian Literatures* 25, no. 2 (Summer 2013): 199.
3. Zitkala-Sa, *American Indian Stories*, 56.
4. Ruth Spack, "Translation Moves: Zitkala-Ša's Bilingual Indian Legends," *Studies in American Indian Literatures* Series 2, vol. 18, no. 4 (Winter 2006): 43–4.
5. Dexter Fisher, "Zitkala-Ša: The Evolution of a Writer," *American Indian Quarterly* 5, no. 3 (August 1979): 229.
6. Zitkala-Sa, *American Indian Stories*, 186.
7. David L. Johnson and Raymond Wilson, "Gertrude Simmons Bonnin, 1876–1938: 'Americanize the First American,'" *American Indian Quarterly* 12, no. 1 (Winter 1988): 34.
8. Johnson and Raymond, "Gertrude Simmons Bonnin," 34.
9. "Gertrude Bonnin (Yankton Sioux)," in *Recovering Native American Writings in the Boarding School Press*, ed. Jacqueine Emery (Lincoln: University of Nebraska Press, 2017), 253.
10. Dexter Fisher, "Zitkala Sa: The Evolution of a Writer," 236, 238.

BIBLIOGRAPHY

Fisher, Dexter. "Zitkala Sa: The Evolution of a Writer." *American Indian Quarterly* 5, No. 3. August 1979.

"Gertrude Bonnin (Yankton Sioux)." Jacqueine Emery, ed. *Recovering Native American Writings in the Boarding School Press*. Lincoln: University of Nebraska Press, 2017.

Hafen, P. Jane. "'Help Indians Help Themselves': Gertrude Bonnin, the SAI, and the NCAI." *Studies in American Indian Literatures* 25, No. 2. Summer 2013.

Johnson, David L., and Raymond Wilson. "Gertrude Simmons Bonnin, 1876–1938: 'Americanize the First American.'" *American Indian Quarterly* 12, No. 1. Winter 1988.

Spack, Ruth. "Translation Moves: Zitkala-Ša's Bilingual Indian Legends." *Studies in American Indian Literatures*, Series 2, 18, No. 4. Winter 2006.

Zitkala-Sa. *American Indian Stories*. Washington: Haysworth Publishing House, 1921.

FURTHER READINGS

Carpenter, Ron. "Zitkala-Ša and Bicultural Subjectivity." *Studies in American Indian Literatures*, Series 2, 16, No. 3. Fall 2004.
Chiarello, Barbara. "Deflected Missives: Zitkala-Ša's Resistance and Its (Un)Containment." *Studies in American Indian Literatures*, Series 2, 17, No. 3. Fall 2005.
Hafen, P. Jane. "Gertrude Simmons Bonnin: For the Indian Cause." In *Sifters: Native American Women's Lives*, edited by Theda Purdue, 127–40. New York: Oxford University Press, 2001.
Hafen, P. Jane. "Zitkala-Ša: Sentimentality and Sovereignty." *Wicazo Sa Review* 12, No. 2. Autumn 1997.
Hardy, Gayle J. *American Women Civil Rights Activists: Bibliographies of 68 Leaders, 1825–1992*. Jefferson, NC: McFarland & Company, Inc., Publishers, 1993.
Kune, Catherine. "Fire of Eden: Zitkala-Ša's Bitter Apple." *Studies in American Indian Literatures*, Series 2, 18, No. 1. Spring 2006.
Mullin, Molly H. "Bonnin, Gertrude Simmons." Carole Barrett and Harvey Markowitz, eds. *American Indian Biographies*. Pasadena, CA: Salem Press, Inc., 2005.
Spack, Ruth. "Zitkala-Sa, The Song of Hiawatha, and the Carlisle Indian School Band: A Captivity Tale." *Legacy* 25, No. 2. 2008.
Susag, Dorothea M. "Zitkala-Sa (Gertrude Simmons Bonnin): A Power(full) Literary Voice." *Studies in American Indian Literatures*, Series 2, 5, No. 4. Winter 1993.
Willard, William. "Zitkala Sa: A Woman Who Would Be Heard!" *Wicazo Sa Review* 1, No. 1. Spring 1985.
Zitkala-Sa. *Dreams and Thunder: Stories, Poems, and* The Sun Dance Opera. Edited by P. Jane Hafen. Lincoln: University of Nebraska Press, 2005.
Zitkala-Sa. *Help Indians Help Themselves: The Later Writings of Gertrude Simmons-Bonnin (Zitkala-Sa)*. P. Jane Hafen, ed. Lubbock: Texas Tech University Press, 2020.

Chapter Eleven

Where Is Victory?
Harriette Shelton Dover (b. 1904–d. 1991)

Richard A. Hanks

When Harriette Shelton Dover was six years old she was walking with her paternal grandmother along a deserted road on a summer evening on the Tulalip Reservation near Marysville, Washington. Her grandmother, *Hat's Kol Litsa*, spoke only *Lushootseed*, the language predominant among the Salish peoples of the Puget Sound. In the middle of an intersection her grandmother stopped and told Harriette, "Now is the time for you to tell the spirits of the earth and Doh-Kwi-Buhch, the great creator, who you are." Grandmother told Harriette to walk very slowly toward the east until told to stop, raise her open palms to the sky, and proclaim her name—her Indian name *Hiahltsa*—loudly her grandmother said, "so that the earth and its spirits can hear you." She repeated this three more times, announcing to the four directions and the spirits, the names of her father, mother, and grandparents as well, "so that the earth would know me."[1] Such a display of traditional belief was prohibited by federal authorities and could have resulted in punishment for Harriette's grandmother and for the little girl as well. Both could have been jailed for the infraction.

Harriette was born in 1904 on Tulalip. The name *Tulalip*—*dxʷlilap* in Lushootseed—is an ancient name meaning "small mouthed bay" after the inlet along its western shoreline. It is home to confederated tribes of Snohomish, Skykomish, and Snoqualmie peoples, among others, as a result of the Treaty of Point Elliott of 1855. The federally recognized confederation was organized under the Indian Reorganization Act of 1934 and has an enrolled Native population of 4,611 people living on over 22,000 acres, thirty miles north of Seattle.

The demonstration of self-recognition, instructed by her grandmother, made a deep impression on Harriette. Years later she remembered that "it never bothered me, 'who am I.' I know who I am."[2] She was the daughter of

Wha-cah-dub, the last hereditary leader of the Snohomish tribe, born at Sandy Point on Whidbey Island in 1868. Her father learned the oral narratives of his people from the elders around him as would his daughter. At the age of seventeen, he entered the Catholic-run school at Tulalip against the wishes of his parents who feared the rampant disease at the school would take his life. There, a priest gave him the name William Shelton. Elders taught William the ways of Indian doctoring and tribal leadership, but he wished to understand the new white world. He learned English but left the school after two years following a brutal beating he suffered for swimming and laughing on a Sunday.[3] Harriette reported that her father never set foot inside a church again and "lived through the teachings of the old times."[4]

William married Ruth (Siastenu) Sehome of Guemes Island (Clallam and Samish) and found employment in the agency's lumber mill where, over a period of years, he honed his skills as a master carver of story totem poles. Those poles preserved the legends of his people, provided instruction for tribal children, and educated non-Native people of the area, exposing them to the rich culture of Tulalip. William also gained the trust of agency superintendent Charles Buchanan. He convinced Buchanan that a longhouse should be built to remember the treaty of 1855. Petitions to the Commissioner of Indian Affairs were approved and the longhouse, long banned by the government, was erected in 1912. Observance of "Treaty Day" commemorated the loss of their land but their culture was again celebrated in their traditional communal house, beginning a long step toward cultural revitalization for the people of Tulalip.

Shelton learned to walk the dual road of being an Indian within a new reality. His efforts and those of his daughter bridged the two worlds and preserved and revived the language, stories, and songs of the Tulalip nations. Harriette, as an adult, became the keeper of the stories which were manifested in the graceful carvings of her father's poles. Those stories told of *squəlalitut*—the powerful guardian spirits whose protection was sought by tribal members of upper-class Salish to which Harriette and her father belonged. Being part of this class demanded certain personal conduct communicated through the parables of the stories—traditional values of appropriate behavior, of living properly, which are at the heart of *xəčusədəʔ* (Huchoosedah)—the cultural knowledge that delineates knowledge of self for Indigenous peoples of the Puget Sound.

Harriette worked with her father to revive their time-honored dances, revealing these to the white society around them. This commitment led to a resurgence of the Lushootseed language, critical to tribal identity, and she took the lead in resurrecting the ancient First Salmon Ceremony honoring the return of these sustainers of life. Accepting the mantle of leadership as instructed by her father, Harriette dedicated her life to reintroduction of traditional practices and, as an activist, battled the bureaucracy of the Bureau of Indian Affairs (BIA) for the rights and protections promised by the treaty of 1855 including the legal maneuvers that stripped Natives of their land allotments. She became only the second woman elected to the Tulalip Tribal Council and the first to hold the office of chairwoman.

Her earliest education came on the knee of her grandmother and other elders who imparted proper moral and ethical behavior to the little girl through telling the oral narratives that marked the time of her people. These included sacred laws that the people followed to be healthy as Tulalip people. Among the stories were "The Fox and Mink," which taught caution with strangers; "The Deer and the Wolves," which stressed restraint, and "The Eagle Brothers and the Mink," which taught honesty. Her grandmother also used the story of "The Red and Blue Stars" to teach Harriette generosity. The youngest in her family, Harriette displayed a typical "me first" attitude her grandmother looked to correct. She learned that ancient heroes worked for the benefit of the community, not the self.

There were two sisters, Hat's Kol Litsa started. "The younger one was selfish; always saying, 'this is mine,' or 'me first.'" One night the girls were sleeping outside looking up at the vast sky full of stars. "The younger sister said, 'I choose the red star; that is the prettiest. It's mine. You can have the blue.'" Her grandmother continued, "All right," said the older sister, "mine is the blue star." The girls fell asleep watching the stars. That night the Great Spirit came and lifted them both into the heights of the sky. He told them that now each one would meet the red star and the blue star. But, explained her grandmother, "the red star was a young man with very sore red eyes, and the blue star was handsome and beautiful." She concluded, "You must remember, not to grab at everything." Her grandmother cautioned: "not to say, 'me first,' 'this is mine.'" Otherwise, she added, "you are going to have a husband with red sore eyes." Years later Harriette wrote about the impression and lessons the story had taught her. Her immature behavior had been addressed not by scolding or anger but by ancient stories detailing how to behave correctly as a Tulalip person. "Little by little we learned," she wrote.[5]

At the age of seven Harriette entered the government's boarding school at Tulalip. The anguish, both physical and emotional, deeply scarred this small girl as it did thousands of Indian children across the country. Her recollections recount times of separation, homesickness, depression, deprivation, illness, abuse, and frequent death that took friends and family, including her older sister who died of tuberculosis. She was forced to live at the school for ten months of the year. Attempts to escape home were met with severe punishment, especially for the boys. School officials shaved their heads and they often had a ball and chain placed on their legs. Stripped of their clothing, they were daily beaten with canes or straps that tore their flesh. Kept on bread and water, the boys were forced to wear girls' dresses as humiliation.

When Harriette was nine, she was caught speaking Lushootseed with other girls in a restroom. The matron had her own heavy leather strap that she used to beat the girls "from the back of our necks down to our ankles."[6] When the matron whipped Harriette, the blow sent the diminutive girl flying across the floor. Harriette had trouble eating or sleeping after that and sometimes prayed for death when faced with returning to school after summer break. Years later Harriette sympathized with many of her generation who turned to alcohol. "Their roots from home were broken," she said. Yet, "we found our way in that strange new culture."[7]

The dominant culture of the United States at boarding school instructed Indians in the ways of Christianity—competing versions. The priest taught Catholic catechism and conducted Sunday mass while Superintendent Charles M. Buchanan, a Protestant, offered a St. James Bible reading Sunday evenings. As a little girl, one song caught Harriette's attention—the lyrics commanding that "we march, we march to Vick-tory." Harriette identified with that since they marched everywhere: they marched to school, to dinner, to church, to the sewing room. But she was terrified, wondering "where are we going?" She wanted to know urgently, "where is Vic-tory?"[8]

Harriette's parents lost three children while the children were only toddlers. Another brother, Alphonsus, collapsed and died while running to fulfill a school duty at the sound of the school's fire drill bell. When Harriette's sister, Ruth, became ill, Harriette returned home with her. Ruth died in 1917. "Tuberculosis is a terrible death," she later wrote, "it's a lingering death."[9] Harriette and her parents kept watch at Ruth's bedside, cradling her as the disease of pain and exhaustion ate away at her body. It took Harriette years to get beyond her sister's death and, as a young woman, it hardened her heart against a white society seemingly indifferent to the misery imposed by government officials on America's First Nations people. Harriette was ill as well; glands in her arm and neck were painfully swollen. She did not return to school for two years. Given all the tragedy and sickness associated with the boarding school, Harriette was surprised when her parents still demanded she go back. Her father had purposely entered the mission school to understand whites and knew education was a vital tool for his people. "You read, read, read, those are white man's words and you read the books . . . everything you can read," he admonished her. Learn new words, he told her; learn how to spell and pronounce them.[10]

Harriette spent another five years at the Tulalip boarding school, graduating in 1922 at the age of seventeen from the eighth grade. She found a different experience at Everett High School. Although challenging, she did well with her studies and graduated in 1926 in the middle of her class. The following year, she assisted her father and brother Robert who, with nineteen other tribes, sued the federal government (*Duwamish et al. v. United States*) for acknowledgment of their fishing rights and promised payments under the treaty of 1855. Jail time for Natives fishing their traditional river systems was commonplace. The treaty gave Indians the right to fish at all usual and accustomed places but the state of Washington ignored federal law. In the end a Washington state court ruled against the Indian claimants. Tribal minutes written by Harriette and her brother, Robert, however, would later play an important part in another federal legal contest with a much better outcome, the court case known informally as the Boldt decision (1974), which recognized the rights of Northwestern Indians to fish in accordance with their treaties.

Harriette became her father's best friend and partner, in their efforts to preserve their besieged culture and treaty rights. Dressed in the full regalia of Indians of the Great Plains, she began accompanying her father on presentations to civic and school groups of the Puget Sound, performing songs and dances of Coast Salish people. Her clothing and that of her father, while not traditional Salish dress, satisfied their white audiences and their common misconception of Native appearance—an ice breaker, according to one historian.

In July 1926, Harriet married Francis Williams of Clallam Coast Salish descent after meeting him at a dance in Seattle. Their son, Wayne, was born two years later. Frank was an assistant engineer on a steam-powered ferry, which often left Harriette on her own for long periods of time after moving to a Seattle apartment. Money was short and so was work for Indians in an intolerant Seattle. As a house servant, she viewed the callousness of the idle rich and the indignity of greeting patrons while in an exaggerated Indian costume at the garish Twin Tepee Restaurant. However, she also sold stories about the legends of her people to the *Seattle Post-Intelligencer* for five dollars apiece, continuing her cultural outreach.

She became quite ill once while waiting to meet Frank along a bitterly cold waterfront. She and Wayne returned to Tulalip where the illness turned into a feverish pneumonia and pleurisy. The doctor expressed doubts that Harriette would survive. Family members took turns holding vigil at her bedside, as they had done for her sister years before. In a fog of unconsciousness, Harriette had a dream. She stood alone at a bay similar to Tulalip Bay as a storm began to rage. Large black waves suddenly turned into menacing animal forms such as alligators and giant lizards, nearly at her feet. As winds moaned and howled, she became frightened and believed the fearsome animals would kill her. Fear gripped her until she heard a drum beat coming from the sky. A song began as well and she started to sing the song and a lightness came upon her as she danced up and down the beach. She told herself that nothing would frighten her and if this be death she would face it as she had been taught—with bravery and dignity. Continuing her dancing, she looked at her feet. The menacing animals had become leaves and wild flowers. The drums got louder and although all alone she began to feel better as she danced.

As she awoke she saw her father sitting alongside her, firmly holding her hand. She told him of her dream and tried to sing the song she had heard but struggled, gasping for breath, and could not finish. Her father then began to sing the song as he had heard it when he was a small boy but had not thought about it for years until Harriette tried to sing it. It was the song of the Mountain Woman telling her vision coming from the mountains. The vision had first appeared to Harriette's great-grandmother, after whom Harriette was named. Still holding her hand, her father told Harriette that she was going to be well. That's going to be your sqəlaitut. It will give you courage to live a long, long time. Live right, he said. This song, from Skykomish country, became Harriette's song, and she would sing it during the First Salmon Ceremony and Treaty Day gatherings.

As a leadership family, her older brother, Robert, received training from his father preparing him for a principal position at Tulalip. Robert's death from peritonitis in 1930 changed that dynamic. A terrible blow to the family, Harriette wrote that her parents seemed to rapidly age overnight. The focus of William Shelton's training now fell upon his last remaining child, Harriette. Living right, presenting herself well in public, and a re-emphasis on education were essential parts of her instruction. Her father's death eight years later was another heartbreak for Harriette who suffered afterward from bouts of self-doubt and depression. "How I long for the sound of his dear voice," she wrote in her diary.[11] Her focus became her son, Wayne. They were forced to go on welfare for a time but with the beginning of World War II, prospects opened at the Boeing plant in Seattle. She and Francis divorced in the mid-1940s. Wayne recalled that his mother's activism began in earnest following the divorce.

Harriette stepped forward to tackle the civic, political, and educational issues that burdened Tulalip members. Shortly after her father's death in 1938, she was elected to Tulalip's Board of Directors, a position she held at different times until 1951. In 1945, she served as the board's chairwoman—the first Indian woman in the state of Washington to hold such a position. During this time, Harriette was also postmaster of Tulalip's U.S. Post Office, and in 1951, she served as a tribal judge.

In 1950 Harriette married George Dover, a white man whose parents leased land on Tulalip. She met George when he picked up mail at her post office. He was eight years her junior and had been a sergeant in the Army Air Corps during World War II. Her mother was deeply opposed to the union and reminded Harriette that her father had warned her never to marry a white man. Criticism came from extended family as well. But George was a stabilizing influence on Harriette and perhaps helped her with her own misgivings about the larger white society. During this time, Harriette gave birth to her second son, William. George Dover, this "dear man" as Harriette referred to him, died in 1969.[12]

While she did not heed her father's warning about marrying a white man, she did live up to his hopes and instruction that she assume a leadership role for the benefit of her tribe and culture. In this way, Harriette followed the instructions taught to her as a child through Tulalip oral traditions. And, as her father had done, she gathered items embodying the material culture of her people—canoes, baskets, cedar-bark clothing, rattles, and other Native curios filled her home, which gained distinction as a private museum, appearing in publications such as *Sunset Magazine*. She answered correspondence from around the world seeking information on her culture. It had been necessary for her father to hide the artifacts, concealing many in his attic away from government agents, to prevent their confiscation. Harriette, however, was able to proudly display them for all who were interested. In 1957, at her own expense, she and her husband, George, initiated salmon bakes at their Tulalip home for the general public, who then could tour her museum. Schoolchildren in particular were always welcome. Years later in 1976, Harriette took the lead in reviving the once-outlawed and long-dormant First Salmon Ceremony.

Harriette compiled stories she had heard and learned as a child. She continued her work with the greater community, especially with the children, white and Native. In 1956, a visit to a Sultan, Washington area campsite of over 100 children and chaperones was met with excited expectation. A newspaper reported that "in a beaded white buckskin gown, she chanted a prayer to the Great Spirit, while she beat a rhythmic accompaniment on a drum. With a beautifully told legend, she forever secured in the hearts of her listeners the glory of her people."[13]

Harriette acknowledged the hardships faced by European immigrants but wrote that they had something different than Indians—they had freedom of choice and opportunity. As taught by her father, she knew that education was the key for her people to succeed. In the mid-1950s that meant securing a new elementary school for Tulalip. The agency school closed in 1932 and reservation students suffered long bus rides to schools in Marysville, paid for with federal money. Harriette confronted the school board and her agitation resulted in a new school at Tulalip that opened in 1959. Education had given her the sophistication to battle white society using its own laws and institutions to fight for Indian rights.

She returned to school in the 1970s and earned her Associate of Arts degree from Everett Community College concentrating on Anthropology and History. She was rightfully proud of such an achievement and was eager that her example would inspire Tulalip's young people to pursue higher education. In 1974, her testimony in the case of *United States v. Washington* (the Boldt decision) helped mark aboriginal fishing areas for the court that finally affirmed the salmon harvesting rights of the signers to the treaty of 1855. Another goal of Harriette's was to produce a book detailing her life and the history of Tulalip as she had learned it from the elders around her. Just before her death in 1991, she worked with anthropologist Darleen Fitzpatrick on her memoirs, *Tulalip, From My Heart*, which was published in 2013.

In the last two years of her life, she also recorded several tapes to preserve the Lushootseed language and songs. In 2011, her hope for a Tulalip museum was realized with the opening of the Hibulb Cultural Center and Natural History Preserve. The facility, with its research library, exhibits, and educational programs, offers a place for all to learn Salish culture of the Puget Sound. At its core is the vast collection compiled by three generations of the family of William Shelton, including his daughter Harriette and grandson, Wayne.

After her death, the Tulalip people and many others praised Harriette Shelton Dover as a tribal ambassador who sacrificed for her people and culture. William Shelton's story poles and his book, *Legends of the Totem Pole* (1923), provided detail knowledge for Indians and non-Indians alike. He wanted others to know that the people of Tulalip were educated, cultured people, his grandson, Wayne, remembered, so they could learn from them. When told by some white Christians that her stories could not be compared to the Bible, Harriette had bristled. The stories of her people were ancient and no less inspired by the Spirit, just like the Bible. Harriette had written: the sacred stories of the Tulalip people are "of a time that is like a curtain of fog or mist that covers our past . . . We have been here a long, long time. We have always been here."[14]

NOTES

1. Harriette Dover, *From My Heart*, 90. *Tulalip From My Heart: An Autobiographical Account of a Reservation Community*, Darleen Fitzpatrick, ed. (Seattle: University of Washington Press, 2013), 90.

2. Lawrence David Rygg, "The Continuation of Upper Class Snohomish Coast Salish Attitudes and Deportment as Seen Through the Life History of a Snohomish Coast Salish Woman" (Bellingham, WA: Western Washington State College, Master's Thesis, 1978), 50.

3. Peter Blecha, "Harriette Shelton Williams Dover (1904–1991)," digital essay, HistoryLink.org.
4. Dover in Rygg, *The Continuation of Upper Class*, 64.
5. Dover, *From My Heart*, 87; Rygg, *The Continuation of Upper Class*, 48.
6. Rygg, *The Continuation of Upper Class*, 139.
7. Rygg, *The Continuation of Upper Class*, 135–36.
8. Rygg, *The Continuation of Upper Class*, 152.
9. Rygg, *The Continuation of Upper Class*, 157.
10. Rygg, *The Continuation of Upper Class*, 147.
11. Harriette Dover Diary, July 1940, Archives of Hibulb Cultural Center, Tulalip Reservation, Washington.
12. Rygg, *The Continuation of Upper Class*, 280.
13. Vanderhyde, "Autos and Buckskins," *Seattle Times*, August 12, 1956.
14. Dover, *From My Heart*, 279.

BIBLIOGRAPHY

Blecha, Peter, "Harriette Shelton Williams Dover (1904–1991)," digital essay, HistoryLink.org Essay 9079, The Free Online *Encyclopedia of Washington State History*, July 27, 2009.
Dover, Harriette. Diary, July 1940. Archives of Hibulb Cultural Center, Tulalip Reservation, Washington.
Dover, Harriette. *Tulalip From My Heart: An Autobiographical Account of a Reservation Community*, Darleen Fitzpatrick, ed. Seattle: University of Washington Press, 2013.
Interview of Anonymous Tribal Historian by Richard Hanks, June 23 and 25, 2016, Tulalip Reservation, Washington.
Interview of Anonymous Tribal Elder by Richard Hanks, May 24, 2016, Tulalip Reservation, Washington.
Rygg, Lawrence David. "The Continuation of Upper Class Snohomish Coast Salish Attitudes and Deportment as Seen Through the Life History of a Snohomish Coast Salish Woman." Bellingham: Western Washington State College. Master's Thesis, 1978.
Vanderhyde, Betty. "Autos and Buckskins, TV and War Drums In Indian Princess' Life." *Seattle Times*, August 12, 1956.

FURTHER READINGS

Hilbert, Vi, ed., *Haboo: Native American Stories from Puget Sound.* Seattle: University of Washington Press, 1985.

Hilbert, Vi and Crisca Bierwert, *The Ways of the Lushootseed People: Ceremonies and Traditions of Northern Puget Sound Indians*. Seattle: United Indians of All Tribes Foundation, 1980.

Ruby, Robert H., John A. Brown, and Cary C. Collins, *A Guide to the Indian Tribes of the Pacific Northwest.* Norman: University of Oklahoma Press, 2010.

Shelton, Chief William, *The Story of the Totem Pole: Early Indian Legends*. Everett: Kane & Harcus, 1923.

Chapter Twelve

Ending Termination in Indian Country
Lucy Covington
(b. 1910–d. 1982)

Benjamin Jenkins

Among the countless Native American women whose activism improved their communities and Indian Country as a whole during the twentieth century, Lucy Covington's name commands great respect. Born into a humble household and brought up as a rancher, by mid-twentieth century, Covington had become one of the most vocal proponents of Native sovereignty in the United States. She played a key role in the battle against termination on the Colville Reservation in Washington State at the national level. Rather than standing by and allowing the federal government to seize resources across Indian Country, Covington implored Indians to improve their communities from within, instead of accepting federal aid in exchange for abandoning their ancestral homelands. Admired by Native and non-Native political activists across the United States, Covington and her coalition of followers demonstrated the viability of tribal sovereignty in the face of federal opposition.

Lucy Friedlander was born in 1910 to Nellie and Louis T. Friedlander Sr. She famously came into the world in a tipi near the city of Nespelem, Washington. Louis Friedlander Sr. descended from Nez Perce and German forebears, and died when Lucy was only two years old. Lucy's mother, however, had more children, and as a result Lucy had siblings of Palus, Sanpoil, Columbia River Sincayuse and Wenatchi heritage. Tragically, Nellie died soon after her husband. This left Mary Moses, the sister of Lucy's grandmother, to raise the young girl. Mary Moses was famous in her own right, having lived through the Plateau Indian Wars of 1850s. Although born into the family of Chief Owhi, *Sanclow* (Mary Moses) married Chief Moses. Thus, Lucy was born into a leadership family and married into another.[1]

During her youth, Lucy ranched on the reservation, and years later recalled spending substantial portions of her life on horseback. While living with Mary Moses, Lucy attended high school, graduating from Haskell Institute in 1931. She matriculated at the boarding school in Kansas and took classes at Kinman Business College in Spokane, Washington.[2] She always retained connections to her Native heritage. Years after Lucy's death, a lawyer who worked with the tribal council to prevent termination recalled her familiarity with the land of the Colville Reservation. Lucy also made her identity visually explicit by wearing Native jewelry and keeping her hair in braids.

Lucy's pedigree prepared her for a strong leadership role in Indian Country. She was related to a number of Indian leaders from the Pacific Northwest, including the powerful leader Kamiakan of the Yakama, Palus and Owhi of the Yakama. Kamiakan had urged his people to reject the Treaties of Walla Walla of 1855 that the government forced on Native peoples of the Plateau. Moreover, Lucy was a direct descendent of Chief Moses, a chief of the Colville Reservation, who had protected his people and their land from American invaders seeking to exploit natural resources. Lucy lived on the land Chief Moses had protected, which strongly connected her with her ancestors. Located on the Columbia Plateau in the north central part of the modern state of Washington, the Colville Reservation was signed into existence by President Ulysses S. Grant in 1872 as a home for eight Native groups that had not signed treaties with the federal government. Chief Joseph, famed leader of the Nez Perce who attempted to lead his people to Canada, eventually came to the Colville Reservation with a number of his people. He spent the last years of his life there and is buried on the reservation. Growing up on the Colville Reservation gave Lucy respect for all Native nations.

In 1935, Lucy married another member of the Colville Reservation, John J. Covington. The couple moved to Portland, Oregon, during World War II, where they worked as welders. John sadly died in an automobile accident in 1958. Lucy never remarried or had any children. However, she remained heavily involved with her community as a political leader. Covington was elected to the Colville Business Council in 1956, making her the first woman in the nation to join a tribal governing body. She served continuously until 1980, including a stint as tribal chair. She was the first woman to become a tribal chairwoman. In addition to using her influence to argue against termination, Covington also led the planning committee.

Fighting termination became the axis on which Covington's legacy turned. Initiated by the federal government of the United States in 1953 under the so-called Termination Resolution, this policy allowed the government to end its relationship with tribes to revoke a tribe's sovereignty, paving the way for the dissolution of Native governments across the country. This also permitted non-Natives to exploit Indian lands. In the seventeen years following adoption of the Termination Policy, the government terminated 109 Indian communities across the United States, often targeting areas with substantial natural resources such as the lumber of the Pacific Northwest.

The debate over termination began in earnest on the Colville Reservation in 1956, when Congress tasked the Colvilles with drawing up legislation for the termination of their tribally held lands. The Confederated Tribes of the Colville Reservation were no strangers to having their resources unduly appropriated. The federal government rescinded millions of acres of land it had previously deeded to the Colvilles in 1872 and 1879. More severely, in the 1890s, the government forcefully took a substantial portion of the reservation, known as the North Half, from the Colvilles. To the Indigenous peoples of the Pacific Northwest, who had suffered military and political depredations throughout the nineteenth century, termination simply represented the latest incursion by the American government into tribal power and resources. However, during the battle to terminate the Colville Reservation, Congress tempered its interference in Indian Country with the prospect of financial reward. To entice the Indian people of the Colville Reservation to accept termination, the federal government restored the North Half of the reservation that it had confiscated in the 1890s, but only allowed Native Americans to hunt and fish there, not to own the land. However hollow, this gesture, and the prospect of further recompense, convinced many members of the Colville Reservation to favor termination—but not Lucy Covington.

The specter of termination haunted Covington during her time on the tribal council. During the 1950s and 1960s, a majority of the members of the Colville Business Council favored termination.[3] Members of the reservation seemed convinced that the federal government would offer them sizable individual payments if they accepted termination, which would allow them to prosper. Covington disagreed, pointing to the impoverishment of groups such as the Menominee, who had suffered after the federal government revoked their sovereignty. She used statistics to demonstrate the substandard education and unemployment among the Confederated Tribes of the Colville Reservation, which would only worsen if the Native peoples voluntarily relinquished their tribal sovereignty. Only economic development on the Colville Reservation could lead to long-term stability, Covington argued. She fervently believed that she could persuade the people of the Colville Reservation to act collectively to preserve their country, sovereignty, and identity.

Lucy Covington's political values emerged from lessons she had learned over the course of her life on the reservation. During Covington's youth, Mary Moses, the great-aunt who had raised her, repeatedly stressed the importance of the Colville Reservation as a tribal land base and resource. It was far more than a collection of assessable natural resources: it was a home, a shelter for Native peoples that the government of the United States had persecuted and warred against in the nineteenth century. "She wanted me to know somehow how much suffering had happened before we got a home base," Covington later recalled of Moses. "If an Indian doesn't have land, he has nothing."[4]

Covington marshaled every resource she had to spread this concept of Indian sovereignty in order to prevent the termination of the Colville Reservation. In 1968, she focused her tribal election campaign around the rejection of termination. She invited speakers from the Menominee and Klamath tribes to share with Colville residents about the difficulties they faced as a result of termination. Covington also established her own news medium. She felt that the *Tribal Tribune*, the tribal newspaper of the Colville Reservation, had become a vehicle to spread propaganda in favor of termination. This spurred her to start *Our Heritage*, which she used as her own bully pulpit to promote traditional values and to argue in favor of tribal sovereignty and against termination.[5] Through this venue, and her personal charisma, Covington attracted many powerful allies to her side, including Native lawyer Paschal Sherman and tribal councilor Mel Tonasket. Finally, in 1968, Covington and a number of members of the Colville Business Council spoke before the Subcommittee on Indian Affairs of the House of Representatives. She persuasively remarked that, because the debate over termination had engulfed the Colville Reservation for fifteen years, the tribe had not focused on other crucial areas, such as education and economic development. Realistically, termination would throw the Colville Tribe into turmoil, she commented. Covington famously remarked, "Termination is something no Indian should dream about. It is like giving your eagle feather away."[6]

Covington's arguments resounded across the Colville Reservation. In 1971, the people of the reservation voted into office an anti-termination majority, and by 1972 the council passed a resolution that officially closed the door to further consideration of termination. On the Colville Reservation, sovereignty trumped termination. Just as importantly, it established a precedent for Native American governments across the country to reject termination in favor of tribal government. In 1970, President Richard M. Nixon formally repudiated termination as the policy of the American government, and in 1975 Congress followed suit by passing the American Indian Self-Determination and Education Assistance Act. On the Colville Reservation, Covington guided the tribal council through a resolution that formally dismissed any consideration of termination.[7] As Covington's successful campaign vividly illustrated, by the 1960s, the days when the federal government of the United States could easily and forcefully manipulate Native Americans had long since passed.

On September 30, 1982, years after her successful anti-termination campaign, Lucy Friedlander Covington died from pulmonary fibrosis in her house in Nespelem, Washington.[8] She was seventy-one years old. To this day, the peoples of the Colville Reservation acknowledge the tremendous impact Covington had on her community. In 2015, Eastern Washington University awarded Covington an honorary Doctor of Humane Letters. Furthermore, the school opened a Lucy Covington Center to groom the next generation of tribal leaders, fittingly named for the woman who best exemplified the enduring power of Native sovereignty against tremendous odds.

NOTES

1. Interview of Mary Moses by William C. Brown, Brown Collection, Manuscripts, Archives, and Special Collections, Holland Library, Washington State University, Pullman, Washington. A transcription of the Mary Moses Interview is found in Clifford E. Trafzer, ed., *Indian War in the Pacific Northwest: The Journal of Lieutenant Lawrence Kip* (Lincoln: University of Nebraska Press, 1999); Alvin J. Ziontz, *A Lawyer in Indian Country: A Memoir* (Seattle: University of Washington Press, 2010), 136.
2. Paulette Running Wolf and Susan Banks, "Covington, Lucy Friedlander," in *Native American Women: A Biographical Dictionary*, 2nd ed., ed. Gretchen M. Bataille and Laurie Lisa (New York: Routledge, 2001), 79.
3. Alexandria Harmon, "Covington, Lucy Friedlander," in *Notable American Women: A Biographical Dictionary Completing the Twentieth Century*, ed. Susan Ware and Stacy Braukman (Cambridge, MA: The Belknap Press of Harvard University Press, 2004), 138.
4. Charles F. Wilkinson, *Blood Struggle: The Rise of Modern Indian Nations* (New York: W.W. Norton & Company, 2005), 181.
5. Laurie Arnold, *Bartering with the Bones of Their Dead: The Colville Confederated Tribes and Termination* (Seattle: University of Washington Press, 2012), 20.
6. Peter Iverson and Wade Davies, *We Are Still Here: American Indians Since 1890*, 2nd. ed. (Malden, MA: Wiley Blackwell, 2015), 141.
7. Arnold, *Bartering with the Bones of Their Dead*, 124.
8. Harmon, "Covington, Lucy Friedlander," 138.

BIBLIOGRAPHY

Arnold, Laurie. *Bartering with the Bones of Their Dead: The Colville Confederated Tribes and Termination*. Seattle: University of Washington Press, 2012.

Harmon, Alexandria. "Covington, Lucy Friedlander." Susan Ware and Stacy Braukman, eds. *Notable American Women: A Biographical Dictionary Completing the Twentieth Century*. Cambridge, MA: The Belknap Press of Harvard University Press, 2004.

Interview of Mary Moses by William C. Brown, Brown Collection, Manuscripts, Archives, and Special Collections, Holland Library, Washington State University, Pullman, Washington.

Iverson, Peter, and Wade Davies. *"We Are Still Here": American Indians Since 1890*, 2nd ed. Malden, MA: Wiley Blackwell, 2015.

Trafzer, Clifford E., ed. *Indian War in the Pacific Northwest: The Journal of Lieutenant Lawrence Kip*. Lincoln: University of Nebraska Press, 1999.

Dahl, Kathleen A. "The Battle over Termination on the Colville Indian Reservation." *American Indian Culture and Research Journal* 18, No. 1. 1994.

Running Wolf, Paulette, and Susan Banks. "Covington, Lucy Friedlander." Gretchen M. Bataille and Laurie Lisa, eds. *Native American Women: A Biographical Dictionary*, 2nd ed. New York: Routledge, 2001.

Wilkinson, Charles F. *Blood Struggle: The Rise of Modern Indian Nations*. New York: W.W. Norton & Company, 2005.

Ziontz, Alvin J. *A Lawyer in Indian Country: A Memoir*. Seattle: University of Washington Press, 2010.

FURTHER READINGS

Scheuerman, Richard D., and Michael O. Finley. "Chief Cleveland Kamiakin and 20th-Century Political Change on the Colville Reservation." *The Pacific Northwest Quarterly* 101, No.1. Winter 2009–2010.

Trafzer, Clifford and Richard D. Scheuerman. *Snake River-Palouse Indians and the Invasion of the Inland Pacific Northwest*. Pullman: Washington State University Press, 2016.

Thrush, Coll-Peter. "The Lushootseed Peoples of Puget Sound Country," digital essay, University of Washington Digital Collections. Web, June 5, 2016. http://content.lib.washington.edu/aipnw/thrush.html.

Chapter Thirteen

Good-Hearted Woman
Cecilia Fire Thunder
(b. 1946)

Joshua Thunder Little

On October 24, 1946, Cecilia Apple-Fire Thunder, a member of the Oglala Lakota Tribe, was born in Kyle, South Dakota, on the Pine Ridge Indian Reservation. The Pine Ridge Reservation is located in the southwest border of Nebraska and South Dakota. This reservation is the home to many of the members of the Oglala Lakota Nation. Cecilia was raised in South Dakota. She grew up speaking her Native tongue, Lakota, and eventually learned to speak English while attending the Red Cloud Catholic High School, located on the Pine Ridge Reservation. Cecilia thought that her time at the Red Cloud High School was a "brain washing experience."[1] Her school forbid the students from speaking their Native language, but she did anyway whenever among her people. Her father, Stephen Apple, was a farmer and worked in agriculture.

When Cecilia was a teenager, her father experienced economic hardships and as a result of such hardships her father relocated their family to California. During the 1960s, the U.S. government funded a program known as the Urban Relocation Program, a policy to encourage Native American people to leave reservations and move to urban centers for jobs. Cecilia's father moved to Los Angeles. The purpose of the relocation program was to offer Indian people the opportunity to seek better employment in cities. This relocation program provided the opportunity for Cecilia's family to find economic prosperity. In 1963, they relocated to East Los Angeles and sought a new life. She completed high school in California and eventually married John Fire Thunder. She gave birth to two children. Unfortunately, she divorced her husband and as a result of that she had to find a means of financially supporting herself and her children. With the assistance of a social worker, Cecilia enrolled in a program to become a nurse. When she completed her nursing program and passed the state board tests, her career in the health field began. This is where her path as a prominent Native American woman activist began.

During her life, Native American people in the United States were not treated equally, and Cecilia was well aware of it. She understood that in order to implement change she had to strategically collaborate with both Native American and non-Native American people. One of the first initiatives she supported aimed at building a Native American health center. She successfully completed a free health clinic for Native Americans in Compton, California. In 1980, Cecilia moved to San Diego, California, and also initiated the establishment of an Indian health clinic there, which became known as the San Diego American Indian Health Center. The Indian health clinics in both Los Angeles and San Diego provided Indians that resided in those two California towns high-quality healthcare. She reached out to doctors, asking for assistance by simply taking out the phone book and calling doctors in alphabetical order. It was a lengthy process but her efforts proved successful. By doing this she was able to come into contact with professors at the University of California, Los Angeles, the University of Southern California and San Diego State University. Her initiatives to build health clinics can be seen in her hard work and ability to organize community-based movements.

In 1986, Fire Thunder moved back to her birthplace on the Pine Ridge Reservation of South Dakota. Upon her return to Pine Ridge, she worked at the Bennett County Hospital. She took a night job there and worked as a nurse. In addition to her nursing, she served on the National Advisory Board of the National Organization on Fetal Alcohol Syndrome (NOFAS). Alcoholism is rampant in many Indigenous communities, and as a community organizer, she wanted to prevent alcoholism from spreading. Cecilia also began a Native American women's society that studied reservation problems, which included helping battered women.

She aided in the establishment of Cangleska Incorporated, a shelter for women who suffer abuse. Violence against Native American women is a significant problem in Indian communities and in response to this rising epidemic, Cecilia helped form Cangleska Inc., a nonprofit agency designed to combat abuse of women and children. Her work served the women of the Oglala Lakota tribe. Her background as a nurse gave her knowledge and experience, and she assisted Indians to ensure healthy lifestyles. As a leader, she improved the living conditions of Indian people in an effort to ensure the continuance of future generations. For Indian people, working with the community is important because it is a traditional value. Cecilia continues traditional practices through the community-based organizations she participates in.

In 2004, Cecilia decided to run for the President of the Oglala Sioux Tribe. During her first campaign for the President of the Oglala Sioux Tribe, she won! Cecilia Fire Thunder was officially elected the first Chairwoman of the Oglala Sioux Tribe and was sworn into the presidency on November 2, 2004. During her term as president, Cecilia became a national figure in the fight to provide women reproductive choices and rights. Throughout her life, her work has been focused on healthcare, an issue she brought to the forefront of the tribe. In addition to her focus on the health of Native people, she attempted to enhance the budget of the tribe. The credit rating of the tribe was terrible and there were significant payments that the Oglala Lakota tribe had not paid. Just as Cecilia did when she was working in California at two Indian health clinics, she reached out to various tribes in an effort to receive financial support. She also wrote letters and eventually the President of the Shakopee Tribe in Minnesota offered to secure a $38 million loan at 6.5 percent interest for fifteen years to the Oglala Lakota Tribe at Pine Ridge. Her community-based skills helped Fire Thunder work with Indian people and bring prosperity to her tribe. Cecilia's dedication to the people of the Oglala Lakota Nation is seen through her leadership skills.

In 2006, the state of South Dakota banned nearly all abortions. This ban encouraged Cecilia to build a clinic for women on the Pine Ridge Reservation. Fire Thunder stated, "I keep thinking about all the times I've worked with women who never had a choice."[2] Cecilia wanted to provide all women the choice to decide whether or not they wanted to have abortions. As a pro-choice woman, she supported the building of the Sacred Choices Clinic. Cecilia understood that not only Native American women desire an abortion or support abortion rights. The clinic was going to be designed to serve all women from South Dakota and Nebraska. She stated that the termination of pregnancies has been in Lakota society for hundreds of years. Fire Thunder also emphasized the availability of sex education for men, women, and youth.

Cecilia wanted people to practice safe sex. She believed it was crucial for young Native American men and women to understand the importance of family planning and the outcomes of choosing to be sexually active. While in office as president, Fire Thunder established a health clinic on the Pine Ridge Reservation. The state of South Dakota and some of the Indian people in her community criticized the health center. Her work in sexual education and approval of abortion led to her unfortunate removal as Tribal Chairwoman in June 2006. She was accused of misappropriating funds to fund the abortion clinic. She was officially impeached by the Oglala Lakota Tribe on June 30, 2006, and Alex White Plume, the tribe's vice president, ascended to the role of the Tribal President/Chairman. Cecilia understood that not only Native American women desire an abortion or support abortion rights. In spite of this setback in her career, she never stopped working within the American Indian community.

Cecilia continues to be politically active in the U.S. government. She has been a Democratic representative for the state of South Dakota. In 2008, she attended the Democratic National Convention with the goal of discussing topics of importance to Native American rights. She was a delegate to the Democratic National Convention where she discussed women's rights. She attended several caucuses and enjoyed discussing women's rights with politicians. Cecilia stated, "There is such a tremendous discussion on women, on healthcare, family, and children."[3] As a political leader and expert in Native American women's health, Fire Thunder chose to represent Native American people at this convention by discussing issues that pertain to Native American people in the United States.

Collaborating with Democratic constituents allowed for Cecilia to have a discussion to take place and the possibility of legislation to be passed. She attended the women's caucuses and as a South Dakota State Representative, she proudly served as a voice for the Oglala Lakota Nation. Cecilia also attended political conferences that discussed Native American issues. The National Congress of American Indians is one of the many groups that she joined. The National Congress of American Indians brings issues to the forefront that are important to American Indians and implements change in their policies. She believes that drafting resolutions through this political group ultimately will lead to positive changes for Indian people. Cecilia understands that tribal people in the twenty-first century must collaborate with both Native American and non-Native American people to create positive change for Indian people. Her actions in the past clearly demonstrate how successful tribes can be when they work alongside people for a common goal.

Cecilia has also been invited to various conferences and has been a keynote speaker many times. She has spoken at women's conferences, including one on Soboba Indian Reservation of California. On October 14, 2016, she talked to Carrie Garcia, a brilliant young Native woman at the Soboba Band of Luisenos Indians Sports Complex at an event titled "Let's Find and Use Your Voice." People and organizations often ask her to speak at these conferences, so she can instill in young Native American women that they must feel empowered. Women are sacred, and Cecilia Fire Thunder does a great job ensuring that women remember their important place in Indian Country. By reaching out to American Indian youth, Fire Thunder is able to educate women at a young age, asking them never to they forget their identity as Indigenous people.

Cecilia Apple Fire Thunder remains an active member of the American Indian community of the United States. She has dedicated her life to the support for Native American men and women. Many Native people in the twenty-first century face health problems and Cecilia continuously finds ways to address health issues that plague Indian Country. Whether Cecilia Fire Thunder is working as a nurse, holding elected office, leading community organizations, speaking at a conference, or actively participating in both tribal and U.S. governments, she has demonstrated her passion for Native American communities and people. Cecilia Fire Thunder's Lakota name means "Good-Hearted Woman."[4] She has earned this honored Lakota name.

NOTES

1. Sam Hurst, "Cecilia Fire Thunder: A Person of Character," *Rapid City Journal*, December 17, 2005.
2. David Melmer, "Oglala President Takes Center Stage in Women's Clinic," *Indian Country Today*, April 12, 2006.
3. "Cecilia Fire Thunder DNC Report," YouTube video, 1:54, posted by BadLandsBlue, September 2, 2008, https://www.youtube.com/watch?v=_w9WInm_o6c&t=11s.
4. Josè Barriero and Tim Johnson, *America is Indian Country: The Best of Indian Country Today* (Colorado: Fulcrum Publishing, 2005), 37.

BIBLIOGRAPHY

Barreiro, José and Tim Johnson. *America is Indian Country: The Best of Indian Country Today.* Golden, Colorado: Fulcrum Publishing, 2005.
"Cecilia Fire Thunder DNC Report." YouTube video, 1:54, posted by BadLandsBlue, September 2, 2008, https://www.youtube.com/watch?v=_w9WInm_o6c&t=11s.
Hurst, Sam. "Cecilia Fire Thunder: A Person of Character." *Rapid City Journal*, December 17, 2005.
Melmer, David. "Oglala President Takes Center Stage on Women's Clinic." *Indian Country Today*, April 12, 2006.

FURTHER READING

Leahy, Todd and Nathan Wilson. *Historical Dictionary of Native American Movements.* Lanham, MD: Rowan and Littlefield, 2016.

Chapter Fourteen

The Necessary Evil

Dolly Smith Cusker Akers
(b. 1901–d. 1986)

Shannon M. Smith

Dolly Smith Cusker Akers described herself a necessary evil and a person prone to stand up for Indian rights and demand Indigenous sovereignty.[1] As a woman and a Native American, Akers flaunted the social conventions of her era by becoming heavily involved in local, state, and, eventually, federal politics. Her work within the government affected major Native American legislation throughout the twentieth century. She worked her entire life determined to make an impact on the U.S. government for her people and all Native Americans.

Akers, an Assiniboine-Sioux woman, was born at Wolf Point, Montana, at a time when her people were relatively new to the reservation system. Before the European-Americans reached the Great Plains, the Sioux people had lived throughout their territory in temporary camps. During the spring-summer season they had followed the bison, and they lived in seasonal villages along the rivers in the winter. In the 1860s, the U.S. government forced many tribes of the Norther Great Pains onto reservations, and the Assiniboine and Sioux peoples were no exception. The national government set up reservations and moved several Assiniboine and Sioux to what became the Fort Peck Indian Agency. With the destruction of the buffalo, more Plains people moved on the Fort Peck Reservations where they lived near and with relatives and friends. The government provided some rations but life was tough. By 1880 the Sioux were permanently living on Fort Peck and the two tribes worked cooperatively to survive during the transitional period of Native American history. Indians leaving the reservation without permission were considered hostile and could be shot on sight.[2]

When Akers was born in 1901, her people were nearly dependent on the federal government for rations as the United States had destroyed their means of living and traditional economy. The old ways were gone after the wars with the American cavalry, removal to the reservation, and the arrival of settlers who used the lands for farming and ranching. American soldiers, settlers, hunters, traders, farmers, and ranchers had destroyed the traditional economy of Dolly's people. No longer allowed to leave the confines of the reservation to hunt or gather for their food, combined with inadequate supply of governmental food rations, rampant starvation occurred. The weakened condition of the people and the harsh winters took a tremendous toll on the tribe, allowing starvation and sickness to decimate the population. Akers grew up in Wolf Point, just outside of Fort Peck, where her mother and father, a man of Irish-American heritage, eked out a living. However, her mother's family remained on the reservation and looked to the future for a better life for their kin. The deprivation experienced by her relatives heavily influenced Dolly's worldview.

Akers' education began at the Fort Peck Indian school, an on-reservation government school in District 1. After the premature death of her mother, Akers attended Sherman Institute in Riverside, California, an off-reservation Indian boarding school where Dolly learned domestic science or homemaking. At school she joined the other students at daily chores of washing clothing, ironing, sewing, cooking, cleaning the buildings, and obeying the strict rules, which forbade children from speaking their native languages. From 1913 to 1916 Dolly attended Sherman Institute, and her school records remain housed at the Sherman Indian Museum on the campus of Sherman Indian High School and in the National Archives in Riverside, California. The Indian school on Magnolia Avenue in Riverside was like the other off-reservation American Indian boarding schools.[3] The school superintendent, teachers, and disciplinarians sought to assimilate Native children into the dominant American society. Sherman Institute was no different. At school, another level of assimilation existed. The school had a gendered curriculum for girls and young women. School officials tried to force Native American girls in to the mold of Victorian women of the United States. Native girls were taught that a woman's proper place was one of servitude in the home. To ensure this, all female students had to enroll into the Arts of Homemaking, consisting of vocational training, academic instruction, and social programs.[4]

It was during this time that Akers acquired the skills she later used to restore independence for Assiniboine-Sioux people. Academic lessons taught her how to read, write, and speak English. Vocational training consisted of several areas: the upkeep of the home, preemptive health care, and the ideology of consumerism in American society, which became the most beneficial to Akers' future. Rounding out the boarding school education was social programs. These social events developed a deep understanding of how Anglo-American culture worked. Akers used this knowledge to her advantage. In addition to all this, Dolly learned to turn the power, to take the harsh experience of her boarding school days and make something powerful and positive out of it. She used her Sherman days to learn about white people and their systems of government, economies, religions, and ways of treating others. She left school determined to use her education for the betterment of herself and her people.[5]

After graduating from Sherman Institute in 1916, Dolly returned home to Fort Peck. While she was away at school, the living conditions for Assiniboine people had deteriorated. Shortly after returning home, Dolly married George Cusker. Her marriage was the trigger of her political career. George Cusker suffered from ailments that kept him from attending tribal executive board meetings, and actively working to provide opportunities for the people. As a result, Dolly Akers attended executive board meetings for her husband and other functions. She served in his place, and she grew as a community-based activist. In 1921, at the age of twenty, Akers traveled to Washington, DC, as an interpreter for two tribal elders, Bear Hill and Dave Johnson. Dolly served as their interpreter. It was in the nation's capita that Akers first began her fight for American Indian citizenship and independence from American oppression.[6]

Akers' first step was to have Native people granted American citizenship. With this goal in mind, she began to lobby for what became the Native American Citizenship Act of 1924. Her fight was not necessarily for citizenship of Indigenous people but for all that came with citizenship, particularly the right to vote and to seek justice in the American court system. Years later she would be seen as an Indian who had the foresight to see the importance of Native American citizenship, which occurred in 1924. Akers strongly supported the Amerian Indian Citizenship Act, and she continued to work throughout the 1920s as an activist. She was elected to the tribal council at Fort Peck, and she earned a reputation as one who worked to benefit tribal members.[7]

When the United States fell into the Great Depression, Akers was concerned that Montana's Native population would not survive during the harsh economic times. As a result, she ran for the Montana State Legislature in 1932 and won by a landslide. She was the first Native American—and the only woman to be elected into this position. During the Depression, President Franklin Roosevelt's administration developed the Indian New Deal. This program provided tribes with the ability to incorporate and make their own financial decisions for their community. In addition, the New Deal developed the Public Welfare Act to assist people in need. In her capacity as a Montana State Legislator, Akers traveled to Washington, DC, to ensure that the act included federal relief for Indigenous people. Recognizing Akers' activism, the Montana governor appointed her the first coordinator of Indian welfare, representing all seven reservations within the state to the secretary of the interior.[8]

In the early 1940s, Akers was living a domesticated life on a farm, with her second husband, John Akers. Even though she had been content living outside the political arena, she remained active in her tribal community. However, the domesticated home life did not last long, and she found herself once again in Washington, DC. This time, she charged the Bureau of Indian Affairs with illegally selling tribal lands, selling mineral rights, and taking away Native American economic sovereignty. In addition, Akers fought BIA policies that prevented tribes from managing the sale of tribal lands and the ability to negotiate deals for natural resources within reservation boundaries.[9]

In 1953, national officials arrested Akers for assaulting a federal officer. She was found guilty and sentenced to a sixty-day suspended sentence and a one-year probation. Akers believed that she was unjustly convicted of a felony and her reputation and integrity were insulted. She continued her work and went back to Washington, DC, more aggressive than ever. This time she became involved in opposing termination. Her hard work and dedication were noticed by her own people. In 1956, they elected her as the first woman to chair the Fort Peck Executive Board. After Akers' term was completed, she returned to Washington, DC, as the Vice President of the National Congress of American Indians, once again fighting on behalf of Native people across the nation. This time she will accomplish one of her proudest achievements, the American Indian Civil Rights Act of 1968.[10]

While Akers was in her seventies, she worked to improve living conditions on reservations across the United States. She was an advisor on behalf of the Native communities to the Federal Home Administration in Washington, DC. Returning to Montana, Akers spent the next decade as Chair of the Fort Peck Tribal Housing Authority. In this position, she ensured that Fort Peck received all the federal funding needed for her people to secure appropriate housing.

Though Akers was wheelchair bound and in failing health, she still continued the fight to remove the disproportion of inequality that hindered the self-sufficiency of Native Americans. At age eighty-two, Akers made her last trip to Washington, DC, where she met with a congressional committee on behalf of her people, the Assiniboine Sioux of the Fort Peck Reservation. Many Indigenous people profited from the activism of Dolly Smith Akers, but not everyone supported her work during her career. Native communities criticized her, and people with her tribe felt she held too much influence with her political positions. Opponents criticized her for her alleged favoritism. Her opponents claimed she had released federal funding only to those who supported Akers throughout her career, leaving those who opposed her without much-needed government relief. However, her determination and perseverance gave the American Indian people the ability to determine their own destinies, free from federal oversight and interference. She encouraged Indigenous people to become assertive and self-reliant once again.

Akers did not allow her gender or ethnic identity to prevent her from working in the realm of local, state, and national politics. She willfully fought to be the one who called out the U.S. government, to be the first one to speak her mind, and to be the one who stood up for all Native people. According to Akers, no solution existed to the so-called Indian problem of the United States, at least not until the Interior Department and Indian Office embraced Indian sovereignty and self-determination as well as modified its policies to support the First Nations of the nation.

NOTES

1. "'I am a very necessary evil': The Political Career of Dolly Smith Cusker Akers," Women History Matters, Montana Historical Society (May 29, 2014), montanawomenhistory.org.

2. Clifford E. Trafzer, *As Long As the Grass Shall Grow and Rivers Flow: A History of Native America* (Belmont, CA: Wadsworth, 2000), 247–55; 280–86.

3. Clifford E. Trafzer, Matthew Sakiestewa Gilbert, and Lorene Sisquoc, *The Indian School on Magnolia Avenue: Voices and Images from Sherman Institute* (Corvallis: Oregon State University Press, 2014), 5–9; Interview of Lorene Sisquoc by Shannon M. Smith, Monday, May 23, 2016, Sherman Indian Museum, Riverside, California.

4. Clifford E. Trafzer, Jean Keller, and Lorene Sisquoc, eds., *Boarding School Blues: Revisiting American Indian Educational Experiences* (Lincoln: University of Nebraska Press, 2006), 13–29, 174–84.

5. Trafzer, Keller, and Sisquoc, *Boarding School Blues*, 237.

6. "'I am a very necessary evil': The Political Career of Dolly Smith Cusker Akers," Women History Matters, Montana Historical Society.

7. Cusker, Dolly Smith Akers Papers, 1927–1985. Biographical Note of Dolly Cusker Akers. archiveswest.orbiscascade.org.

8. "'I am a very necessary evil': The Political Career of Dolly Smith Cusker Akers," Women History Matters, Montana Historical Society; Phone Interview of Jody Foley, Montana State Archivist, by Shannon M. Smith, May 10, 2016, Montana Historical Society, Research Center Archives.

9. Shawn White Wolf, "Montana's 1st Indian lawmaker fought her entire life to keep intact her people and their way of life," *Independent Record*, January 26, 2003; "'I am a very necessary evil': The Political Career of Dolly Smith Cusker Akers," Women History Matters, Montana Historical Society.

10. "'I am a very necessary evil': The Political Career of Dolly Smith Cusker Akers," Women History Matters, Montana Historical Society; Liz Cantarine, "She's Dolly Akers, 69-Year-Old Dynamo." *Billings Gazette*, July 18, 1971.

BIBLIOGRAPHY

Beazley, Freda Augusta. Beazley Collection, 1960–1975. Manuscript Collection 187. Montana Historical Society Research Center, Helena.

Cantarine, Liz. "She's Dolly Akers, 69-Year-Old Dynamo." *Billings Gazette*, July 18, 1971.

Cusker, Dolly Smith Akers Papers, 1927–1985: http://archiveswest.orbiscascade.org/ark.

Fort Peck Assiniboine & Sioux Tribes History, http://www.fortpecktribes.org.

"Fort Peck Tribal Board Orders General Election." *Great Falls Tribune*, February 5, 1959.

"'I am a very necessary evil': The Political Career of Dolly Smith Cusker Akers," Women History Matters, Montana Historical Society (May 29, 2014), montanawomenhistory.org.

Interview of Lorene Sisquoc by Shannon M. Smith, Monday, May 23, 2016, Sherman Indian Museum, Riverside, California.

Phone Interview of Jody Foley, Montana State Archivist, by Shannon M. Smith, May 10, 2016, Montana Historical Society, Research Center Archives.

Trafzer, Clifford E. *As Long As the Grass Shall Grow and Rivers Flow: A History of Native America* (Belmont, CA: Wadsworth, 2000), 247–55; 280–86.

Trafzer, Clifford E., Matthew Sakiestewa Gilbert, and Lorene Sisquoc. *The Indian School on Magnolia Avenue: Voices and Images from Sherman Institute*. Corvallis: Oregon State University Press, 2014.

Trafzer, Clifford E., Jean Keller, and Lorene Sisquoc, eds. *Boarding School Blues: Revisiting American Indian Educational Experiences*. Lincoln and London: University of Nebraska Press, 2006.

White Wolf, Shawn. "Montana's 1st Indian lawmaker fought her entire life to keep intact her people and their way of life." *Independent Record*, January 26, 2003.

Wotanin Wowapi, June 19, 2006.

FURTHER READINGS

Miller, David, Dennis Smith, Joseph McGeshick, James Shanley, and Caleb Shields. *The History of the Assiniboine and Sioux Tribes of the Fort Peck Indian Reservation, 1800–2000*. Poplar, MT.: Fort Peck Community College, 2008.

Fourstar, Odessa Jones. Letter to the editor, March 5, 1976. *Wotanin Wowapi*, March 11, 1976. "Indian Relief Setup Organized for Peck." *Helena Daily Independent*, December 21, 1934, 5.

Palmer, Tom. "My People, My Life: Indian Elder Still Serving Her Tribe." *Helena Independent Record*, March 3, 1985, 2, 3.

Trafzer, Clifford E., Jeffrey A. Smith, and Lorene Sisquoc. *Shadows of Sherman Institute: A Photographic History of the Indian School on Magnolia Avenue*. Pechanga: Great Oak Press, 2016.

"Woman Indian Leader Finds Liberation Movement 'Old Hat.'" *Farmington Daily Times*, July 14, 1971.

Chapter Fifteen

Champion of the National Congress of the American Indian

Ruth Muskrat Bronson
(b. 1897–d. 1982)

Julia Coates

"To search for the determined historical objective of the American Government in its dealings with Indians since their pacification seems to me like searching on a dark night for a black cat that isn't there."[1] So wrote Indian rights activist Ruth Muskrat Bronson in 1948. At the time, Muskrat Bronson was midway through her tenure as Executive Secretary of the National Congress of American Indians (NCAI), an organization she helped establish. Her professional title is misleading—she was far more than a secretary. In fact, the title was the one bestowed on the individual who held the organizational reins, an exceptional role for a woman of her era. Muskrat Bronson was the only woman among the six individuals usually credited as being the organization's founders. But she did not remain the NCAI's only woman for long. Under her mentorship, a dozen more from tribes across the country became influential as well, including a subsequent Executive Secretary, Helen Peterson. But none was as instrumental to the NCAI's inception and indeed its very survival in the early years as Ruth Muskrat Bronson.

By 1948, descriptive and forthright communications were increasingly typical of her. Although she had spent decades working within the federal Indian bureaucracy and certainly knew when and how to express herself in more politic ways, at that moment she was in a fully resistant mode. Not only was she battling unrelenting and often underhanded congressional and corporate attempts to exploit tribal resources and communities, but Muskrat Bronson was under vicious political and personal attack as well. Her exasperation was on display, but she was at the height of her own formidable strength and others also had to reckon with *her*. She was a savvy strategist and a potent fighter on behalf of the tribes and the people. Had she not been, the attacks on her might not have been so aggressive. The fledgling NCAI was battered as a result, but Muskrat Bronson defended it and herself just as aggressively, and almost through the sheer force of her own will rebuilt it even stronger before finally handing the reins to her successor in 1950.

Who was Ruth Muskrat Bronson and what were the forces that shaped her? She was born in 1897 at Cowskin Prairie in the Delaware district of the Cherokee Nation. At the time, her tribal government was in the fight of its life. For sixty years the Cherokee Nation had operated a bona fide republic in the Indian Territory (presently northeastern Oklahoma) after their forced removal to that location on the Trail of Tears in 1838 and 1839. But at the time of Ruth Muskrat's birth, the Nation's landholding and government were being forcibly dismantled by the United States. Allotment was carried out between 1898 and 1906, and various aspects of tribal government and jurisdictional authority were being systematically eliminated. Her earliest memories were of a national conversation of dispossession and occupation, heard in her family and throughout the community. Although her own family managed to retain their allotments, most others did not and became deeply impoverished as a result. The impacts of these events left a deep impression in her consciousness. Her earliest writings from her teenage years reflect a strong, dignified awareness of the injustice.

Ruth displayed other aspects of the Cherokee national character that shaped her beliefs and actions. She was born to a Cherokee father who was of high enough blood degree that he was "restricted" in his landholding, meaning he could not manage his allotment without first gaining the permission of the Bureau of Indian Affairs.[2] The authoritarian federal requirement was intended as a protection of the more racially identifiable Indians, who it was presumed had little experience or ability to deal with land as a real estate commodity. As was the case for many high-quantum Indians, the Muskrat family was, in fact, entirely capable of managing their land, and the paternalism that limited them rankled.

The marriage of her parents caused consternation within Ruth's mother's family, the Kellys. Of Irish descent, their objection was almost certainly along racial lines. As a result, Ruth's mother, Ida Kelly Muskrat, was driven to ensure that her Indian children were "just as good as"—a quality that is admirable, but which may also display an underlying acceptance of the American society's presumed superiority.[3] Certainly the characteristic was shared by most Indian intellectuals of the time, even as many of them also insisted on respect for tribal tradition. As she matured, Ruth adopted this perspective as well—she firmly believed in the ability of Indian people to adapt and excel at the standards of the dominant American society. But she also refused to tolerate any denigration of Indian values, behaviors, or culture.

One of the values espoused within the Muskrat family was a reverence for education. In this, the family also reflected the Cherokee national disposition.

Having become a widely literate people in their own language as a result of the invention in the early 1820s of a written language system by the native genius Sequoyah, the Cherokees had established about 150 day schools which offered to its citizens free compulsory education to the eighth grade, as well as the renowned Cherokee Male and Female Seminaries. Although those school systems had been appropriated by the state by the time Ruth Muskrat was ten years old, that reverence for the power of education and literacy remained within the people. And as she matured, this reverence became a defining quality within her as well. From the moment her career began until the moment her life ended, she remained firm in the belief that education could make the difference for Indian people.

And as were her people, she was oriented toward the larger world and toward service. Throughout their existence the Cherokees had been an outward-looking and incorporative people. They had displayed interest in different technologies, peoples, languages, cultures, and religious beliefs. They had long engaged in foreign relations and their political sophistication in dealing with the United States was respected and their advice sought by other tribes. Their political rhetoric was well-honed and largely focused on the subject of human rights and the American moral imperative in relation to tribal governments, and is the subject of scholars in the present day. Along with rights came obligations, and the Cherokee tradition of "ga-du-gi," which superficially translates as "coming together to work" but which communicates deep values of collectivity and responsibility, required contributing to one's community and tribe.[4] As Ruth Muskrat moved into maturity, she was thoroughly a Cherokee woman, a citizen of an effective tribal government, with a reverence for education, an interest in the larger world of which her people were a part, and a strong sense of obligation.

Ruth Muskrat fought for her higher education. Funding was always a problem and Ruth was already twenty-two years old before she was able to enter the University of Oklahoma in 1919. However, she had to leave after her first year when she was no longer able to finance her studies. She was hired to work for the Young Women's Christian Association (YWCA) on the Mescalero Apache reservation that was essentially a re-entry program for Indian girls returning home from boarding schools. Ruth's compassion and advocacy on behalf of the girls were noteworthy, and she was moved by both the challenging conditions these young women faced as well as their resilience in meeting the trials. It contributed to her lifelong hope and belief that when Indians became educated they would return to their home communities and dedicate themselves to improving the lives of others.

Ruth's ability to work well with tribal communities was recognized by the YWCA. The coordinator of the project, Edith Dabb, began to actively mentor her. The 1920s were a very active decade that shaped Ruth Muskrat for the rest of her life, and Edith Dabb can be credited with opening many of the opportunities that Ruth was able to take advantage of. It was a close relationship that lasted a lifetime. After two summers at Mescalero, the YWCA was instrumental in awarding Ruth a three-year scholarship to the University of Kansas in Lawrence. While a student, Ruth was recruited in 1922 to be a representative to the World Student Christian Federation conference, an event with which the YWCA was closely affiliated. That year it was held in China, and Ruth was the first American Indian representative to the conference. The weeks spent in China resulted in a profound revelation for her as she began to make associations between the experiences of many ethnic minorities within that country and those of American Indians.

The conference brought national recognition to Ruth as one of the bright young leaders of the next generation of Indian intellectuals and activists. In 1923, Ruth received a full scholarship to Mt. Holyoke in Massachusetts where she would attend her last two years of college, and in 1924, she was invited to the White House to meet President Calvin Coolidge, as well as established Indian leaders such as Charles Eastman and Henry Roe Cloud. Ruth was developing what today would be regarded as a "pan-Indian" identity, encouraging alliance between peoples of different tribal nations to emphasize similarities while self-defining as American Indians within the federal context. Upon graduation in 1925 she accepted a position as a teacher at Haskell Indian Institute and returned to Lawrence, Kansas, where she remained for the next five years.

Ruth only taught for two years before becoming the registrar at Haskell, which was operated by the Bureau of Indian Affairs. Much of her work during the next three years was for the Outing program, which placed students in unskilled summer employment. She was able to expand the program to also identify employment opportunities at resorts and national parks for some of the students, but finding anything better than domestic work and manual labor remained difficult. She continued to make outreach and speak on behalf of the YWCA's programs and those of other Christian organizations, to recruit Indian youth and place them in various educational and employment programs, to mentor still others to go on in higher education, and generally as a public advocate and speaker on behalf of Indian people.

In 1928, Ruth married a Connecticut Yankee, John Bronson. It was another fortuitous outcome of the mentorship of Edith Dabb since Bronson was Dabb's cousin. He was the perfect husband for Ruth, as she had already dedicated herself to working on behalf of Indian people, a commitment he supported. John Bronson, perpetually clad in Pendleton shirts and wire spectacles, "loved the west as only a Connecticut guy could," according to their great-nephew, and throughout their life together John was entirely willing to relocate whenever Ruth might need to.[5] This trait may have seemed entirely appropriate to a Cherokee woman, but was remarkable in a non-Indian man of Bronson's time.

The Meriam Report of 1928 acknowledged a need for reforms of Indian education policy. As a new decade dawned in 1930, with a new Indian Commissioner, Charles Roads, at the helm and increased congressional funding, Ruth Muskrat Bronson's role at Haskell was re-titled Guidance and Placement Officer as she expanded post-graduation training possibilities into skilled, professional, and higher education realms under a new federal mandate. In 1930, she left Haskell to become a full-time employee of the Bureau of Indian Affairs, and her role expanded to eight states as she began to administer a loan program to help fund postsecondary training for increasing numbers of students. She and John moved to Kansas City, and then to Vinita, Oklahoma, to be closer to her family.

Ruth's job entailed a great deal of travel and she regularly crossed the region alone by car to visit Indian schools throughout the west, conducting surveys and assessments, recruiting, and providing funding information. Within a short time, she transitioned to working exclusively with loans and development. That promotion took the Bronsons to Washington, DC, in 1935, which brought even greater visibility to Ruth's work. She was a prolific speaker and a relentless fundraiser, and was often called on by agencies, reformers, and bureaucrats alike to share her ideas on Indian education. Among the reforms she sought were changes in the institutional attitudes of many of the administrators of Indian schools, which often expected little of Indian students and offered them even less in encouragement or support. This sort of constant messaging, Muskrat Bronson asserted, quashed spirits and abilities and left little possibility for Indian students to fulfill their capacities or aspirations.

She also sought reforms in the methods by which the Bureau of Indian Affairs (BIA) Agency Directors disbursed the scholarship monies to schools, which was lackadaisical and often jeopardized the student's ability to stay in school. She persuaded the BIA to forego some of its security requirements for disbursing the loans to students, particularly the one that forced them to put up their allotments as collateral. She promoted culturally relevant teaching not only to assist student achievement, but to provide validation of their own cultural traditions. And she made it a personal cause to specifically recruit qualified young Indian women as candidates for the loans that were offered.

The years in Washington were fruitful for Muskrat Bronson. She earned accolades from many of her peers and other Indian leaders for her work and had the opportunity to meet some of the most influential leaders in the country, including D'Arcy McNickle, Arthur C. Parker, Louis Bruce Sr., and

David Owl, all of whom would become influential alongside her in forming the National Congress of American Indians. She completed the coursework for a master's degree in Education at George Washington University, but did not write the required thesis to be actually awarded the degree. And in 1939, Ruth and John adopted a toddler, a little girl from Laguna Pueblo, Dolores, whose mother had been one of Ruth's most successful student recruits. When Dolores' mother passed away, the Bronsons stepped in to care for the child.

In 1943, at the age of forty-six, Ruth retired from the BIA after all its operations were being moved to other states in order to free up office space in DC for the war effort. Initially Ruth intended to spend more time with her family and took the opportunity to write her only book, *Indians Are People, Too*, which was published in 1944. It was written at the request of a Protestant ecumenical mission to study American Indians, and reflects the tone also taken by Ella Cara Deloria in her work from the same era, *Speaking of Indians*. In many respects, the tone of these works seems assimilative to contemporary audiences, so it is important to remember that they were intended to give a human face to Indians for a non-Indian audience—an audience that in past decades had done much damage to Indians despite their reformist intentions. The works were also explanatory, but unapologetic, of Indian beliefs and customs to that same audience that had often tried to eradicate Indian cultures.

As she remained in Washington after her retirement, Muskrat Bronson's home became "the American Indian lobbying center in Washington" according to family recollections, and the National Congress of American Indians was started "around Ruth's kitchen table" according to Yeffe Kimball.[6] Technically, the NCAI began in 1944 from a conference in Denver at which board leadership was designated, but Kimball's remark is probably accurate in regard to the actual development and growth of the organization. Ruth's home address was the first used by the organization that emerged, the National Congress of American Indians.

Initially the NCAI focused on several issues: securing Indian voting rights, particularly in Arizona, New Mexico, and Maine, where those rights had been expressly denied in seeming contradiction to federal law, and guaranteeing Social Security benefits to Indians in states that had denied them. More general struggles were also taken up by the National Congress of American Indian (NCAI), such as tribal claims against the United States which the NCAI soon began to litigate on behalf of some tribes, and lobbying for the protection of Indian lands and resources. Ruth's initial contribution to the new organization was to cover Indian Affairs in Washington, DC, and report them as the founder of NCAI's legislative news service. This was a critical service since treaty-making had ended in 1871 and afterward, Congress had often legislated matters of interest to the tribes without any input from them. Often they were not even informed of legislative changes that impacted them. The NCAI became the "watchdog" in Washington on behalf of tribes across the country.

Ruth also put to work on behalf of the NCAI the formidable skills she had acquired while a BIA employee. She volunteered her time and recruited others, often Indian students. She went back to the list of donors she had cultivated over many years in new fundraising efforts. And perhaps most importantly, she established the Legal Aid and Service Bureau of the NCAI from inside her home in Washington, DC. In 1946, Ruth Muskrat Bronson's efforts were recognized and she was made NCAI's Executive Secretary, its director. Until she stepped down from this post in 1950, Ruth worked indefatigably during an era when there was an onslaught of proposed federal legislation designed to terminate Indian rights and lands. She defended Indian tribalism in the era of the Red Scare and the comparisons between Native communalism and Marxist-style communism. The role of the NCAI was critical in this hostile political climate.

However, Muskrat Bronson also became embroiled in what some saw as the questionable practice of urging tribes represented by NCAI to award attorney's contracts to one of her closest colleagues at the organization. While she defended the recommendations on the basis of wanting to provide tribes with the best legal advice she knew of, others saw it as cronyism that benefitted the NCAI. Many Indian leaders regarded it as a minor issue and believed that Congress was trying to undercut tribal sovereignty by using the issue to give itself the right to approve all tribal contracts with attorneys. It was also a mechanism to eviscerate the influence of Ruth Muskrat Bronson, whose organization was one of the strongest and most vocal advocates on behalf of Indian rights. The attacks on her were often vicious and underhanded, and she fought back with tremendous strength. She survived the political onslaught, but the NCAI was wrought with internal divisions over its leader and whether she should continue in the role given the notoriety that now surrounded the organization, whether justified or not.

Ultimately, the attempt to extend congressional oversight of tribes was beaten back, but Ruth was sullied from the battle and soon stepped away from leadership of the NCAI. However, the very seasoned Ruth Muskrat Bronson continued to volunteer through 1956, including another stint as interim Executive Secretary. Finally, when Helen Peterson was chosen to be the NCAI's leader, the two women worked together to rebuild the organization at the critical time of the Termination policy. That Indians were able to limit the impact of this devastating policy to any degree was assisted immeasurably by the efforts of the NCAI under Muskrat Bronson and Peterson.

Ruth continued to be a prolific fundraiser, particularly for ARROW, Inc. (Americans for the Restitution and Righting of Old Wrongs), the NCAI's fundraising arm, and as one of the founders of American Indian Development (AID), a self-help community development project. Health education, scholarship assistance, and land policy became Ruth's work again, as well as travel to work in reservation communities across the country. By the late 1950s, John Bronson was wanting to retire and relocate permanently to the southwest. Ruth actively began looking for ways in which to establish herself in that region on a more permanent basis, and in 1963 became one of the first Indian health educators assigned by the Indian Health Service (IHS) for the San Carlos Apache reservation. Dedicated to San Carlos by IHS, she and John moved onto the reservation, where she expanded her activities through a collaboration with the Save the Children Federation (SCF) and was bestowed the Olivia Culp Hobby award from the U.S. Department of Health, Education, and Welfare for her service.

After she and John retired, they moved to Tucson, Arizona, where Ruth moved fully into local, self-determined tribal community development in the last phase of her long career. Continuing as a part-time consultant with SCF, she helped to extend its work with village- and community-based groups not only at San Carlos, but also with the Tohono O'odham and Pascua Yaqui. She was also involved with the federal recognition process of the Tonto Apache and with Pascua Yaqui health programs.

Ruth's expertise and previous work among Alaska Native villages as part of her stint at NCAI led to her selection as a commissioner in the process of developing ANCSA (Alaska Native Claims Settlement Act), but she had to withdraw due to John's health, and he passed away in 1966. In 1969–1970, her great-nephew, Jim Crouch, having just finished college, came to live at her home and become her typist and driver. He paints a lively picture of his elderly aunt, who had an elaborately hand-painted, Mexican cane that she used to point or pound on the ground to get attention, what he called "working her cane." In particular, he remembered her mentorship and support of emerging tribal leaders of that time, and the strong friendships she had with many of the O'odham women, in particular. She was, as he stated it, "wonderfully at home in the Tohono O'odham villages."[7]

Ruth never lost sight of the tribal individual living the life on the ground. Her own experience had taken her from the corridors of power in Washington, DC, and all across the country, even the world. But she had a great gift for "working with people where they were at," according to her great-nephew.[8] Despite all her achievements, Jim states that her proudest moment came when, while at the BIA, she had met the young Cherokee artist Lloyd New who was studying at the Chicago Art School. He confided in her that his biggest burden was often the severe acne that he suffered from. She arranged for him to have state-of-the-art treatment, recognizing the impact that the simple ability to confidently display one's face can have on a person. New became one of the most respected Native artists of his era.

Ruth and Jim clicked as well. Both were political people, but she "gave him permission," in his words, to care about Indian affairs and championed his own burgeoning identity as a Cherokee.[9] Although she had implemented many programs and had witnessed their impacts and successes, as an elder she still recognized that change is inevitable and helpful. She strongly understood that what worked yesterday may not be tomorrow's solution. To her last day, she continued to mentor those who were coming up and to invest her all into the betterment of life for Indians in their home communities.

Ruth Muskrat Bronson suffered a stroke in 1972 that curtailed her activities but not her passions. She lived for another ten years and passed away in 1982 at the age of eighty-four. For her family members, Ruth is still that Cherokee woman who was just one of the aunties, alongside her sisters Jewel and Thelma. Despite her accomplishments, this Cherokee woman was at heart still the self-deprecating teaser seeing the absurdities in life, rooted deeply in the rural community history and ways of her people that she loved, ways she had found were mirrored among Indian people everywhere.

NOTES

1. Ruth M. Bronson to John R. Nichols, undated letter in 1948, National Congress of American Indians Records, Box 72, Nichols, John R., Correspondence 1948–49, Smithsonian Institution, National Museum Archive Center, 4220 Silver Hill Road, Suitland, Maryland, 20746.

2. Interview of James (Jim) Crouch, July 17, 2016, by Julia Coates, Sacramento, California. I would like to express my gratitude to Jim Crouch of Sacramento, California, for speaking with me at length about his Aunt Ruth. During his interview with me, Jim graciously shared about his great-grandmother Ida Kelly Muskrat. For many years Jim served as director of the California Rural Indian Health Board assisting many California Indian communities.

3. Jim Crouch Interview, July 17, 2016. Jim Crouch is the great-nephew of Muskrat Bronson. Jim related the information on Ida Kelly Muskrat. The analysis of the characteristic is my own, with which he may or may not agree.

4. Tradition: Gadugi is a Cherokee concept of working together. www.knowitall.org.

5. Jim Crouch Interview, July 17, 2016.

6. Jim Crouch Interview, July 17, 2016. Yeffe Kimball, long respected as a Native American artist, presented herself as Osage and was acquainted with many of the Indian leaders of the day who apparently accepted her claims. Subsequent investigation has revealed that Ms. Kimball did not have Indian heritage, and her work has been removed from many collections and displays of Native American artists. Neverthe-

less, her comment is pertinent as coming from someone who was in the social circles of prominent Indians at that time and who had firsthand knowledge of the gatherings at Muskrat Bronson's home.
7. Jim Crouch Interview, July 17, 2016.
8. Jim Crouch Interview, July 17, 2016.
9. Jim Crouch Interview, July 17, 2016.

BIBLIOGRAPHY

Bronson, Ruth M. to John R. Nichols, undated letter, 1948. National Congress of American Indians Records, Box 72, Nichols, John R., Correspondence 1948–49, Smithsonian Institution, National Museum Archive Center, 4220 Silver Hill Road, Suitland, Maryland, 20746.

Interview of James (Jim) Crouch by Julia Coates, July 17, 2016. Sacramento, California.

Tradition: Gadugi is a Cherokee concept of working together. www.knowitall.org. Author's Collection.

FURTHER READINGS

Brown, Kirby. *Stoking the Fire, Nationhood in Cherokee Writing 1902–1970.* Norman: University of Oklahoma Press, 2018. Chapter 4, "Cherokee Trans/National Stateswomanship in the Nonfiction Writings of Ruth Muskrat Bronson." 168–210.

Cowger, Thomas W. *National Congress of American Indian: The Founding Years.* Lincoln: University of Nebraska Press, 2001.

Denson, Andrew. *Demanding the Cherokee Nation.* Lincoln: University of Nebraska Press, 2004.

Harvey, Gretchen G. "Cherokee and American: Ruth Muskrat Bronson, 1897–1982." Tempe: Arizona State University, PhD Dissertation, 1996.

Harvey, Gretchen C. "Bronson, Ruth Muskrat." Gretchen M. Bataille and Laurie Lisa, eds. *Native American Women: A Biographical Dictionary.* New York: Garland Publishing, 1993, 42–44. Reprint by Routledge, 2002.

Muskrat Bronson, Ruth. *Indians Are People, Too.* New York: Friendship Press, 1944.

Chapter Sixteen

Seeking Justice through Storytelling
Leslie Marmon Silko
(b. 1948)

Amanda K. Wixon

Leslie Marmon Silko is an internationally acclaimed writer and poet, whose work has earned her numerous accolades in the literary world. As an essayist, she advocates for land rights, tribal sovereignty, and reform through her essays. As a novelist, she uses traditional Native storytelling to restructure the novel, grounding many in Laguna culture. As an activist, she seeks justice for those who have lost their land, culture, and way of life. While her work as an activist addresses the continuing struggle for many Native peoples, as well as racism and women's issues, Silko has made it clear that she is a person of mixed-blood ancestry but there should be no doubt that she is a citizen of Laguna Pueblo.[1]

Leslie Marmon (Silko) was born in Albuquerque, New Mexico, to Leland Howard Marmon and Mary Virginia Leslie. In the 1880s, Robert (Silko's great-grandfather) and his brother, Walter, came to Laguna from Ohio and married Laguna women. As valued members of the Laguna community, both of the men served as Governor of the Pueblo. Robert's wife, Marie Anaya Marmon, a full-blooded Laguna, attended Carlisle Indian Industrial School and was an accomplished storyteller, while their son, Henry, attended Sherman Institute in Riverside, California. Her father, Leland, was a photographer and managed the Marmon Trading Post in Old Laguna Village, and her mother was from Montana. Leslie was raised on the Laguna Pueblo reservation and began her education at home with her aunts, grandparents, and great-grandparents who took care of her and her sisters while her parents worked. Under their care, she learned her family's history and many stories of Laguna people, stories that she later incorporated into her writing. From preschool to fourth grade, she attended Laguna BIA (Bureau of Indian Affairs) School and later, Albuquerque Indian School. She attended a Catholic school in Albuquerque.[2]

Although she was acutely aware of her Indian, Mexican, and white ancestry, she did not allow this conflict to interfere with her deep desire to know the landscape and stories of Laguna people. Silko pointed out that she grew up under the influence of strong women. "I grew up," she reported, "with women who were really strong, women with a great deal of power." She explained, "If someone was going to thwart you or frighten you, it would tend to be a women." Fathers were "the soft touch," Silko remembered, but "you could see it coming from your mother, or sent by your mother."[3] No question existed in Silko's mind that her great-grandmother, grandmothers, aunties, and mother significantly influenced her childhood as did the female characters she knew as a children from the ancient stories of Laguna people.

As a child, Silko often roamed the land on horseback, seeking the solitude of the hills located to the southeast of Laguna. Through her solitary wanderings she learned to trust the land and felt safe in the embrace of the hills, among familiar plants and animals. This feeling led to a lifelong relationship with the land, instilling a reverence for the environment that colors much of her writing and visual art. Silko drew on the wellspring of her youth and the environment around her at Laguna, and she listened to the stories told by her elders, which influenced her writing. She once explained that "our identify is formed by the stories we hear when we're growing up. Literature helps us locate ourselves in the family, the community and the whole universe."[4]

At the age of five, Leslie's father was elected tribal treasurer. During his term, the Pueblo of Laguna filed a lawsuit against the state of New Mexico for six-million acres of stolen land. The lawyer hired to represent the Laguna often met expert witnesses at Marmon's house to prepare for court. The elders, as the expert witnesses, told stories of the land that made them cry, affecting young Leslie with their sense of loss and anger. In high school, Silko decided to pursue law as a way to seek justice for her people. She studied English at the University of New Mexico, earning a Discovery Grant from the National Endowment of the Arts for her short stories. Despite this award, she remained focused on law school. While completing three semesters in the American Indian Law School Fellowship Program, Silko began to recognize the inherent injustice of the Anglo-American legal system. Disturbed by the relationship between money, power, and justice, she abandoned her law studies, deciding to combat injustice with the power of stories. She enrolled in a photography class and took graduate courses in English. In 1971, she left school to teach on the Navajo Reservation in Chinle, Arizona. Silko's professional life as a writer began in 1968, while still at the university. In the next six years, she wrote several short stories and poems later featured in *Laguna Woman*, published in 1974.[5]

In her personal life, Silko married Richard C. Chapman in 1965 and soon gave birth to a son, Robert. Her marriage to Chapman ended in 1969. In 1971, she married John Silko and gave birth to another son, Casimir. In 1973, the family moved to Ketchikan, Alaska, for John Silko's work. The cold, rainy weather and lack of sunshine took a toll on Leslie, and she was unable to immediately resume her writing. After several months, and with a writing space of her own, she began her novel, *Ceremony*. In the novel, Silko explored many of the issues concerning Native American soldiers returning home from war: alcoholism, poverty, racism, and healing. To tell her story, Silko incorporated traditional storytelling to contextualize the protagonist's experiences and to describe the world he lived in as a Laguna man. Published in 1977, this critically acclaimed novel pushed Silko into the literary spotlight.[6]

Laguna Woman, Ceremony, and *Storyteller*, a collection of short stories published in 1981, earned Silko the recognition of the MacArthur Foundation in Chicago, and she became one of the first recipients of the "genius" award.[7] Over the next two decades, Silko continued to write and publish collections of short stories and poems, letters of correspondence, essays, two novels, and a memoir. Though her work earned her both praise and criticism, Silko remained a committed activist and wrote several essays that demonstrate her dedication to fighting injustice.

In *Yellow Woman and the Beauty of the Spirit,* published in 1996, Silko's activism is expressed through essays about a variety of topics, including immigration, U.S. Border Patrol policies, tribal sovereignty, land rights, federal Indian policy, and tribal council politics. This collection also features Pueblo migration stories, family histories, and essays on visual arts and the role of the photographer. However, this seemingly random collection of thoughts and writings beautifully illustrates Silko's perspective on activism. Controversial and thought-provoking essays about the Native American experience should not be separated from essays about Laguna culture, relationships, migrations, and families. For Silko, these sensitive topics are all part of knowing Laguna. As she pointed out in the beginning of *Laguna Woman*, "I suppose at the core of my writing is the attempt to identify what it is to be a half-breed or mixed blooded person; what it is to grow up neither white nor fully traditional Indian." In an interview, she stated, "I am of mixed ancestry, but what I know is Laguna."[8]

In 2010, *The Turquoise Ledge: A Memoir*, Silko uses the structure of Native storytelling to explore her own history as a Laguna woman. As a person of mixed ancestry, Silko often used her work to describe her unique experiences, good and bad. As a child, white Euro-Americans considered her to be Indian enough to attend an exclusively Indian school, yet Pueblo people barred her from attending Laguna ceremonies. In her memoir, Silko explores her Laguna, Cherokee, Mexican, and European roots while ruminating on the environment and her relationship with the spiritual world. As with her other work, Silko uses storytelling to forcefully comment on issues like environment exploitation, attacking the parties responsible for destruction of the land.

Silko also uses her voice to critique her contemporaries, accusing some authors of profiting from Native culture while taking others to task for not addressing Native issues like tribal sovereignty in their work. For Silko, creative fiction is not excused from work of activism. Much of her writing is also concerned with healing. In *Ceremony*, the protagonist, Tayo, seeks spiritual solace after the trauma of World War II. The novel is essentially Tayo's journey of healing. Like Silko, Tayo is of mixed-ancestry, and his journey reflects Silko's own struggles with identity and her path to global citizenship.

For fifty years, Silko has been a significant voice in Native American activism. Her writing is considered an essential part of many literature courses and she continues to produce important works that advocate for Native rights and seeks to correct historical injustices committed by Euro-Americans against Native peoples. Her work has earned her recognition and prestigious awards within the Native community and beyond. In 1980, she received the American Book Award for Outstanding Literary Achievement for her novel, *Ceremony*. 1988, the New Mexico Humanities Council named Silko as a Living Cultural Treasure. In 1994, she received the Third Wordcraft Circle of Native Writers and Storytellers Lifetime Achievement Award. In 2000, she received the Lannon Literary Award for Fiction. Weaving justice with words, Leslie Marmon Silko honors her elders and her community through her work as a writer, poet, artist, and activist.[9]

NOTES

1. Laura Cotelli, "Silko, Leslie Marmon," Gretchen M. Bataille, *Native American Women: A Biographical Dictionary* (New York: Garland Publishing, 1993), 233.

2. Annette Van Dyke, "Leslie Marmon Silko: Laguna Pueblo Novelist and Poet," Sharon Milinowski, ed., *Notable Native Americans* (Detroit: Gale Research, Inc., 1995), 396.

3. Van Dyke, "Leslie Marmon Silko," 396.

4. "Leslie Marmon Silko," Duane Champagne, ed., *North American Indian Almanac* (Detroit: Gale Research, Inc., 1994), 1160.

5. Leslie Marmon Silko, *Laguna Woman: Poems by Leslie Marmon Silko* (Tucson: Flood Plain Press, 1974), 1–2.

6. Leslie Marmon Silko, *Ceremony* (New York: Penguin, 1977).

7. Leslie Marmon Silko, "Biographical Sketch," www.poets.org.

8. Butlerbanner.com.

9. Van Dyke, "Leslie Marmon Silko," 396–97.

BIBLIOGRAPHY

Bataille, Gretchen M. *Native American Women: A Biographical Dictionary*. New York: Garland Publishing, 1993.

Champagne, Duane, editor, T*he Native North American Almanac.* Detroit: Gale Research Inc., 1994.

Malinowski, Sharon, ed. *Notable Native Americans.* Detroit: Gale Research, Inc., 1995.

Silko, Leslie Marmon. "Biographical Sketch." www.poets.org.

Silko, Leslie Marmon. "Biographical Sketch." Butlerbanner.com.

Silko, Leslie Marmon. *Ceremony.* New York: Penguin Books, 1977.

Silko, Leslie Marmon. *Laguna Woman: Poems by Leslie Marmon Silko*. Tucson: Flood Plain Press, 1974.

FURTHER READINGS

Silko, Leslie Marmon. *The Turquoise Ledge: A Memoir.* New York: Viking Press: 2010.

Silko, Leslie Marmon. *Yellow Woman and a Beauty of the Spirit: Essays on Native American Life Today*, New York: Simon and Schuster, 1996.

Trafzer, Clifford E., Matthew Sakiestewa Gilbert, and Lorene Sisquoc, eds. *The Indian School on Magnolia Avenue: Voices and Images From Sherman Institute*. Corvallis: Oregon State University Press, 2012.

Chapter Seventeen

Native American Scholar Activist
Bea Medicine
(b. 1923–d. 2005)

Elvia Rodriguez

On June 2, 1924, President Calvin Coolidge signed the Indian Citizenship Act, granting Native Americans full citizenship in the United States. Two months later, on August 1, at the Standing Rock Reservation in Wakpala, South Dakota, Anna Medicine gave birth to a baby girl. The newborn's Lakota name was *Hinsha Waste Agli Win*, which translates to "Returns Victories with a Red Horse Woman," but most people came to know her simply as Bea.[1] Her father, Martin, served in the American military during World War I and was a full-blood Lakota who instilled his ancestral traditions in his children. Bea recalled that "Being Lakota was seen as the most essential aspect of living."[2] Her colleagues later wrote that "Bea Medicine was trained as a cultural anthropologist, but she was first and foremost a Lakota (Sihasapa) woman whose chosen career path was education."[3]

Bea was a gifted teacher, and in her lifetime served as an educator at many levels, ranging from kindergarten to college. According to one account, "Since childhood, Bea has been a natural teacher and dedicated mentor. She enjoyed telling the story that as a youngster, she gathered her siblings into a shed on her family's land in order to teach them what she had learned in school, whether they liked it or not."[4] As in the case of her teaching, Medicine became involved in anthropology from an early age. Medicine remembers observing renowned anthropologist, Ella Deloria, conducting research at Standing Rock.[5] Even as a child, Bea realized she would one day interact with society outside of the reservation, but anthropology enabled her to maintain a connection with her Native roots.

In 1945, Bea graduated from South Dakota State University with a bachelor of science degree. Nine years later, she earned a Master's degree in sociology and anthropology from Michigan State University. In the decades that followed, Bea developed as a professional in the world of academia and by 1983, she earned her doctorate in cultural anthropology from University of Wisconsin-Madison.

Medicine's teaching career spanned more than fifty years. Faye V. Harrison, a friend and colleague, described Bea's career as "professional nomadism."[6] Medicine served as a lecturer, professor, or visiting professor in colleges and universities throughout the United States and Canada. The American institutions at which she held posts include Stanford, Dartmouth, University of Washington, San Francisco State University, California State University at Northridge, and University of South Dakota. In Canada, Bea worked at the University of New Brunswick, University of Calgary, and University of British Columbia. Medicine continued teaching even after her retirement, serving as visiting professor at schools such as Humboldt State University in California, Colorado College, University of Minnesota, and University of Toronto.

From 1982 to 1985, Bea was the coordinator of the Interdisciplinary Program in American Studies at Northridge. When her tenure in California concluded, Medicine became the director at the University of Calgary's Native Center. She remained at this post until 1988. Medicine "worked to dispel anthropological myths that have tended to oversimplify and homogenize Native American cultures ... She sought to depict the diversity of historical and present-day Native American life."[7]

In addition to teaching anthropology, Medicine was an active researcher and prolific writer. Her research interests centered primarily in Native American women's roles and family dynamics. Throughout Medicine's academic career, she researched important issues of Native American religion, issues of social justice, families, clans, moieties, Indian education, gender, substance abuse, and mental health developments. Medicine published her research in a number of venues, including books, book chapters, articles, and reviews. Her publications have appeared in over sixty scholarly journals. In addition, she authored and coedited three books, *The Native American Woman: A Perspective* was published in 1978, *The Hidden Half: Studies of Plains Indian Women* in 1983, and in 2001, *Learning to be an Anthropologist and Remaining "Native."*

The Native American Woman deals with the stereotypes, partly perpetuated by anthropologists, and everyday challenges American Indian women encounter. Medicine also addressed sexual roles, sexual rites, and taboos among Plains Indians, as well as examined issues regarding marriage, identity, education, and religion. She coedited *The Hidden Half: Studies of Plains Indian Women* with Patricia Albers based on a compilation of papers presented at a symposium in 1977 on "The Role and Status of Women in Plains Indian Cultures." The author's objective was to offer a critique on "past evaluations of Plains Indian women and to reassess the realities of their lives. . . . In addition, the essays stress the need for creative thinking regarding substantive knowledge, methodology and theory relating to Indian women."[8] *Learning to Be an Anthropologist and Remaining "Native"* are collected works written by Medicine. The book's themes include Native American education, gender roles, families, language, and culture. *Learning to Be an Anthropologist and Remaining "Native,"* as the title itself suggests, also highlights the duality of Medicine's career as both a scholar of Native peoples and of being an American Indian herself.

Bea's Lakota heritage propelled her to be a diligent advocate for Native American peoples, especially students. In 1974, Medicine served as translator for non-English speaking Lakota elders, and as expert witness in the Wounded Knee trials.[9] Following her retirement as a professor, Medicine returned to her hometown and served on the board of the Wakpala School District. Bea's efforts led to the construction of another public school to serve the community. A. LaVonne Brown Ruoff, a close friend of Medicine's, recalled that Bea "greatly enjoyed visiting classes [in Wakpala's schools] to talk to the students about Lakota culture and history and to encourage them to complete their education."[10] Moreover, Medicine "viewed Indigenous community-based education, especially the school-based promotion of tribal languages, as essential for Indigenous self-determination and cultural survival."[11]

Medicine's academic achievements and community involvement earned her numerous awards, which included several honorary doctorates, the Ohana Award from the American Counseling Association, the Outstanding Woman of Color Award from the National Institute of Women of Color, an Honoring Our Allies Award from the National Gay and Lesbian Task Force, the Bronislaw Malinowski Award for Lifetime Achievement from the Society for Applied Anthropology, and the George and Louise Spindler Award for Education in Anthropology from the American Anthropological Association. Another less formal award of which she was perhaps prouder was having been the Sacred Pipe Woman at the Sun Dance at Sitting Bull's Camp in 1977.[12]

Medicine touched the lives of countless families while simultaneously building her own. In 1957, Bea welcomed her son into the world. Ted Sitting Crow Garner was raised as a traditional Lakota Sioux and always maintained close ties with the Standing Rock Reservation. Today, Garner is a renowned sculptor based in Chicago. Bea was married to Ted's father for over ten years, but the marriage ended in divorce.

On January 3, 2006, *Rapid City Journal* reported Medicine's passing. The article noted that Medicine passed away on December 19, 2005, during emergency surgery in Bismarck, North Dakota. The website also informed readers that "Medicine's family asks that donations in lieu of flowers be made to the American Indian College Fund."[13] The request was a testament to Bea's generous and caring nature. Medicine was a distinguished author, tireless advocate, poet, role model, and friend. Though many felt her loss, Medicine's legacy will live on, for in her lifetime, she went to great lengths to safeguard the rights granted to her people by the Indian Citizenship Act.

NOTES

1. Donna Deyhle and Teresa L. Mccarty, "Beatrice Medicine and the Anthropology of Education: Legacy and Vision for Critical Race/Critical Language Research and Praxis," *Anthropology and Education Quarterly* 38 (August 2007), 209.
2. Beatrice Medicine, *Learning to Be an Anthropologist and Remaining "Native:" Selected Writings* (Urbana: University of Illinois Press, 2001), 7.
3. Donna Deyhle and Teresa L. Mccarty, *Beatrice Medicine and the Anthropology of Education,* 209.
4. A. LaVonne Brown Ruoff, "Beatrice Medicine: A Strong Lakota Woman, Pioneering Anthropologist, and Dedicated Mentor," *Meeting Ground* No. 49 (Fall 2006), 4.
5. Beatrice Medicine, *Learning to Be an Anthropologist and Remaining "Native,"* 6.
6. Beatrice Medicine, *Learning to Be an Anthropologist and Remaining "Native,"* xvi.
7. Gretchen M. Bataille and Laurie Lisa, ed. *Native American Women: A Biographical Dictionary* (London: Routledge, 2001), 204–05.
8. Glenda Riley, "Review of *The Hidden Half: Studies of Plains Indian Women,*" *Journal of American Ethnic History* 4 (Spring 1985), 116–117.
9. Beatrice Medicine, *Learning to Be an Anthropologist and Remaining "Native,"* 7.
10. A. LaVonne Brown Ruoff, *Meeting Ground*, 4.
11. Donna Deyhle and Teresa L. Mccarty, "Beatrice Medicine and the Anthropology of Education: Legacy and Vision for Critical Race/Critical Language Research and Praxis,"*Anthropology and Education* 38 (August 2007), 209.
12. "Human Rights Advocate Beatrice Medicine Dies," *Rapid City Journal*, January 3, 2006,
13. "Human Rights Advocate Beatrice Medicine Dies," *Rapid City Journal*, January 3, 2006,

BIBLIOGRAPHY

Bataille, Gretchen M. and Laurie Lisa, ed. *Native American Women: A Biographical Dictionary*. London: Routledge, 2001.

Deyhle, Donna and Teresa L. Mccarty, "Beatrice Medicine and the Anthropology of Education: Legacy and Vision for Critical Race/Critical Language Research and Praxis." *Anthropology and Education Quarterly* 38 (August 2007): 209–20.

Glenda Riley, "Review of *The Hidden Half: Studies of Plains Indian Women*," *Journal of American Ethnic History* 4 (Spring 1985): 116–17.

"Human Rights Advocate Beatrice Medicine Dies," *Rapid City Journal*, January 3, 2006.

Medicine, Beatrice. *Learning to Be an Anthropologist and Remaining "Native:" Selected Writings.* Urbana: University of Illinois Press, 2001.

FURTHER READINGS

Arnold, Laurie, ed. *Meeting Ground* (D Arcy McNickle Center for American Indian History. *Newsletter* No. 49 (Fall 2006): 1–10.

Chapter Eighteen

Literary Activist, Political Voice of Native America
Elizabeth Cook-Lynn
(b. 1930)

Susan M. Wood

Elizabeth Cook-Lynn was born Elizabeth Bowed Head Irving on November 17, 1930, in the government hospital on the Sioux Reservation at Fort Thompson, South Dakota. Raised on the reservation, she was a member of the Crow Creek Sioux Tribe. Poet, novelist, essayist, editor, and scholar, Cook-Lynn, now deceased, commented that "writing is an essential act of survival for contemporary American Indians."[1] She did not view the activity as "some kind of melancholy reminiscence . . . I'm interested in the cultural, historical, and political survival of Indian nations, and that's why I write and teach."[2] Elizabeth Cook-Lynn was a leading figure in the twentieth-century Native American literary renaissance and one of the founding scholars of Native American Studies Programs in North America. She pursued literary, scholarly, and political interests that connected deeply with her heritage.

Cook-Lynn was raised in a traditional household and knew its oral traditions well. Her family names are familiar in Native American history and their collective contribution and dedication to their culture had a lasting impact on her political and social views, as well as on her writing. Her grandfather and namesake, a Yankton Sioux, Joseph Bowed Head Irving, was an accomplished tribal politician. Bowed Head Irving and other tribal leaders traveled to Washington, DC, with Sitting Bull in the nineteenth century to negotiate treaties on behalf of the Sioux and Lakota people. Cook-Lynn's father, Jerome Bowed Head Irving, a Sisseton Sioux, served on the Crow Creek Tribal Council for many years. Her mother, Hulda Irving, was a school teacher and Cook-Lynn followed her mother into the world of American Indian education. As for her dedication to the written word, Cook-Lynn followed in the literary footsteps of her father, Gabriel Renville, a native linguist who was instrumental in developing early Dakota language dictionaries. Her grandmother and namesake, Eliza Renville Irving, was from a well-known

French and Indian family of the Sisseton-Wahpeton Sioux Reservation near the border between North Dakota and Canada. Eliza Renville Irving was respected in her own right as a bilingual writer who worked in the Dakota language of her people and published in some of the early Native Christian newspapers. During Cook-Lynn's childhood, she lived only a few miles from her grandmother, and the two spent a great deal of time together.

As a young girl, although well versed in her oral traditions, Cook-Lynne remembers being fascinated by the written word and read anything she could. In the course of her reading, Cook-Lynn became aware that she never saw mention of her own people. In an autobiographical essay in 1987, she discussed the effect this had on her, the realization that she was purposefully excluded from a world as a *persona non grata,* first breeding distrust and then anger. She wrote "that anger is what started me writing."[3] After graduating high school, Cook-Lynn attended South Dakota State College, and in 1952, she earned a bachelor of arts degree in journalism and English. In 1953, she married Melvin Traversie Cook with whom she had four children before they divorced in 1970. In 1975, she married Clyde J. Lynn and adopted the surname of Cook-Lynn, an amalgamation of her two married names.

While raising her family, Cook-Lynn worked as a journalist, editor, and high school teacher. In 1966, she returned to school and received a master's degree in educational psychology and counseling in 1971 from the University of South Dakota in Vermillion. Cook-Lynn taught English and Native American Studies at Eastern Washington University (EWU) from 1971 to 1989. In 1985, while at EWU, she founded *The Wicazo Sa Review* along with her colleagues Roger Buffalohead, Beatrice Medicine, and William Willard. Translated as "Red Pencil," *Wicazo Sa* is a journal focusing on the scholarship associated with Native American studies as a developing academic discipline. For many years, Cook-Lynn served as the journal's editor and contributed numerous articles on topics ranging from land issues to Native American literature. In 1976, she was a fellow for the National Endowment for the Humanities at Stanford, and between 1977–1978, she enrolled in a doctoral program in comparative literature at the University of Nebraska. In 1991, EWU granted Cook-Lynn *Emeritus* status. She has also served as a visiting professor at University of California, Davis, and writer-in-residence at universities around the United States. In 1993, N. Scott Momaday and Cook-Lynn held a workshop for Sioux writers at South Dakota State University, and from this came a journal, *Woyake Kinikiya: A Tribal Model Literary Journal.*

Cook-Lynn acknowledged three primary influences on her creative writing. These were her rich, family-tribal heritage; the northern plains landscape with its strong visual imagery of land, skies, rivers, and powerful animals; and the writing of Pulitzer Prize winning Kiowa author N. Scott Momaday.

Momaday's novel in 1968, *House Made of Dawn*, began what critic Kenneth Lincoln termed the "Native American Renaissance." The label, which some critics now consider controversial because they argue that it privileges the written word over oral tradition, was Lincoln's attempt to explore the explosion in literary works by Native Americans in the decade and a half since the publication of Momaday's novel. Gender was a fourth influence evident in Cook-Lynn's writing. Often the narrative voice in her poems and fiction is feminine, and strong female perspectives are present in her writing.

Cook-Lynn began writing poetry and fiction in college, and although her early work appeared in numerous literary magazines and journals, she did not gain national recognition of her work until the age of forty with the publication of her first two books. Although her writing was born of anger and frustration, she sustained an obligation, writing "it is the responsibility of a poet like me to 'consecrate' history," as well as "survival and joy and sorrow, the significance of ancestors and the unborn."[4] It is from this perspective that readers can interpret her books. The first, published in 1978 and titled *Then Badger Said This*, is a short collection of stories, songs, and poems that explore the sources of Dakota life, values, and the relationship between contemporary Dakotas and their past, using a juxtaposition of poetry, myth, personal and cultural history. Cook-Lynn's use of the multiple-genre techniques, inspired by Momaday, inserts her own voice into the voices of the Sioux, expressing a Native American worldview through fiction. The second, *Seek the House of Relatives* (1983), addressed history through a more direct approach, exploring her pride in her tribe's oral and spiritual traditions and the social issues that threaten them. Biographer Norma C. Wilson described Cook-Lynn's works, writing she "searches for what is real and lasting amid the false history she exposes."[5] Her themes of life on the reservation and the intrusive role of the federal government of the United States further strengthen her messages of tribal unity and sovereignty. She expands the presence of these themes in her third book, *Power of Horses and Other Stories* (1990).

Cook-Lynn's novel, *From the River's Edge* (1991), consciously took the reader into the political nature of Native American life in the United States, exploring the imposition of white values and justice on Native American cultures. It does so by using the story of a Native American man who enters the white justice system to seek compensation for stolen cattle and lost land due to development and ends up facing persecution himself. Through the exploration of these themes, Cook-Lynn advances, "a clear recognition of the sovereign nature of America's Indian nations."[6]

In subsequent books, Cook-Lynn's commitment to speaking critically became even more evident. In *Why I Can't Read Wallace Stegner and Other Essays: A Tribal Voice* (1996), which received the Myers Center award for the Study of Human Rights in North America in 1997, she addressed issues she encountered as a Native American woman in academia. She raised issues of critical importance to Native Americans, such as who is telling their stories, where cultural authority lies, and most important, how is it possible to develop an authentic tribal literary voice within the academic community. In *The Politics of Hallowed Ground* (1998), collaboration with Oglala Sioux attorney Mario Gonzalez, they chronicled the persistent legal struggles of the Sioux on the reservation.

Cook-Lynn continued her prolific output of thought-provoking literature. In *New Indians, Old Wars* (2007), she addressed Native American studies in the context of the past, present, and future. Her essays in this volume confronted the discipline head-on and, in addition, presented a radical revision of the popular view of the history of the American West in the process. Disclaiming the widespread historians' view of the West as a shared place, Cook-Lynn argued that the American West was, in essence, stolen. She further claims that the Indian wars of resistance against the colonial effort to seize land and resources was part of continuing imperial narrative in America, and the terror the world now suffered might be the direct consequence of events perpetuated against Native Americans generations ago.

Cook-Lynn claimed the story of the American West taught the political language of land theft and tyranny. As a corrective measure, she proposed that the academic field of Native American Studies must be set apart as its own discipline, not a division of history or anthropology. She claimed that such a shift, not merely an institutional or theoretical change, could allow Native American studies to play an important role in defending the sovereignty of Indigenous nations today.

In an excerpt from one speech on "The Decolonization of American Indians" given at an Indian Studies Conference, posted to the website *Indian Country Today* in February 2007, Cook-Lynn discussed political dialogue, which spoke to her body of work. She claimed that "It is in the political dialogue that I have centered much of my work . . . because it is in the political dialogue that we can disrupt the rules of the game. It is in the political dialogue that we urge ourselves toward practices that can expose a vast critical examination of what has happened to us and how we must go forward. . . . Politics are about power relations and how we are governed. I can think of no subject more useful to those of us who want to culturally affirm our survival; how to define and create Indigenous realities; how to rise above oppression and how to value our laws."[7] In her essay, "*You May Consider Speaking about Your Art,*" she stated that she wrote to defy the dominant society's effort to make the Indian population invisible. She declared "writing is an act of defiance born of the need to survive. It is the quintessential act of optimism born of frustration. It is an act of courage, I think. And, in the end, it is an act that defies oppression."[8] Her mission as a writer is best summed in her own words: "The final responsibility of a writer like me . . . is to commit something to paper in the modern world which supports this inexhaustible legacy left by our ancestors."[9] To use her own professional jargon, she kept the plot moving.

NOTES

1. Liz Sonneborn, "Cook-Lynn, Elizabeth," *A to Z of American Indian Women* (New York: Infobase Publishing, 2007), 51.
2. Sonneborn, "Cook-Lynn, Elizabeth," 51.
3. Elizabeth Cook-Lynn, "You May Consider Speaking about Your Art," in *I Tell You Now: Autobiographical Essays by Native American Writers,* Brian Swann and Arnold Krupat, eds. (Lincoln: University of Nebraska Press, 1987), 57.
4. Cook-Lynn, *You May Consider*, 59.
5. Norma C. Wilson, "Elizabeth Cook-Lynn," *Dictionary of Literary Biography: Native American Writers of the United States 175* (Detroit: Gale Research, 1997), 40.
6. Wilson, "Elizabeth Cook-Lynn," 40.
7. Elizabeth Cook-Lynn, "Decolonization of American Indians." Excerpt from a speech given by Cook-Lynn at the Indian Studies Conference, February 2007, *Indian Country Today*, February 2007, http://intercontinentalcry.org/decolonization-of-american-indians.
8. Cook-Lynn, *You May Consider*, 57–58.
9. Cook-Lynn, *You May Consider*, 63.

BIBLIOGRAPHY

Elizabeth Cook-Lynn, "Decolonization of American Indians." Excerpt from a speech given by Cook-Lynn at the Indian Studies Conference, February 2007, *Indian Country Today*, February 2007, http://intercontinentalcry.org/decolonization-of-american-indians.
Cook-Lynn, Elizabeth. "You May Consider Speaking About Your Art," In *I Tell You Now: Autobiographical Essays by Native American Writers*, eds. Brian Swann and Arnold Krupat. Lincoln: University of Nebraska Press, 1987.
Sonneborn, Liz. "Cook-Lynn, Elizabeth." *A to Z of American Indian Women.* New York: Infobase Publishing, 2007.
Wilson, Norma C., "Elizabeth Cook-Lynn." *Dictionary of Literary Biography: Native American Writers of the United States.* Volume 175. Detroit: Gale Research, 1997.

FURTHER READINGS

Cook-Lynn, Elizabeth. *Notebooks of Elizabeth Cook-Lynn*. Tucson: University of Arizona Press, 2007.

Cook-Lynn, Elizabeth. *New Indians, Old Wars*. Champaign: University of Illinois Press, 2007.

Cook-Lynn, Elizabeth. *I Remember the Fallen Trees: New and Selected Poems*. Cheney: Eastern Washington University Press, 1999.

Cook-Lynn, Elizabeth. *Why I Can't Read Wallace Stegner and Other Essays: A Tribal Voice*. Madison: University of Wisconsin Press, 1996.

Liz Sonneborn, "Cook-Lynn, Elizabeth," *A to Z of American Indian Women* (New York: Infobase Publishing, 2007).

Index

Aataentsic (Woman Who Fell From the Sky), 10, 11
Adams, Hank, 19
Adams, Robert, 52
Advancement of Maori Opportunity, 66
Agnew, Spiro, 60
Akers, Dolly Smith Cusker, 129, 131
Akers, John, 132
Alaska Native Claims Settlement Act (1971), 48, 142
Alcatraz, 12, 21, 28, 67, 70, 95
Alcatraz Island, 12, 21, 28, 70, 95
Alvitre, Cindi, 12
American Book Award, 148
American Friends Service, 19
American Indian Citizenship Act, 1924 131, 151, 154
American Indian Development (AID), 142
American Indian Movement, 25, 26, 27, 28, 29, 31, 32, 33, 35, 47
American Indian Press Association, 51, 53, 93, 96, 97
American Indian Religious Freedom Act, 1978 52
American Indian Review Commission, 47
American Indian Stories, 101, 103

American Indian Women's Services League, 17
Americans for Indian Opportunity (AIO), 42, 45, 61
Ames Moot Court (Harvard University), 89
Anderson, Clinton, 63
Andreas, Mary Ann, 12
Apache, 58
Arapaho, 53, 59
Arlington Cemetery, 103
Armstrong, Jeannette, 13
Army, 42, 51, 58, 99, 112
ARROW, 141
As Long as the Rivers Run, 20

Banks, Dennis, 20, 31, 94
Bean, Lou, 29
Bear, Bull, 53
Bell Community Revitalization Project, 72
Bennett County Hospital, 124
Bennett, Ramona, 17, 18, 19, 20, 21, 22, 23
Bernal, Paul, 62
Bible, 110, 114
Big Meadows, 93
Bird, Gloria, 13

Bissonette, Gladys, 29
Blackfeet, 10
Blackhorse v. Pro-Football, 53
Blue Lake (*Ba Whyea*), 61, 62, 63, 64, 65, 67
Boarding schools, 7, 17, 110, 130, 137
Boldt Decision, 1974   20, 21, 111, 114
Boldt, George, 20
Brant, Molly, 12
Brave Bird, Emily, 26
Bridges, Allison, 21
Bridges, Valerie, 21
Bronislaw Malinowski Award, 153
Bronson, John, 138, 142
Bronson, Ruth Muskrat, 135, 136, 139, 141, 143
Bruce, Louis, 139
Buchanan, Charles M., 108
Bureau of Indian Affairs (BIA), 12, 17, 20, 28, 41, 42, 43, 44, 47, 65, 66, 70, 72, 86, 102, 103, 109, 132, 136, 138, 139, 140, 141, 142, 145, 152

Cabazon v. California, 88
Cache Creek, 58
Caddo, 59
Cahuilla, 8, 10
Cangleska Inc., 124
Carson National Forest, 62
Carter, Jimmy, 52, 66
Catholic Church, 7, 27, 47, 102, 108, 110, 123, 145
CBS, 19, 20
Ceremony, 147
Chacon, Martha Manuel, 8, 9
Chamberlin, Joseph Edgar, 100
Chambers, Reid, 67
Chapman, Richard C., 147
Cherokee, 10, 12, 13, 69, 70, 71, 72, 73, 136, 137, 139, 142, 143, 148
Cherokee Nation, 12, 69, 72, 136
Cheyenne, 13, 51, 52, 59, 99
Chicago Art School, 142

Chicago Conference, 11, 95
Chickasaw, 103
Chinook, 10
Choctaw, 2, 3, 10, 37
Christian, 4, 7, 30, 58, 59, 100, 102, 114, 137, 138, 158
Citizens Association for the Advancement of Menominee People (CAMP), 45
Civil Rights, 9, 28, 30, 32, 132
Civil Rights Act, 1968 132
Clallam, 108
Clinton, William Jefferson, 41
Cloud, Henry Roe, 138
Colorado River, 7
Columbus, 4
Colville, 21, 117, 118, 119, 120, 121
Colville Business Council, 118
Colville Reservation, 21, 117, 118, 119, 120, 121
Comanche (*Numunuu*), 45, 57, 58, 59, 62, 45
Confederated Tribes of the Colville Reservation, 119
Cook-Lynn (Elizabeth Bow Head), 32, 33, 34, 35, 37, 157, 158, 159, 160
Cook, Melvin, 158
Coolidge, Calvin, 138, 151
Council of Energy Resources Tribes (CERT), 65
Covington, John J., 118
Covington, Lucy Frielander, 117, 119, 121
Crawford, Donald, 58
Crouch, Jim, 142
Crow Dog, Anwah, 29
Crow Dog, Bernadette, 29
Crow Dog, Ina, 29
Crow Dog, Jennifer, 30
Crow Dog, June Bug, 30
Crow Dog, Leonard, 25, 26, 27, 29, 30, 31, 32, 33, 34, 35, 36, 37
Crow Dog, Mary (Mary Moore/Mary Brave Bird/Mary Olquin), 25, 26,

27, 28, 29, 30, 31, 32, 33, 34, 35, 36, 37
Crow Dog, Paradise, 29, 30, 34, 35
Crow Dog, Richard, 29
Crow Tribe, 10, 48
Crownpoint, 85, 87
Cushman Medical Hospital, 17, 22
Custer, George, 99

Dabb, Edith, 137
Dakota, 32, 99, 101, 104, 157, 158, 159
Davids, Sharice, 15
Dawes Severalty Act (General Allotment Act), 99, 103
Daybreak Star, 21, 167
Deer, Ada, 41, 42, 44, 45, 46, 47, 48, 65, 119, 120
Deer, Constance, 41, 45
Deer, Joseph, 42
Delaware (Lenape), 10, 136
Deloria, Ella Cara, 140, 151
Deloria, Vine, Jr., 11, 52
Determination of the Rights and Unity of Menominee Share Holders (DRUM), 46, 47, 65
Diné bi beenahaz'aanii, 86
Discovery Grant, 146
Dixon, Patricia, 12
Dixon, Lorena, 12
Doh-Kwi-Buhch, 107
Domestic Policy Committee, 62
Domestic Science, 130
Domestic Violence and the Consideration of Cultural Factors in Criminal and Civic Court Cases, 87
Dover, George, 112, 113
Dover, Harriette Shelton (*Hiahl-tsa*), 107
Drake, Barbara, 12
Duamish et. al. v. United States, 111

Eastman, Charles, 138
El Palacio, 63

Erdoes, Richard, 25, 31, 32, 33, 34, 35, 36
Evergreen State College, 18
Everett Community College, 114
Extermination, 93

Fabens, Charles H., 103
Family Violence Prevention Program, 87
Federal Bureau of Investigation (FBI), 28, 30, 31
Federal Home Administration, 132
Fire Thunder, Cecilia Apple, 123
Fire Thunder, John, 123
First Nations, 11, 110, 133
First Salmon Ceremony, 108, 112
First Wisconsin Trust, 45
fish-ins, 17, 18, 19, 20, 21, 22, 111
Fitzpatrick, Darlene, 114
Five Civilized Tribes, 70, 103
Fonda, Jane, 21, 25
Fort Berthold Reservation, 75, 76, 77, 78, 79
Fort Lawton, 17, 21
Fort Peck, 129, 130, 131, 132
Fort Sill, 58
Fort Thompson, 157
Fort Yuma, 7
Frielander, Louis, T., 117
Frielander, Nellie, 117
From the Rivers, 159
Fuller, Reba, 12

Garcia, Carrie, 126
Garner, Ted Sitting Crow, 153
Garrison Dam, 75, 81
General Federation of Women, 103
Genocide, 7, 35, 93, 96
Ghost Dance, 30
Glancy, Diane, 13
Goldwater, Barry, 52
GOON squad, 28
Grant, Ulysses S., 118
Great Western Power Company, 93, 94

Haaland, Debra Anne, 15
Hanson, William, 102
Harjo, Joy, 14
Harjo, Suzan Shown, 12, 51
Harjo v. Pro-Football, 53
Harmonization Project, 86
Harper's Magazine, 101
Harris, Brian, 60
Harris, Fred, 45, 60, 62, 63, 64
Harris, Kathryn, 60
Harris, LaDonna, 45, 57, 58, 59, 60, 61, 62, 63, 64, 65, 66, 67
Harris, Laura, 60
Harrison, Faye V., 152
Harvard Law School, 89
Haskell Institute, 117, 138, 139
Hat's Kol Litsa, 107
Heye Foundation, 52
Hibulb Cultural Center and Natural Historical Preservation, 114
Hill, Bear, 131
Hinsha Wast Agli Win (Returns Victories with A Red Horse), 151
Hogan, Linda, 13
Hopi, 10
House Made of Dawn, 159
Hugo, Feliia, 70
Hugo, Gina, 70
Hugo, Hector, 70
Human Rights Youth Advisory Board, 42
Hupa, 10

Indian, 101 59, 63, 67
Indian Child Welfare Act, 17, 22
Indian Claims Commission, 43, 63, 94
Indian Country Today, 10, 160
Indian Newsletter, 103
Indian Reorganization Act, 1934 (Wheeler-Howard Act), 107
Indian Self-Determination and Educational Assistance Act (1975), 46, 47, 48, 66
Indian Territory, 54, 58, 136
Indians Are People, Too, 140

Inouye, Daniel, 14, 52
Irving, Eliza Renville, 157, 158
Irving, Hulda, 157
Irving, Jerome Bow Head, 157
Irving, Joseph Bow Head, 157

Jackson, Henry, 63
Jaimes, M. Annette, 31, 32
Johnson, Dave, 131
Johnson, Lyndon Baines, 60, 61
Johnson, Wally, 67
Jones, Flora, 13

Kamiakin, 118
Keahanie-Sanford, Angela, 87, 88
Kennedy, John F., 11
Kennedy, Ted, 52
Kerr, Robert, 60
Kidwell, Clara Sue, 46
Kilberg, Bobbie Green, 62, 63, 67
Kimball, Yeffe, 140
Kiowa, 58, 59, 158
Klamath Reservation, 44, 120
Kumeyaay, 10
Kuralt, Charles, 19

Laguna Pueblo, 145
Laguna Woman, 15, 140, 145, 146
Lakota, 10
Lakota Woman, 25, 26, 27, 28, 29, 30, 31, 32, 33, 34, 35, 36, 37
Lame Deer, John Fire, 31
Lamont, Buddy, 29
Lamont, Cheyenne, 29
Lannon Literary Prize, 148
Laurie, Nancy, 45
Learning to be an Anthropologist and Remaining Native, 152
Leslie, Mary Virginia, 145
Little Big Horn, 99
Little Soldier, Nathan, 75
Longhouse, 108
Los Angeles American Indian Health Center, 124
Louise Spindler Award, 153

Lummi, 10
Lushootseed, 107
Lynn, Clyde, 158
Lyons, Barbara, 12

Mahjo, Juana, 12
Mahto, Mark, 75
Maidu, 93, 94, 96, 97
Mankiller, Charlie, 69
Mankiller, Donald Louis, 73
Mankiller, Wilma Pearl, 12, 69, 70, 71, 72, 73
Mann, Henrietta, 13
Marmon, Leland Howard, 145
Marmon, Marie Anaya, 145
Martinez, Audrey, 12
McCloud, Janet, 19
McNickle, D'Arcy, 139
Means, Danyelle, 32
Means, Russell, 31, 32, 33, 44, 88, 89, 123
Medicine, 3, 10, 13, 25, 26, 29, 30, 32, 33, 53, 54, 58, 76
Medicine, Anna, 151
Medicine, Beatrice, 13, 151
Medicine Lodge Treaty, 1867 53, 54
Menkiller (*Ah nee-ska-yah-di-hi*), 69
Menominee, 41, 42, 43, 44, 45, 46, 47, 48, 65, 119, 120
Menominee Enterprise Inc. (MEI), 45, 46, 47
Menominee Reservation, 41, 42, 43, 44
Meriam Report, 139
Mescalero Apache Reservation, 137, 138
Mewuk, 10
Miami Tribe, 10
Mihesuah, Devon, 33, 37
Mills, Sid, 21
Modoc, 10
Mohawk, 12, 36
Mojave, 10
Momaday, Scott, 158, 159
Mondale, Walter, 47

Montana State Legislature, 131
Montezuma, Carlos, 101
Moore, Bill, 26 35
Morning Star Institute, 51
Morris, Sherry, 71
Moses, Chief, 117, 118
Moses, Mary (*Sanclow*), 117, 119, 120
Mount Lassen, 93
Mount Rushmore, 28
Mount Shasta, 13
Mourning Dove, 8
Moves Camp, Ellen, 29
Ms. Magazine, 73
Muskrat, Ida Kelly, 136
Myasthenia Gravis, 71

Nation to Nation (Exhibit), 52, 54
National Association of Mental Health, 61
National Committee Against Discrimination in Housing, 61
National Congress of American Indians (NCAI), 51, 95, 126, 132, 135, 137, 140
National Football League (NFL), 51, 52
National Organization of Women (NOW), 66
National Organization on Fetal Alcohol Syndrome, 124
National Steering Committee on the Urban Coalition, 61
National Women's Advisory Council of the War on Poverty, 61
National Women's Political Caucus, 61
Native American Church, 25, 30, 36, 103
Native American Graves and Repatriation Act (NAGPRA), 14, 53
Native American Rights Fund (NARF), 47
Navajo (*Diné*), 10, 36, 85, 86, 87, 88, 89, 146
Navajo Nation v. Russell Means, 88
Navajo People's Legal Services, 85

Navajo Reservation, 36, 85, 87, 88, 146
New England Conservatory of Music, 100
New Indians, Old Wars, 160
Nez Perce (*Nimipuu*), 10, 117, 118
Nighthorse Campbell, Ben, 14, 52
Nisqually, 17, 19, 21, 22
Nixon, Richard M., 45, 46, 60, 61, 62, 63, 64, 65, 66, 67
Nu'eta, 75
Numakshi Mihe (Lead Woman), 75, 76, 77, 78, 79, 80, 81

Obama, Barack H., 51, 53, 79
Ocean Woman (*Hutsipamamau'u*), 3
O'Donnell, Jim, 63
Office of Indian Education, 7
Oglala Lakota, 123
Ohana Award, 153
Ohiya, 102
Ohlone, 10
Oklahoma Women's Hall of Fame, 73
Oklahomans for Indian Opportunity, 58, 60
Oklahoma's Poor Rich Indians, 103
Olguin, Rudi, 25, 36
Omaha, 10, 34
Oto, 10
Our Heritage, 120
Oury Reservation, 102
Owhi, Chief, 117, 118
Owl, David, 140

Paiute, 2, 3, 10, 12, 37, 163
Palouse (Palus), 10, 117, 118
Paris Exhibition, 100
Parker, Arthur C., 139
Patterson, Bradley, 67
Pearson, Maria (*Hai-Mech-Eunka*), 13, 14
Pedro, 25, 29, 30
Peltier, Leonard, 21, 31
Phillips, Madonna, 32, 33, 34
Pictou-Aquash, Anna Mae, 30, 32

Pine Ridge, 25, 28, 29, 123, 124, 125
Peacemaker, 86
Pocahontas, 12
Power of Horses and Other Stories, 159
Pratt, Richard Henry, 7
Public Law, 91-550 63, 64
Public Welfare Act, 131
Puha, 3, 57, 58, 59
Puyallup, 17, 18, 19, 20, 21, 22
Puyallup River, 19, 20

Quechan, 7, 10

Rainbow Youth and Family Services, 22
Ramah, 85
Rangle, Charlie, 52
Rapid City Journal, 154
Ray, Carol, 12
Red Cloud Catholic High School, 123
Red Panther, 27
Red Power, 17, 95
Red River Wars, 58
Red Scare, 141
Redskins, 53
Relocation, 9, 32, 70, 123
Reneville, Gabriel, 157
Rice, Julian, 35
Richard Nixon Presidential Library and Museum, 66
Romero, Jesus, 62
Roosevelt, Eleanor, 42
Roosevelt, Theodore, 62, 76
Rosebud Reservation, 26, 27, 29, 34, 35, 41
Ruoff, A. LaVonne, 153

Sacajewea, 12
Sacred Choices Clinic, 125
Sacred Places, Sacred Lands Coalition, 52
Samish, 108
San Carlos Apache Reservation, 142
San Diego American Indian Health Center, 124

San Poil, 117
Sanchez, Georgiana, 12
Satiacum, Robert, 21
Save the Children Federation, 142
Scheirbeck, Helen, 11
Seattle Post-Intelligencer, 111
Seek the House of Relatives, 159
Sehome, Ruth, 108
Self-Determination, 11, 14, 18, 32, 35, 46, 47, 48, 64, 65, 67, 93, 95, 96, 97, 103, 120, 132, 133, 153
Self-Determination Act, 46 48
Serrano, 8, 10
Sequoya, 137
Seventh Cavalry, 28, 99
Shanley, Kathryn, 13
Shasta Dam, 13
Shawano High School, 42
Shelton, William, 108
Sherman Institute, 130, 131, 145
Sherman, Paschal, 120
Sierra Nevada Mountains, 93
Silko, John, 147
Silko, Leslie Marmon, 145, 146, 147, 148
Silko, Robert, 145
Silko, Walter, 145
Simmons, David, 99
Simmons, Ellen (*Tate-I-Yohin-Win*), 99
Sincayuse, 117
Sioui, Eleonore, 10, 11
Sioui, Georges, 10, 11
Sisk-Franco, Calleen, 13
Sisquoc, Lorene, 12
Sitting Bull, 64
Sitton, Clara Irene, 69
Sitton, Pearl Halady, 70
Slaish, 107, 108, 111, 114
Smoke Signal, 93, 94, 95, 96, 97
Sniffen, Matthew, 103
Snohomish, 107
Snoqualmie, 107
Soap, Charlie Lee, 73
Soboba Indian Reservation, 126
Society of American Indians, 102, 103

Sovereignty, 9, 10, 11, 14, 25, 27, 33, 35, 41, 44, 46, 47, 51, 58, 64, 65, 66, 67, 75, 76, 77, 81, 89, 90, 117, 118, 119, 120, 121, 129, 132, 133, 141, 145, 147, 148, 159, 160
Spotted Bear, Alyce, 81, 75, 76, 77, 78, 79, 80
Spring Rancheria, 8
Squaw, 5, 12
Standing Rock Reservation, 13, 64, 77, 78, 151, 153
Stone, Oliver, 25
Storyteller, 147
Sun Dance, 27, 30, 36, 102, 153
Sunset Magazine, 113
Supreme Court of Navajo Nation, 86
Survival of the American Indian Association, 17, 19, 20
Swimmer, Ross, 72

Tabbytite, LaDonna (Harris), 58, 59, 60
Tabbytite, Lily, 58
Taos Pueblo, 61, 62, 63, 64, 65, 67
Tax, Sol, 11
Termination, 32, 35, 41, 42, 43, 44, 45, 46, 47, 48, 64, 65, 67, 117, 118, 119, 120, 125, 132, 141, 153
The American Indian Magazine, 102
The Doors, 25
The Hidden Half, 152
The Native American Woman, 152
The Northern Maidu, 93, 94
The Politics of Hallowed Ground, 160
The Sun Dance Opera, 102
The Turquoise Ledge, 147
The Wicazo Sa, 158
Then Badger Said This, 159
Thorpe, Grace, 21
Three Affiliated Tribes, 75, 76, 77, 78, 79, 80
Tipospaye, 26, 30
Tohono O'odham, 10, 142
Toledo, Irene, 85, 86, 87, 88, 89, 90
Tonasket, Mel, 120
Toronto (The Meeting Place), 10, 152

Townsend, Celeste, 12
Trail of Broken Treaties, 25, 28
Treaty of 1855, 111
Treaty of Point Elliott, 18
Treaty of New York, 53
Treaty of Wolf River, 1854   43
Tulalip From My Heart, 114
Tulalip Reservation, 107, 108, 109, 110, 111, 112, 113, 114
Turner, Sarah E., 37
Turner, Ted, 25, 37
Twin Tepee Restaurant, 111

Uintah Reservation, 102
Uncommon Controversy, 19
United Indians of All Tribes, 21
United Keetoowa Band of Cherokee, 72
United Nations, 66
United Nations Education, Scientific, and Cultural Organization (UNESCO), 66
United States Army, 42, 51, 58, 99, 112
United States Department of Justice, 85
United States Forest Service, 61, 62
United States Supreme Court, 44, 86, 88, 89
United States v. State of Washington, 20, 21, 114
University of Oklahoma, 60, 137,
Upward Bound, 42

Valbuena, Lynn, 12
Vance, Cyrus, 66
Vietnam War, 87

Wa-He-Lut Indian School, 22
Walla Walla Treaties, 1855, 118
War on Poverty, 61
Warrior, Clyde, 52, 158
Warrior Society, 47
Washington Football Teach, 53

Washington State Department of Fish and Game, 19
Wasicu, 27
WBAI Radio, 53
Wenatchi, 117
Wha-cah-dub, 108
White, Jim, 46, 65
White Plume, Alex, 125
Whitebear, Bernie (*Sin-Aikst*), 21
Whitmer, Carl, 75
Why I Can't Read Wallace Stegner, 159
Wilkinson, Bud, 60
Williams, Francis, 111
Wilson, Dick, 28
Wilson, Norma, 159
Winnemem Wintu, 13
Winnemucca, Sarah, 12
Wolf Point, 129
World Student Christian Federation, 138
World War II, 8, 9, 42, 43, 44, 51, 112, 113
Wounded Knee, 1973 25, 28, 29, 31, 32, 33, 34, 36, 67, 153
Woyake Kinikiya, 158
W. W. Hastings Hospital, 69

Yakama, 118
Yankton Sioux, 12, 13, 99, 100, 101, 102, 104, 157
Yankton Sioux Reservation, 100, 102
Yazzie, Herb, 86
Yellow Woman and the Beauty of the Spirit, 147
Young Women's Christian Association (YWCA), 137, 138
Youngbird, Ben, 75
Yuwipi, 36

Zitkala-sa (Gertrude Bonnin), 8, 99, 100, 101, 102, 103

About the Editors

Clifford E. Trafzer holds the titles of Distinguished Professor of History and Rupert Costo Chair in American Indian Affairs at the University of California, Riverside. In 1973, he earned his PhD in History at Oklahoma State University. He has worked as a farm worker, ranch hand, archivist, museum curator, and professor. He has taught Native American History, Culture, Oral Narratives, and Public History at Navajo Community College (Diné College), Washington State University, and San Diego State University. For the past thirty years, he has taught at the University of California, Riverside. He has served on the Chancellor's Native American Community Advisory Committee, California Native American Heritage Commission, Board of the California Indian Heritage Center, University of California President's Native American Advisory Council, and as a Trustee of the California Historical Society. Trafzer has published several books, including *Native Universe* (2004), the inaugural book of the Smithsonian's National Museum of the American Indian, *Exterminate Them!* (1999), *Willie Boy & The Last Western Manhunt* (2020), *Fighting Invisible Enemies: Health and Medical Transitions of Southern California Indians* (2019), and *Strong Hearts and Healing Hands: Southern California Indians and Field Nurses, 1900–1950* (2021).

Donna L. Akers is Choctaw and has been a professor at California State University, Northridge, University of Nebraska, and University of Texas, Arlington, where she has been Chair of Ethnic Studies/Native American Studies for many years. She is the author of several articles and *Living in the Land of Death: The Choctaw Nation, 1830–1860*.

Amanda K. Wixon is Chickasaw and is completing her PhD in History at the University of California, Riverside. For the past four years, Wixon has served as an Assistant Curator and Researcher at the Sherman Indian School Museum and the Gene Autry Western Center. She is currently writing a book-length manuscript on Sherman Institute as a site of Native American incarceration.

About the Contributors

Daniel Archuleta is a PhD student in history at the University of California, Riverside. He is a member of the Tohono O'odham Nation of Southern Arizona. His research focuses on tribal sovereignty through his people's religious and spiritual beliefs, and he is writing on Staying Sickness among O'odham people. His interest in Spotted Bear stems from his own belief in education and educational opportunities for Native American people of all ages. He lives with his wife and children in Hemet, California, near the Soboba Indian Reservation.

Renae M. Bredin is professor of women and gender studies at California State University, Fullerton. For many years, Bredin has led the development of women's studies and guided her department in 2000 to create the field as a university major. She is known internationally for her publications about Native American women, feminist history, and Indigenous women.

Julia Coates is a citizen of the Cherokee Nation. Born in Pryor, Oklahoma, she holds BAs in anthropology and English from San Francisco State University. She earned the PhD in American studies from the University of New Mexico. Coates was a delegate to the Cherokee Nation Constitutional convention and the project director for the award-winning Cherokee Nation History Course. She is presently serving her third term on the Cherokee Nation Tribal Council while teaching American Indian studies at Pasadena City College and California State University, Northridge.

Theodor Gordon, PhD is a visiting assistant professor in the Sociology Department at the College of Saint Benedict and Saint John's University. He is the author of *Cahuilla Nation Activism and the Tribal Casino Movement*, published by the University of Nevada Press. He earned his PhD in sociocultural anthropology from the University of California, Riverside.

Richard A. Hanks worked as a journalist and public historian after earning his bachelor's and master's degrees from the University of California, Riverside. Upon receiving his PhD in Native American studies, he taught for several years researching a work on resistance by Southern California Indians and their fight to protect their culture. He has published *This War is for a Whole Life*. A move to Washington State led to his work with Tulalip people and production of this essay.

Benjamin Jenkins is archivist and assistant professor at the University of La Verne. He oversees archives and special collections at Wilson Library as well as the Public History Program. He is writing two books on the citrus industry in California, one for Arcadia Publishing's prolific *Images of America* series titled *California's Citrus Heritage*.

Thomas Long received his PhD in Native American and public history at the University of California, Riverside. He is professor of history and assistant dean at California State University San Bernardino, where he also serves as the Coordinator of Public History and the Social Science BA program. Long has published books on California History and Constitutional History of the United States. He has curated museum exhibitions on American Indian History and Culture. Long also serves as Board Secretary for the Dorothy Ramon Learning Center, an institution dedicated to educational outreach and programming on Southern California Native American Studies.

Michelle Lorimer earned her BA at California State University, San Bernardino, and both her MA and PhD in history from the University of California, Riverside. Her research focuses on the history of the United States, California, and Native American history, including Native American women. She is the author of *Resurrecting the Past: The California Mission Myth* (2016) as well as several publications focusing on the representation of Native people in popular culture. As a central part of her work, Dr. Lorimer actively engages with local and statewide education initiatives.

Vera Parham joined the faculty of American Public University System as associate professor of history in 2014. She earned her PhD in Native American history from the University of California Riverside. Her research and publications focus on the use of protest by various Native American groups and individuals of the Pacific Northwest in the quest to preserve and protect culture and heritage. In 2018, Lexington Books published her latest book titled, *Pan-Tribal Activism in the Pacific Northwest: The Power of Indigenous Protest and the Birth of Daybreak Star Cultural Center*. She is also the president of the World History Association of Hawaii and has presented papers on Indigenous struggles for survival at numerous conferences. Her publications appear in several anthologies as well as journals focusing on Native American and public history.

Elvia Rodriguez received her PhD in history from the University of California, Riverside, in 2013. Her dissertation on the print culture of the Chicano Movement gives special attention to the contributions of Chicanas in this civil rights struggle. Since 2015, Rodriguez has taught at Fresno City College and California State University, Fresno (Fresno State University). At Fresno State, she primarily teaches courses related to women's history. In 2020, Rodriguez received Fresno State's College of Social Sciences Outstanding Lecturer Award.

Michael Seager earned his PhD in history from the University of California, Riverside. He has taught many year in the Department of History at California State University, Fullerton. Most recently, he has taught history at Riverside Community College. He has researched the history of Indigenous peoples, including peoples of the Philippine Islands and continental United States.

Jeffrey Allen Smith, PhD is an associate professor of American history and chair of the History Department at the University of Hawaii at Hilo. He has published historical analyses of nineteenth-century American history including Native American history, military mental health, psychology, and suicide in books, academic journals, and commentaries on his research in the *New York Times, Time,* and *Washington Post*; and has been quoted in *U.S. News & World Report*, NBC News, *Reuters, Stars and Stripes,* and other media outlets.

Shannon M. Smith graduated from the University of California, Riverside, in 2007 with a bachelor of arts degree in American history and a bachelor of science degree in anthropology. She is as an independent scholar and a contract Native American archaeologist. She lives with her family in San Jacinto, California, near the Soboba Indian Reservation.

Daniel Stahl-Kovell is an independent scholar and instructor of history at California State University, San Bernardino. He is a PhD candidate in history at the University of California, Riverside. His research focuses on American Indian education and how Native American leaders and organizations used the mainstream press and periodicals of Native origin to convey their message to Indigenous and the larger communities of the United States.

Joshua Thunder Little is an Oglala Lakota scholar and PhD student in history at the University of California, Riverside. His research interests include activism, Indigenous sovereignty, environmental history, and public history. Thunder Little's interest in Celia Fire Thunder developed out of his interest in Lakota leaders

Susan M. Wood received her MA and PhD in public history from the University of California, Riverside. She received her bachelor of science degree in anthropology from the California State Polytechnic University, Pomona. Wood is a professional scholar in historic preservation and cultural resource management and has conducted extensive ethnohistorical and community-based research with tribal elders focused on decolonization and prehistoric archaeology in the San Bernardino National Forest

www.ingramcontent.com/pod-product-compliance
Lightning Source LLC
Chambersburg PA
CBHW020122010526
44115CB00008B/932